Nebraska Historical Tour Guide

By D. Ray Wilson

ON THE COVER

The three persons featured in the insets, left to right, are Gerald R. Ford, 38th President of the United States (1974-77), born in Omaha; Author Mari Sandoz, born and reared in the Sandhills; and Col. William F. "Buffalo Bill" Cody, noted frontiersman and showman, who made his headquarters in North Platte for several years. The photo below shows the remains of an Alloraus, a dinosaur that once roamed on what is today the Nebraska prairies. This reconstruction, and others like it, are displayed in the State Museum on the campus of the University of Nebraska in Lincoln.

i

Other Books in this Series by D. Ray Wilson
"Wyoming Historical Tour Guide"
"Iowa Historical Tour Guide"
"Kansas Historical Tour Guide"
"Missouri Historical Tour Guide"

ABOUT THE AUTHOR—D. Ray Wilson, a former Nebraska weekly newspaper editor and publisher, is the author of "The Folks," "Fort Kearny on the Platte," and "Episode on Hill 616." He is married to the former Beatrice J. Daffer of Lebanon, Nebraska. Wilson, who received his journalism degree from Northern Illinois University, is publisher and editor of two Illinois daily newspapers and several weeklies. In 1985 he received an honorary Doctor of Letters degree from Judson College, Elgin, Illinois. He is listed in several editions of "Who's Who" and is founder and Chairman of the Board of the DuPage Heritage Gallery, Wheaton, Illinois.

Author: D. Ray Wilson
NEBRASKA HISTORICAL TOUR GUIDE
1st Edition, 1983
2nd Edition, 1988

Published by Crossroads Communications
Carpentersville, IL 60110-0007
Manufactured in the United States of America

Library of Congress Catalog Number: 88-070028
International Standard Book Number: 0-916445-21-6

*This book is dedicated to
my Nebraskan, Vicky Joy Wilson.*

Table of Contents

Legend
N-92: Nebraska Highway 92
US 30: United States Highway 30
I-80: Interstate Highway 80
Population totals are based on 1980 U.S. Census figures for consistency

Photo Credits

D. Ray Wilson—5, 7, 35, 37, 41, 65, 67, 79, 81, 95, 100, 102, 109, 113, 114, 125, 133, 137, 140, 143, 145, 153, 159, 163, 172, 179, 181, 189, 190, 192, 198, 199, 200, 221, 224, 226, 228, 232, 235, 239, 248, 249, 250, 251, 252, 263, 265, 273, 289, 290, 291, 294, 295.

Omaha Visitors Bureau—18, 21 (bottom), 26, 28, 29, 33.

Nebraska State Historical Society 21, 43, 44, 47, 51, 75, 92 (bottom), 98, 119, 123, 136, 161, 162, 165, 171, 188, 203, 207, 211, 225, 237, 238, 256, 259, 285, 286, 287.

Nebraska Game and Parks Commission—73, 91, 135, 257.

Daily Courier-News—28 (top), 57, 71, 204.

Lincoln Convention and Tourist Bureau—31, 49.

Wyoming State Archives and Historical Department—92 (top).

Miscellaneous—24, 27, 117, 39, 55, 63, 69, 88, 105, 127, 144, 150, 151, 169, 174, 176, 177, 186, 255, 271, 275, 288, 292, 293, 296.

Introduction

Nebraska has a very unique place in American history. It served as the principal gateway to the western frontier for thousands of emigrants.

First, the great roads, the Oregon and Mormon Trails, crossed the territory beginning in the 1840s as the first wagon train picked its way through relatively uncharted land for Oregon Country.

The Oregon Trail was the route of most emigrants heading for California or Oregon Country for a new start and new land. It was the route of the thousands of 49'ers who flocked to California with high hopes of becoming rich. It was the route of the Overland Stage Company, freighters and the colorful Pony Express. The Mormon Trail was the main road for the members of the Church of Jesus Christ of Latter Day Saints (the Mormons) whose destination was the Great Salt Lake Valley in Utah.

Second, two developments occurred at Omaha in the 1860s that brought swift change to the opening of the West—the development of the telegraph to open instant communications from coast to coast followed by the transcontinental railroad which brought fast, cheap transportation to the frontier.

The completion of the telegraph to the West Coast in 1861 brought an end to the Pony Express. The telegraph line followed the general route of the Oregon Trail to the west coast.

The Union Pacific launched its part of the building of the transcontinental railroad from Omaha immediately after the Civil War. The railroad followed the Mormon and Oregon Trails through most of the state before taking off in a more direct line across the country. It was the railroad that bound the great land mass together, linking East with West. Settlement of the country became a reality with the coming of the railroads.

As settlers began to arrive they found the land hard and the weather harsh. The winters were bitterly cold and the summers dry and usually hot. With crude tools and great human effort they wrested a living from the prairie, made it productive and rich. The land developed a special breed of Americans.

Nebraska has developed a unique heritage. It has produced a variety of hardy and special sons and daughters.

Since 1947, when I became a Nebraskan through marriage, I have been fascinated by the many stories, some not yet pub-

1

lished, about this land and its people. When I completed my book, *Fort Kearny on the Platte* in 1980 I knew I would write more about Nebraska. In 1983 came the first edition of the *Nebraska Historical Tour Guide*. That printing has been sold out leading to this second edition. Dozens of individuals and organizations have assisted in revising and upgrading this new edition.

I am particularly grateful for the assistance of the Nebraska State Historical Society, the Nebraska Game and Parks Commission and Division of Travel and Tourism, Nebraska Department of Economic Development. Also very helpful have been the many chambers of commerce, county historical societies and special individuals contributing to this effort.

Some of our stories and accounts of certain events may be questioned. In most cases we have had people from the geographic areas read our material for accuracy. In some instances we have had two or more stories about a given event. Sometime the printed materials available were in conflict and it took hours of research to reach our conclusions of how it may have been.

We also realize other stories and information about other places and events could have been included. We realize this but it is also necessary to end a work at some point or another and we elected to end ours as we have.

This book is written for Nebraskans as well as visitors to the state. It is always surprising how little we know of our own areas and Nebraskans are no different.

My special thanks and appreciation to Alice McCoy for her research efforts and assistance in the production of the book and to Jeri Salzmann for proof reading and editing. My thanks also go to my wife and daughters for their patience and understanding during our many Nebraska "detours."

We hope you enjoy your next exploration of Nebraska.

D. Ray Wilson
Sleepy Hollow, Illinois
January 30, 1988

Nebraska's Early Days...

Prehistoric Indians may have been the first settlers in the area now known as Nebraska. Archaeological evidence indicates that these first pioneers hunted big game over 10,000 years ago in this region of the United States. These early hunters were followed by tribes of Indians who raised crops of corn, other vegetables and sunflowers. Between 1750 and 1800, the dawn of recorded Plains history, the tribes living in the area included the farming tribes of eastern Nebraska—the Otoe, Omaha, Ponca and Pawnee. These groups made their homes in permanent earth-lodge dwellings where they cultivated crops. It was still necessary, however, for these tribes to engage in buffalo hunts for a large portion of their food supply.

Western Nebraska was under the control of the horse-riding buffalo-hunting, semi-nomadic groups—the Sioux, Cheyenne, Arapaho and Potawatomi. These groups lived in tepees made of animal skins which could be dismantled and moved with them as they pursued the majestic buffalo. Approximately 40,000 Indians were living in Nebraska, speaking three distinct languages, when the first white man came along.

In 1913 only 4,784 Indians, including non-indigenous tribes, remained; other survivors had been removed to reservations in surrounding states. At present there are approximately 14,500 Indians in the state.

In Knox County there are approximately 424 Santee-Sioux. On separate tracts in Thurston County live 800 Winnebago and 1,100 Omaha Indians. About 100 Sauk and Fox are found in southeastern Nebraska, the site of their former reservation.

Strange animals ranged the Nebraska plains more than 20 million years ago. Many fossils of a number of extinct animals have been found in many parts of the state over the years. **Diceratherium**, a fleet-footed, two-horned rhinoceros, once roamed the Nebraska plains in numbers as great as those of buffalo before the middle of the 19th century. Many other prehistoric animals once lived off the land—the **Moropus**, a large mammal with a horse-like head and the body of a tapir; the **Dinohyus**, a ferocious beast called the "terrible pig" because of its appearance; and the **Stenomylus**, small graceful mammals standing just over two feet tall; as well as the **Teleceros**, a species of rhinoceros;

the **Pliohippus**, the three-toed horse; and the elephant-like **Gomphoterium**, all flourishing during the Miocene Epoch, which spanned the period from 26 to 12 million years ago. The largest mammoth fossil found in Nebraska was unearthed near North Platte in 1922. It stands 13 feet, 4½ inches tall.

University of Nebraska State Museum Palcontologist **Michael R. Voorhis** led a group of students and researchers on a dig eight miles north of **Oakland**, in Antelope County in the northeastern section of the state. Here, in 1978-79, the Voorhis party found many fossils of mammals and other life believed to be choked to death in volcanic ash which swept over the plains from some unknown source some 10 million years ago. It is believed the weather in Nebraska during that period was warmer than now and without snow. Among the many fossils found in this discovery were those of rhinos, horses, camels and tiny saber-toothed deer. They found parts of the bodies of mammals—tongue bones, cartilages, tendons and tiny bones of the inner ear—in excellent condition. Many of the discoveries were exhibited at the state museum.

Nebraska's pre-territorial history saw French trappers and traders as the first known white visitors. The **Mallet brothers**, **Paul** and **Pierre**, who named the Platte River, were among the daring mountain men traveling into the Nebraska wilderness. The frenchmen traveled through Nebraska in 1739-40.

In 1714, **Etienne Veniard de Bourgmont**, a French adventurer, ascended the Missouri River to the mouth of the Platte, referring to this river as the Nebraska or "flat water." In 1720 a Spanish expedition, led by **Col. Pedro de Villasur**, was massacred by hostile Pawnees along the Platte River.

The area that was to become Nebraska was claimed by Spain, France and England, but the Spanish claim was recognized by the other two countries in the Treaty of 1763, signed in Paris February 10 of that year. During the Spanish reign, fur traders ascended the Missouri River from time to time to trade with the Indians. A small, temporary trading post was established in what is now the northeastern corner of the state in 1795.

Captains Meriwether Lewis and **William Clark** mapped the eastern boundary of Nebraska during their expedition west in 1804. In 1806 **Lt. Zebulon M. Pike** visited south central Nebraska as part of a government program to explore the newly acquired Louisiana Purchase.

Other explorers included expeditions led by **Maj. Stephen H.**

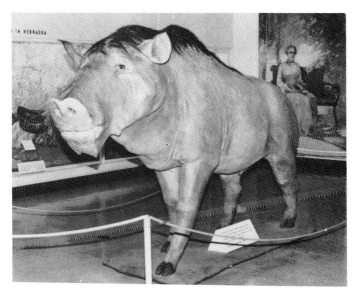

THE TERRIBLE PIG—The Dinohyus, referred to as the "Terrible Pig," was a hog-like animal that lived on the plains 15 million years ago. This large mammal was a swift runner and an aggressive fighter. Fossilized remains of the Dinohyus have been found at Agate Springs Fossil Quarries in western Nebraska. Other fossil remains have been discovered in several sections of the state and several are exhibited at the State Museum at the University of Nebraska.

Long (1819-20), Col. Henry Dodge (1835), Lt. John C. Fremont (1842-44), and Lt. G. K. Warren (1855-57). Most of the reports were unfavorable and Major Long in particular believed much of this new land was a great desert, unfit for agriculture of any kind. American fur traders, men such as Manuel Lisa and William H. Ashley, pioneered travel on the Missouri River and through the Platte Valley. Among the early trading groups was the St. Louis Missouri Fur Company. Manuel Lisa established a post for this company in 1812 in today's Washington County.

The Platte Valley developed as an important road to the Rocky Mountains and the Pacific Coast. It was first used by Robert Stuart, returning from Astoria in 1812-13. In 1824 William Ashley led a group of fur traders and trappers through the Platte Valley to the Rocky Mountains. His group was followed by other traders and trappers for the next several years as the fur trade flourished.

It was in 1820 that a camp, on the Missouri River north of pre-

5

sent-day Omaha, became a permanent Army post called **Fort Atkinson**. The post was established to discourage British encroachment and to protect America's western frontier and its interests in this vast expanse of land. Fort Atkinson operated until 1827.

The first permanent settlement in Nebraska was founded in 1823 and given the name of **Bellevue**. Bellevue was an important fur trading post, missionary center and administrative headquarters for those involved in Indian affairs.

Missionaries to the Oregon country began using the route in the early 1830s. American Methodist missionaries, led by **Nathaniel J. Wyeth** and others, were sent to Oregon in 1833. **Dr. Marcus Whitman**, an ardent Congregationalist, and **Henry Spalding**, a Presbyterian minister, went to Oregon in 1835 and sent back glowing reports on "this new country."

The "great migration" was recorded in 1843 when more than 900 persons with over 1,000 head of livestock went to Oregon through the Platte Valley route. Traffic along the Oregon Trail started as a trickle and within a few years had developed, at times, into a flood.

In 1847 the Mormons, led by **Brigham Young**, went along the north bank of the Platte River enroute to the Valley of the great Salt Lake. Thousands of Americans trekked westward over the Oregon and Mormon Trails in the Great California gold rush of 1849-50 and to Colorado in 1859.

The name "Nebraska" had been used to designate the Platte River Valley and surrounding area as suggested by Lieutenant Fremont in 1843. The name was adopted by **Stephen A. Douglas** who introduced the bill for the organization of the territory in 1844, 1848 and 1852.

Wagon trains could be seen moving west along the Platte Valley trails as the United States expanded. Gold seekers, Mormons and other emigrants on their way to California and Oregon were among the thousands of pioneers using the overland trails between 1840 and 1860. Protection was needed for these brave men and women so Fort Kearny was established, first at Nebraska City in 1846 and then on the Platte River, about six miles southeast of present-day Kearney, in 1848, by a Missouri mounted regiment.

Nebraska City and other towns on the Missouri River became shipping centers and supplied both the military outposts and the new settlers. From April 3, 1860 to October 24, 1861, Pony Express riders carried the mail across the area. The Missouri and

CAMELS ONCE ROAMED NEBRASKA—Camels were among the many prehistoric animals that once roamed the plains of Nebraska in great herds during the Miocene Epoch. The photo here is one of the exhibits of these early day camels on display at the State Museum in Lincoln.

Western Telegraph Company, a subsidiary of Western Union, crossed Nebraska Territory in 1860-61 and was credited with the early demise of the famed Pony Express.

Congress passed the Kansas-Nebraska Act in 1854, organizing the Nebraska Territory. This act opened lands west of the Missouri, previously reserved for the Indians, to settlement.

Until 1864 the Indians in the Nebraska Territory had been

fairly peaceful. There had only been a few isolated, hostile acts until the summer of 1864 when the Sioux and Cheyenne, who had become fearful their hunting lands would soon be destroyed by the white emigrants passing through, went on the warpath. In early August they raided along some 400 miles of the Oregon Trail and literally brought traffic on the trail to a standstill for about six weeks as they destroyed settlements and killed a number of whites. Two major raids, one on Plum Creek near Lexington and the other on the Little Blue River near Oak, occurred Sunday, August 7. At Plum Creek, an oxen train was destroyed and several men killed. A woman and a small boy were taken captive. On the Little Blue, Indians raided several small settlements and stage stations, killed a number of settlers and took two women and two children captive. Most of the hostile Indians were driven from Nebraska in 1870, however, there continued to be Indian "problems" in the Pine Ridge country in the northwest corner of the state. Fort Robinson played an important role in the Indian problems in the 1870s and 80s.

Of course railroads made a great contribution to the early development of the state. The Union Pacific was completed across Nebraska in 1867, and the lines of the Burlington system crisscrossed most of the state by the mid-1880s. Many early railroads received land grants from the state and federal governments to offset the costs of construction. These lands were sold to settlers through extensive advertising campaigns, with some companies sending representatives to Europe to encourage emigrants to come to America and then emigrate westward to Nebraska.

Growth was prominent in Nebraska until the farm depressions of the 1890s. By 1900 most of the prime land in the state was settled and larger claims were needed for profitable farming and ranching.

Nebraska Congressman **Moses Kinkaid** introduced an act in 1904 increasing the size of homesteads from 160 to 640 acres. The Kinkaid Act was quickly ratified. A new population swell occurred in the 20,000 square mile Sandhills area of the state as a result.

The farm depressions of the 1920s and 1930s again arrested the economic growth of the state. Since World War II, however, Nebraska's development has been consistently upward.

Although Nebraska is one of the nation's leading agricultural states, a growing proportion of the state's income is derived from non-agricultural sources. A wide variety of commodities are manufactured in Nebraska. As could be expected, food processing, such as noodles, cereals, dairy products and meat products, is Nebraska's largest manufacturing industry.

Nebraska's Hall of Fame

The Nebraska Hall of Fame Commission, appointed by the governor for six year terms, is permitted to nominate one person to the Hall of Fame every two years. In 1976, the nation's bicentennial year, the commission selected four persons to be honored. Secretary of the Commission is the Director, Nebraska State Historical Society. The Nebraska Hall of Fame is located on the second floor of the state capitol building in Lincoln.

1961—*George W. Norris* (1861-1944), U.S. Congress 1903-1913; Senate 1913-1943; Initiator of reform of House Rules, Anti-Injunction Law for Labor, Tennessee Valley Authority, Rural Electrification, 20th Amendment to the United States Constitution, and sponsor of Nebraska's Unicameral Legislature.

1962—*Willa Cather* (1873-1947), author. "The life of pioneers she described, a literature of Nebraska she created."
"The history of every country begins in the heart of a man or woman."—Pioneers

1963-64—*John J. Pershing* (1860-1948), soldier. Commandant of Cadets, University of Nebraska 1891-1895; Founder, Pershing Rifles; Service, Indian Wars, Cuba, Philippines; Commander, Mexican Border 1916; Commander, American Expeditionary Forces, France 1917-1919; General Armies of the United States 1919, and Army Chief of Staff 1921-1924.

1965-66—*Edward J. Flanagan* (1886-1948), founder of Father Flanagan's Boys Home, Boys Town, Nebraska.
"I have never found a boy who really wanted to be bad."

1967-68—*William Frederick Cody* (1846-1917), "Buffalo Bill," soldier, buffalo hunter, Army scout, actor, rancher, irrigationist, showman of the West.
"More than a Scout—An American Legend."

1969-70—*William Jennings Bryan* (1860-1925), three-time nominee of Democratic party for United States president, congressman, U.S. Secretary of State, orator, religious leader, author.
"You shall not crucify mankind upon a cross of gold."

1971-72—*Bess Streeter Aldrich* (1881-1954), author and writer. Bess Streeter Aldrich, narrator of Nebraska, gave literary life to Nebraska pioneer memories, honored the trials and dreams of the settlers that all may realize and cherish their heritage. One Aldrich novel, "A Lantern in her Hand," was translated into many languages.

1973-74—*John Gneisenau Neihardt* (1881-1973), Nebraska Poet Laureate 1921-1973. Epic poet of the West, historian, philosopher, friend of the American Indian.
"My God and I shall interknit as rain and ocean, breath and air; and O, the luring thought of it is prayer."—From L'Envo

1975-76—*Grace Abbott* (1878-1939), social reformer and social worker. A native Nebraskan internationally honored for her courageous and effective championship of children and mothers and for her promotion of pioneer social legislation of enduring benefit to Americans.

J. Sterling Morton (1832-1902), father of Arbor Day, U.S. Secretary of Agriculture, editor, farmer, legislator, Nebraska territorial secretary.

"Other holidays repose upon the past, Arbor Day proposes for the future."

Nathan Roscoe Pound (1870-1964), botantist, pioneer ecologist, dean of the University of Nebraska Law College, dean of Harvard Law School. "Philosopher of Law."

Mari Sandoz (1896-1966), novelist, historian, friend of the Indian.

"A serious concern for man upon this earth."

"The real frontier lies in the stimulation of the creative mind of man."

1977-78—*Standing Bear* (1829-1908), Ponca chief, symbol for Indian rights.

"I have found a better way; an Indian is a person within the meaning of the law." —Judge Elmer Dundy.

1979-80—*Robert W. Furnas* (1824-1905), newspaperman, soldier, historian, governor 1873-75, agriculturist.

"The state's outstanding agricultural spokesman."

1981-82—*Edward Creighton* (1820-1874), telegraph pioneer and banker.

1983-84—*Susette LaFlesche Tibbles* (1854-1903), daughter of Ponca chief Standing Bear and a prominent 19th century journalist and advocate of Indian rights.

1985-86—*Senator Gilbert M. Hitchcock* (1859-1934), born in Omaha, educated in Europe and practiced law from 1881-1885. Founded the *Omaha World-Herald* after entering the newspaper profession in the late 1880s, later represented Nebraska in the U.S. Congress.

1987-88—*Loren Eiseley* (1907-1977), poet, humanist, philosopher, naturalist, anthropologist, essayist and thinker. Professor of Anthropology at several universities following his graduation from the University of Nebraska.

Section 2

Interstate 80, dedicated October 19, 1974, is the major
motor route through the "Cornhusker" State, replacing the
old "Lincoln Highway" US Highway 30. A brass plaque,
near Sidney commemorates the dedication site.

This interstate begins at the Missouri River in Omaha
and runs south 55 miles to Lincoln before heading westward. From Lincoln I-80 follows the general route of the
Nebraska City-Fort Kearny Cutoff, established in 1861 as
a short cut from Nebraska City on the Missouri River to
Fort Kearny on the Platte River 160 miles west.

At Grand Island, 89 miles west of Lincoln, the interstate
runs parallel to the Platte River to North Platte 142 miles
west. At North Platte I-80 follows the South Platte to a
point near Julesburg, Colorado, before heading west again.

Just west of Grand Island I-80 follows the old Oregon
Trail and Pony Express route. Thousands of wagon trains
traveled over this route between 1845-1865. The Oregon
Trail route ran along the south side of the Platte River;
the Mormon Trail, along the north side of the river.

At North Platte, the Oregon Trail and Pony Express
routes generally followed the South Platte River to
Julesburg then turned back north into Nebraska,
to the Chimney Rock area on the south side of the North
Platte River. The Mormon Trail followed along the north
side of the North Platte River just east of present day
North Platte all the way to the Wyoming line.

Nebraska's sculpture garden, "a museum without walls",
features metal and stone diversions for motorist at nine rest
areas across the state, five westbound and four eastbound.
The rest areas are located near the Platte River, Blue
River, York, Grand Island, Kearney, Brady, Ogallala,
Sidney and Kimball.

The Asphalt Trail Across Nebraska: I-80

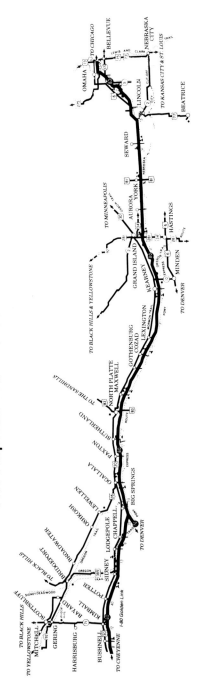

The major highway across Nebraska is Interstate 80, 455.3 miles in length and formally completed and dedicated October 19, 1974. Work began on the project March 8, 1955. This ribbon of concrete cuts through the center of the state until it reaches the panhandle area in the west where it follows a southern route. To fully appreciate Nebraska's rich heritage it is recommended travelers arm themselves with a good map of the state and then take a little time to see some of its most historic attractions.

OMAHA

Founded with the opening of the Nebraska Territory to settlement in 1854, OMAHA (pop. 312,929) was incorporated in 1857. The city was named for the Omaha Indians of the Hokan-Siouan linguistic stock, who ceded all their lands west of the Missouri River to the United States in 1854.

The Territory of Nebraska included the present states of Nebraska, North and South Dakota, all that part of Montana east of the Rocky Mountains, about three quarters of Wyoming and parts of Colorado. The entire population of this vast area was 2,732.

Even before 1854, what was to become Omaha played an important role in history.

Beginning in February 1846, and through the rest of the year, about 18,000 Mormons (members of **The Church of Jesus Christ of Latter Day Saints**) crossed Iowa by ox-drawn wagons enroute to the Great Salt Lake Basin after being driven from Nauvoo, Illinois. Led by **Brigham Young**, the vanguard of this migration reached the Missouri River June 14th near the future site of Council Bluffs, Iowa. Here they established a camp and named it Kaneville (probably for **Thomas L. Kane**, an unofficial agent for the U.S.).

The Mexican War erupted in the spring of 1846 and an Army recruiting officer was sent to recruit a battalion from the Mormon camps. Five hundred men, some wives as laundresses and boys as aids, volunteered and marched to Fort Leavenworth where they were outfitted to march to San Diego, California—the longest infantry march in history.

The departure of this contingent of able-bodied men, known in military history as the **"Mormon Battalion,"** greatly weakened the traveling ability of the Mormons by creating a shortage of manpower in their camps. The rainy weather of the previous four months had slowed their pace and it was too late in the year to push on to the Great Salt Lake region.

A campsite was selected on the west side of the river, across from Kaneville, on a high ridge in what is now the north section of Omaha. An agreement was reached with the chiefs of the Potawatomi and Omaha Indians and provided that this headquarters camp, Winter Quarters, would be used for only one winter.

Omaha was founded in 1854 by **William D. Brown, Dr. Enos Lowe, Jesse Lowe, Jesse Williams** and **Joseph H. D. Street**. The new town's name was suggested by Jesse Lowe. Omaha is an

Gateway City
Trail Map

Mormon Bridge

2. Mormon Cemetery, 4.1 miles to. . .

State Street

USS Hazard displayed in Freedom Park Marina, 2000 North 25E

Pershing

52nd Street

Florence

Eppley Airport

3. Omaha Home for Boys, 2.1 miles to. . .

30th Street

4. World War II Memorial Park, 7 miles to. . .

Dodge Street

1. Josyln Art Museum, 8.6 miles to. . .

5. Boys Town, 8.4 miles to. . .

Creighton University

13. Union Pacific Museum.

132nd Street

University of Nebraska at Omaha

Old Market

President Ford's Birthplace, 33rd and Woolworth Ave.

12. Henry Doorly Zoo, 3.3 miles to. . .

Center Street

6. Ak-Sar-Ben Field, 5.3 miles to. . .

42nd Street

Hanscom Park

Municipal Stadium

13th Street

L Street

7. Union Stock Yards, 7.3 miles to. . .

11. Mount Vernon Gardens, 1.8 miles to. . .

How To Use This Trail Guide

(1) Interesting places marked by Gateway City Trail signs.

Those places unnumbered on this map are not on the trail but are easily reached.

● Actual street locations.

Note: Please realize this map is not in scale. Total miles 1 to 13 = 58.8 miles.

Fontenelle Forest

US Highway 73-75

10. Bellevue Log Cabin, 5.6 miles to. . .

Mission

9. Oldest Church in Nebraska, 3/10th miles to. . .

8. SAC Headquarters and Aerospace Museum, 4 miles to. . .

14

Gateway City Trail Index

1. JOSLYN ART MUSEUM, 22nd and Dodge Sts. $10 million cultural center. Permanent and traveling art exhibits.

2. MORMON CEMETERY, 32nd and State Sts. Site of Brigham Young's encampment during the brutal winter of 1846 where more than 600 died.

3. OMAHA HOME FOR BOYS, Happy Hollow Blvd. A 70-acre tract with extensive 4-H program.

4. MEMORIAL PARK, 63rd and Dodge Sts. Omahans' dimes and dollars created this $500,000 memorial to the men and women who gave their lives in service during World War II.

5. BOYS TOWN, 10 miles west of downtown Omaha on 136th and West Rd. (US 30). Founded in 1917 by Father Edward Flanagan.

6. AK-SAR-BEN, 63rd and Shirley Sts. Ak-Sar-Ben, Nebraska spelled backwards, is nationally known for its rodeo, livestock shows and thoroughbred horse racing.

7. THE OMAHA LIVESTOCK MARKET, 29th and N Sts. One of the world's three largest markets for livestock receipts and processing. Overhead walkways provide an interesting view of this 100 acre operation.

8. SAC HEADQUARTERS AND AEROSPACE MUSEUM, 2510 Clay St., south of Bellevue on US 73 and 75.

9. OLDEST CHURCH IN NEBRASKA, Franklin and Mission Sts., Bellevue. Constructed in 1856 by Presbyterian missionaries.

10. BELLEVUE LOG CABIN, 1805 Hancock St. Built in the 1830s.

11. MOUNT VERNON GARDENS, 13th and Y Sts., Omaha. Replica of George washington's formal gardens overlook Missouri River.

12. HENRY DOORLY ZOO, 10th and Deer Park Blvd. Lions, tigers, buffalo, elk, deer and monkeys may be seen daily.

13. UNION PACIFIC HISTORICAL MUSEUM, 1416 Dodge St. Tells the story of the Great West. A large Abraham Lincoln exhibit.

There are many other attractions as indicated in the Historical Tour guide. The Gateway City Trail is designed to give the visitor a general overview of Greater Omaha. For more information about this and other Omaha attractions, contact the Greater Omaha Convention and Visitors Bureau, Omaha/Douglas Civic Center, 1819 Farnam St., Suite 1200, Omaha, NE 68183. Toll-free: 800-332-1819 or 800-334-1819 (in Nebraska).

Indian word meaning "above all others upon a stream." The ferry company operating between Iowa and Nebraska was responsible for laying out the town. Lots were sold for $25 each.

By July 1854 the first building was erected at what is now 12th and Jackson Sts. The building, best known as the Claim House, was Omaha's first hotel. Roman Catholics built the first church, St. Mary's, on Howard St. between 8th and 9th, in 1856. The Congregationalists built the first Protestant church at 16th and Farnam.

The Nebraska Territorial capital was located in Omaha from 1854-67. The first Territorial legislature met in Omaha January 16, 1855 in a small two story brick building on 9th St., between Douglas and Farnam. This building was used for the 1855-57 legislative sessions before being moved to 20th and Dodge Sts. This building was used until the capital was moved to Lincoln in 1868. The site of the old territorial capitol is currently the site of Omaha's Central High School, constructed in 1912. The central court of the school represents the approximate area of the original capitol.

The first telegraph line between Omaha and St. Louis was completed October 5, 1860. The Western Union Telegraph Company, under the leadership of **Edward Creighton**, strung the first telegraph wires west from Omaha. The transcontinental telegraph line was completed July 4, 1861.

Omaha's first bank opened and closed in 1857. St. Joseph's Hospital is the oldest hospital in the city, founded in 1870.

Upon completion of the transcontinental railroad in 1869, Omaha became an important rail center developing into a trading, processing and shipping point for the Midwest's agricultural empire. In 1871 a meat packing plant was opened and five years later the Union Stock Yard Company was formed. Omaha continues to be one of the nation's major livestock markets and meat packing centers.

Eugene C. Eppley (1883-1958), a hotel empire builder, was one of Omaha's benefactors through the **Eugene C. Eppley Foundation**. For example, land for Omaha's Civic Center was donated by the foundation. The city's airport is named in honor of Mr. Eppley.

Two brothers, **Edward** and **John A. Creighton**, involved in numerous business enterprises in the West, including the building of the telegraph across the plains, are memorialized in Omaha's **Creighton University**, founded in 1878.

16

Other colleges and universities include the **University of Nebraska at Omaha, College of St. Mary, University of Nebraska Medical Center, Bellevue College, Metropolitan Technical Community College** and **Grace College of the Bible**.

The **Woodmen of the World Life Insurance Society** was founded in Omaha in 1890. Today the city is headquarters for more than 30 insurance companies, including **Mutual of Omaha** —the world's largest health and accident insurance company.

The city was host to the Trans-Mississippi and International Exposition of 1898.

Today Omaha serves as a major distribution center in the midwest, undergirded by a strong and diversifed economic base. Among some of the major companies represented in the city are the Union Pacific, Western Electric, Northwestern Bell Telephone Company, Bozell and Jacobs Advertising Agency, Cudahy Foods, InterNorth Guarantee Mutual Life and Peter Kiewit and Sons.

Popular actor **Marlon Brando** was born April 3, 1924 in Omaha. He received Academy Awards for his performances in "On the Waterfront" (1954) and "The Godfather" (1972).

Other personalities born in Omaha include **Melvin Laird** (1922-), Secretary of Defense under President Richard Nixon; **Max Baer** (1909-1959), who became the world heavyweight boxing champion in 1934; **Paul Williams** (1940-), singer, composer and actor; **Montgomery Clift** (1920-66), screen actor; **Nick Nolte** (1942-), screen and TV actor; and **Dorothy McGuire** (1919-), screen actress. Baseball star **Bob Gibson** (1935-) is also a native of Omaha.

Omaha has preserved much of its history. There are several historic places in the city open to the public.

WINTER QUARTERS, North 30th and State Sts., where the Omaha waterworks are today, was occupied from September 1846 to June 1848. The Mormons built a town of log houses, complete with streets and house names, to provide for 3,600 people during the winter of 1846-47. It was the largest settlement in the region. The mill built by the Mormons to grind their wheat into flour still stands. So does the Winter Quarters (Mormon) Cemetery with an impressive monument to the pioneers and its 600 graves, testifying to the hardships suffered by these people. Mormon records indicate more than 340 deaths in Winter Quarters during the harsh winter of 1846-47.

MORMON MONUMENT AT WINTER QUARTERS—The line draw-
ing here depicts the Winter Quarters Monument, located in the Mormon Cemetery in North Omaha. The monument shows sorrowing
Mormon parents at their infant child's grave and commemorates the
hardships suffered by the Mormons here in 1846-48.

Various illnesses of epidemic proportions ravaged the camp.
One was called "black canker" or "inflammation of the bowels,"
probably a form of scurvy since there was a lack of fresh fruits
and vegetables. Many deaths were attributed to this illness.

18

Other deaths were caused by "brain fever," probably typhoid fever; "inflammation of the lungs" and "lung fever," probably pneumonia; and "congestive fever," probably tuberculosis, according to Mormon church records of those times.

The spring of 1848 marked the departure of three Mormon companies from Winter Quarters, each with about 1,000 persons. Only a few hundred remained behind and because permanent settlement on Indian lands was prohibited, they abandoned the camp and moved back across the river into Iowa.

In 1854 a group of merchants and real estate promoters from Council Bluffs acquired title to the former Winters Quarters and organized the city of Florence. Florence competed with Omaha and Bellevue a few years later for the Nebraska Territorial capital, losing to Omaha which finally annexed Florence during World War I.

The Mormons had constructed and operated a ferryboat connecting the Iowa settlements with Winter Quarters. Each spring, into the late 1850s, parties of Mormons bound for the Great Salt Lake Basin used this ferry and organized their wagon trains for their western trek of more than 1,000 miles. Today the Pioneer Memorial (Mormon) Bridge (I-680), connecting Iowa with the Florence suburbs of Omaha, is situated approximately where the old Mormon ferry operated. The bridge was dedicated in 1953.

THE WINTER QUARTERS CEMETERY MONUMENT, the heroic sized monument at Winter Quarters Cemetery, was dedicated by **The Church of Jesus Christ of Latter-Day Saints** September 20, 1936. The sculptor was **Avard Fairbanks**, an internationally known artist from Salt Lake City. It shows sorrowing parents at the open grave of their infant child. The father is shown with his arm and cloak around his mourning wife, protecting her from the chilling wind and sharing with her his physical and spiritual strength in this time of mutual crisis. The stone rectangular forms near the monument indicate the location of graves found when the monument base was set in place. In front of the monument, cast in bronze, are the names of the known dead who are buried here.

The cemetery is owned by the City of Omaha and is leased and maintained by the Mormons. The cemetery and visitors' center is open daily 9 a.m. to 9 p.m.

HOW TO REACH MORMON PIONEER CEMETERY—From I-80, north on I-480 to US 73 (also designated as 30th St.), north on US 73 to State St. (at Florence Park) and turn west for three blocks. Distance is approximately 10 miles. From I-680, turn off at Canyon Road, drive south to 30th St., south on 30th St. for seven blocks to State St., west on State St. for three blocks. Distance is approximately one mile.

FORT OMAHA, 30th and Fort Sts., construction began November 20, 1868 when Omaha was described as "two or three blocks of warehouses, shops and offices, among them a theatre. It boasted a two or three half blocks in brick, a number of frame shops, as well as bar rooms and cheap eating houses, all ending at the Herndon House, at the edge of the steep bluffs which stand well above the highest floods of the Missouri."

Sherman Barracks, the original name of the post, was four miles northwest of the city and almost two miles from the Missouri River. Ten 30' x 80' wooden barracks and 14 officers' quarters were arranged around a rectangular parade ground. The name of the post was soon changed to **Omaha Barracks** and in 1878 again changed to **Fort Omaha**.

The post was headquarters for the Army's Department of the Platte, whose mission was to keep the frontier safe from Indians. The main offices were in downtown Omaha until 1870 when a number of buildings were added. **Brig. Gen. George Crook** established his headquarters here when he was appointed commanding general of the Department of the Platte in 1875.

In 1877 six companies from Fort Omaha were sent to Chicago during a bitter railroad strike. In 1879 a company of troops was sent to Hastings to convince a mob that it was unwise to threaten a federal court during a murder trial involving cattlemen and homesteaders.

Fort Omaha was closed in 1896 but reopened in 1905 as a training center for non-commissioned officers of the Signal Corps. With the installation of a balloon house and hydrogen-gas-making facility, the first balloon flight was made in April, 1909. This flight inaugurated the beginning of the Army's first regular lighter-than-air center. It closed again in 1913 but reopened in 1916 as a training center for crews of Army observation balloons —the first military balloon school in America. About 16,000 men were trained here during World War I.

During World War II the fort served as a support installation for the 7th Service Command, an induction center, and a work camp for Italian war prisoners. After the war the post was turned over to the U.S. Navy and became the Naval and Marine Corps Reserve Center until 1974. The fort's grounds are now largely oc-

AN INDIAN FIGHTER—Brig. Gen. George Crook (1828-1890), famous Civil War cavalry leader and an Indian fighter, made his headquarters in Omaha for several years while serving as commander of the Department of the Platte. At the time of his death in 1890, Crook, with the rank of major general, commanded the Division of Missouri.

GENERAL CROOK HOUSE MUSEUM—This restored residence was built in 1878 for Brig. Gen. George Crook, commander of the Department of the Platte. The museum is located at Fort Omaha, 30th and Fort Sts., and is open to the public.

cupied by Metropolitan Community College, which began classes in 1975.

GENERAL CROOK HOUSE, at Fort Omaha, was built in 1878 to serve as the residence for the commander of the Department of the Platte. Since its completion it has been known as the General Crook House in honor of its first occupant, **Brig. Gen. George Crook**, who with his wife, Mary, came to live in the house in the fall of 1879. The house is one of the few surviving examples of Italianate style architecture in Omaha.

Crook graduated from West Point in 1852 at the age of 23. At the outbreak of the Civil War, he took command of an Ohio regiment with the rank of colonel. He soon commanded a brigade and by 1863 was a cavalry division commander. He was one of Gen. Philip H. Sheridan's corps commanders in the Shenandoah Valley campaign and directed a cavalry division in the final fighting around Richmond.

After the Civil War, General Crook gained fame as an Indian fighter. He operated successfully against the Paiute and Snake Indians in Idaho and then against Apaches in Arizona. As head of the Department of the Platte, he was engaged in the hard-fought Sioux War of 1876. Back in Arizona, in 1883, General Crook led an expedition against a Chiricahua band of Apaches and was finally able to persuade **Geronimo**, their leader, to return to the reservation in 1884.

General Crook served as commanding general of the Department of the Platte from 1875 to 1882 and from 1886 to 1888. The same year he moved into his new quarters at Fort Omaha he became involved in the trial of **Standing Bear**, a Ponca chief. Standing Bear and 30 of his tribe were arrested when they left their reservation in Indian Territory (Oklahoma) and returned to Nebraska to bury Standing Bear's son. As head of the Department of the Platte, Crook was named defendant for the government, although his sympathies were with the Indians. The plight of the Poncas was brought to light in an interview by newspaper correspondent **Thomas Tibbles**, who enlisted the aid of two prominent Omaha attorneys, **Andrew Poppleton** and **John Lee Webster**, to defend Standing Bear. The resulting court decision ruled, for the first time in the history of the United States, an Indian was a "person" within the meaning of the law and the act of habeas corpus applied to him.

In 1886 Crook was promoted to the rank of major general and given command of the Division of Missouri two years later, a post he held until his death in 1890.

As you enter the Crook House, Quarters No. 1, you step back in history at a time in which Omaha was home to pioneers, Indians, cowboys, mule trains, and the United States Army. Restored is a living history, "touch" museum by the Douglas County Historical Society. The house is used for classes, meetings, tours, and social events. Authentic antiques appropriate to the period embellish the lovely rooms and complement the original oak and walnut flooring. Crook, with his usual disdain for ostentation, rejected and altered the original $10,000 plan, building the house for $7,716. The soldiers did the work.

Imagine the sumptuous buffet served in November, 1879 to honor former President Ulysses S. Grant and his wife. The occasion came so soon after completion of the house that the Crook's household furnishings had not yet arrived from the East. China, silver, furniture—all were borrowed from Omaha residents to entertain the Grants. The Grant reception and one held the following year for President and Mrs. Rutherford B. Hayes have since been described as "two remarkable events" in Omaha's social history.

Crook House, the last outpost on the western plains, was formal, a residence built to house generals and entertain dignitaries. Today the General Crook House Museum is listed on the National Register of Historic Places.

The General Crook House is open 10 to 4 p.m., Monday through Friday and 1 to 4 p.m., Sunday or by appointment, (402) 455-9990. Closed on major holidays. Admission is charged.

HOW TO REACH THE GENERAL CROOK HOUSE— Dodge St. to 30th; north to Fort St. or I-680 30th St. exit south to Fort St. Fort Omaha is at 30th and Fort Sts.

UNION PACIFIC HISTORICAL MUSEUM, 1416 Dodge St., through displays of documents, maps and pictures, along with thousands of exhibits, tells the story of the settling of the West and the role of the railroad in that settlement. The transcontinental railroad was completed in 1869.

This herculean feat was accomplished by the Union Pacific, builders from the east, and the Central Pacific, the builders from the west, in three years, six months and 10 days after construction actually got underway in 1865.

The transcontinental railroad had been envisioned and talked about as early as 1830. **Daniel Webster** argued in Congress for a Pacific railroad that year and several journalists urged for a rail-

FOCUS ON RAILROAD WESTERN HISTORY—Railroads played an important part in the development of the West and the Union Pacific was one of the major lines. An excellent railroad history is found in the exhibits and displays in the Union Pacific Historical Museum in Omaha.

road to span the country at the same time.

It was **President Abraham Lincoln** who pressed for the construction of a transcontinental railroad and gained support in Congress. **The Pacific Railroad Act of 1862** was signed into law by Lincoln July 1, 1862.

There were heavy politics involved in the selection of the route west and heavy pressures to start the transcontinental railroad from St. Joseph, Missouri, and St. Louis. The matter was settled December 2, 1862 when President Lincoln sent this telegram to **Peter Dey**, the chief engineer for the Union Pacific, at his Omaha headquarters:

"Fulfilling the responsibility placed upon me by the Act of July

1, 1862, I have affixed the initial point of the Pacific Railroad on the western boundary of the State of Iowa, opposite Omaha—opposite Section 10, in Township 15, north of Range 13, east of the sixth principal meridian, in the Territory of Nebraska."

The Union Pacific Railroad was organized that year. Construction of the railroad did not begin until 1865 because of the Civil War.

The Union Pacific Historical Museum has had more than a million visitors since its inception in 1921. Along with the story of railroad locomotives and equipment, the museum boasts one of the most complete Lincolniana displays in the country, including an executive order signed by the President in 1863 with **"Abraham Lincoln"** rather than **"A. Lincoln"** which became his familiar signature.

There is a section devoted to the Indians, whose presence was strongly felt during the opening of the American West. Another section highlights the outlaw period and their impact on the railroad as well as their frontier settlements.

The free museum is open daily 9 a.m. to 5 p.m., Monday through Friday and 9 a.m. to 1 p.m., Saturday.

HOW TO REACH THE UNION PACIFIC HISTORICAL MUSEUM—From I-80, north on US 75 (13th St.) to Dodge St. The distance is approximately 2.1 miles. From I-680, south on Canyon Road to 30th St. (also US 73) and follow US 73 south to Dodge St. The distance is approximately 7.5 miles. From I-480, off on Dodge St. just after crossing the Missouri River into Nebraska, west on Dodge St. to 13th St.

BOYS TOWN, 136th and West Dodge Road, an unincorporated village on a 1,500 acre site west of Omaha, provides a home and education for approximately 500 boys between the ages of 10 and 18. The charter now permits the Home to care for girls as well as boys.

A young Irish emigrant priest, **Father Edward J. Flanagan**, became discouraged with his work with the "lost men" of Workingmen's Hotel and changed his life's direction during the Christmas season of 1917. He gave a home to three youthful wards of the court and two homeless newsboys at that time. He began his home for the homeless by borrowing $90 to pay the rent on a large rooming house on the edge of downtown Omaha.

Soon his home was filled with homeless, neglected and troubled young boys and larger quarters were sought. In 1921 Father Flanagan found Overlook Farm on the rolling prairies west of

The celebrated Boys Town statue in Omaha.

CULTURAL CENTER HOUSES WESTERN ART—The $10 million Joslyn Art Museum in Omaha houses one of the most comprehensive collections of Western art in America.

Omaha. He made his down payment on the farm and moved his Boys' Home there in October 1921. Father Flanagan's motto: *"There is no such thing as a bad boy. There is only bad environment, bad training, and bad example, bad thinking."*

Father Flanagan gave his boys a town, a **Boys Town**, which inspired the founding of similar homes around the world.

Boys Town was the subject of a 1938 movie starring **Spencer Tracy** and **Mickey Rooney**.

After World War II Father Flanagan was asked to serve as a consultant for our government in dealing with the problems of the war orphans in post-war Europe. During a visit to Berlin in the spring of 1948 he suffered a fatal heart attack and died May 15th. His body was brought home and now rests in the Father Flanagan Shrine on the Boys Town campus.

Monsignor Nicholas H. Wegner, a long time friend of Father Flanagan and who had dedicated St. James Orphanage in Omaha, was chosen to be his successor. Monsignor carried on an ambitious building program at Boys Town. After 25 years at Boys Town, Monsignor Wegner retired in 1973.

Father Robert P. Hupp, a Navy chaplain during World War II and founding pastor of Omaha's Christ the King Parish, succeeded Monsignor Wegner. He has continued to expand the work at Boys Town and it was under his leadership that the charter was changed to permit the Home to care for girls as well as boys.

Half a million visitors tour Boys Town annually. Hours: 8 a.m. to 4:30 p.m., Monday through Saturday; 8:30 a.m. to 4:30 p.m., Sunday.

27

A TRIPLE CROWN WINNER NAMED OMAHA—1935 Triple Crown winner, Omaha, died in 1959 and is buried at Ak-Sar-Ben race track in Omaha.

HOW TO REACH BOYS TOWN—From downtown Omaha, west on Dodge St. (US 6) to 136th St. From the east, I-80 to I-680, north to W. Dodge St., west on Dodge St. to 136th St. From the west, I-80 to I-680, north to W. Dodge St., west on Dodge to 136th St. or west from Lincoln or Wahoo on US 6. The distance is approximately 10 miles from downtown Omaha.

WESTERN HERITAGE MUSEUM/OMAHA HISTORY MUSEUM, 801 South 10th St., Omaha, is operated by the Western Heritage Society, organized in October 1973 to establish a museum in Omaha's Union Station. The building was constructed between 1929-31 and is considered one of the finest examples of Art Deco architecture in the world. It is listed on the National Register of Historic Places.

The museum houses exhibits that present the area's regional history with an emphasis on Omaha.

The museum is open year-round. The hours are 10 a.m. to 5 p.m., Tuesday through Saturday; 1 to 5 p.m., Sunday. It is closed Mondays and major holidays. Admission is charged.

HOW TO REACH THE WESTERN HERITAGE MUSEUM/OMAHA HISTORY MUSEUM —From I-80, north

A FAMOUS SON—Gerald R. Ford, 38th President of the United States, was born in Omaha July 14, 1913. His parents were Leslie and Dorothy King, who were divorced when their son was still a baby. Mrs. King moved to Michigan and married Gerald Rudolph Ford who adopted the small boy and changed his name.

BIRTH SITE OF A PRESIDENT—A rose garden in Omaha marks the site of President Gerald R. Ford's birthplace.

on US 73 (13th St.) to Pacific, east two blocks on Pacific to 10th St., north two blocks. The distance is approximately two miles. From I-480 (just after crossing over from Iowa) turn west on Douglas St. (US 6) to 10th St., south on 10th St. The distance is approximately one mile.

JOSLYN ART MUSEUM, 2200 Dodge St., is a $10 million cultural center completed in 1931 as a memorial to Omaha businessman **George A. Joslyn** by his wife, Sarah. The three-level structure houses representative works reflecting man's artistic achievements during the past 2,000 years. The museum also includes one of the most comprehensive collections of Western American art in the country.

Featured is an on-going series of temporary exhibitions, educational activities and performing arts events. Museum hours are 10 a.m. to 5 p.m., Tuesday through Saturday; 1 to 5 p.m., Sunday. Admission is charged.

HOW TO REACH THE JOSLYN ART MUSEUM—From I-80, turn north on I-480, exit at Dodge St. and drive east four blocks. The distance is approximately 2¼ miles.

PRESIDENT GERALD R. FORD'S BIRTH SITE, 32nd St. and Woolworth Ave., is commemorated in a rose garden with a fountain. The house in which the President was born as **Leslie King** was razed in 1975 after a fire partially destroyed it in 1971. **James Paxton**, president of the Standard Chemical Manufacturing Co., Omaha, purchased the site and has paid for the memorial. The property has been turned over to the City of Omaha. The hours are 8 a.m. to 9 p.m., year-round. Admission is free.

The 38th president of the United States was born **Leslie Lynch King**, July 14, 1913. His father operated a family wool business in Omaha. His parents were divorced when he was about two years old. His mother, Dorothy, moved to Grand Rapids, Michigan, and in 1916 she married **Gerald Rudolph Ford**, who owned a small paint company in the city. Ford adopted the three year old boy and gave him his name.

FREEDOM PARK MARINA, 2000 North 25E, East Omaha, has a floating naval museum. Visitors experience actual conditions aboard the minesweeper, *U.S.S. Hazard*, which was launched May 21, 1944, and still has all systems in operating condition. A miniature aircraft carrier, the *Enterprise Junior*, and training submarine used by the U. S. Navy, the *U.S.S. Marlin*, complete the naval museum.

MOUNT VERNON GARDENS, 13th & Y Sts., overlooks the

A RHINO 25 MILLION YEARS AGO—This gigantic, hornless rhino, which ranged over Asia 25 million years ago, has been reproduced and is displayed in the University of Nebraska's State Museum's "Elephant Hall" with hundreds of other exhibits. This prehistoric rhino stood 17 feet tall. Other exhibits feature the mastodants which once roamed over Nebraska.

Missouri River from a site passed by the explorers, **Captains Meriwether Lewis** and **William Clark**, in 1804. The garden is a replica of George Washington's formal gardens at his Virginia estate at Mount Vernon.

HOW TO REACH MOUNT VERNON GARDENS—From I-80, exit south on 13th St. (US 73) and drive south to Mandan Park. The distance is approximately 2.1 miles.

GREAT PLAINS BLACK MUSEUM, 2213 Lake St., highlights the history of black people west of the Mississippi River through a collection of artifacts and exhibits. The hours are 9 a.m. to 5 p.m. weekdays. Admission is charged.

HISTORIC MILL, in historic Florence, 9200 N. 30th St. (US 73), Omaha, is the oldest mill in Nebraska, constructed by the Mormons at Winter Quarters the winter of 1846-47. It cannot be toured but is open year-round for viewing.

HISTORIC DEPOT, in historic Florence, 9000 N. 29th St., is a railroad museum featuring relics from the late 1800s. It is open Sunday, 1 to 5 p.m., from May to September. For private tour information, call (402) 453-4462. Admission is free.

BANK OF FLORENCE, in historic Florence, 8505 N 30th St. (US 73), has been restored and houses artifacts and relics from the mid-1800s. The bank was chartered January 18, 1856 and closed in 1859. It is open Sunday 1 to 5 p.m. from May to September. For private tour information, call (402) 453-4462. Admission is free.

TOLL HOUSE, in historic Florence, 8500 N. 30th St. (US 73), is an original toll booth from the Mormon Bridge. It is open Sunday 1 to 5 p.m. from May to September. For private tour information, call (402) 453-4462. Admission is free.

VALLEY HISTORICAL MUSEUM, Alexander and Park Ave., Valley, features historical artifacts, clothing, war and railroad mementos. It is open Sunday, 2 to 4 p.m., from May to September. Admission is free.

Other Omaha Attractions

WORLD WAR II MEMORIAL, Dodge St. and Happy Hollow Blvd., is a $500,000 memorial dedicated to the men and women who gave their lives in military service during World War II.

OMAHA'S CHILDREN'S MUSEUM, 18th St. and St. Mary's Ave., is open the year-round, closed on Mondays. June 1-September 20: 10 a.m. to noon and 1 to 5 p.m., Tuesday through Friday; and 1 to 5 p.m., weekends. September 20-June 1: 2:30 to 5 p.m., Tuesday and Wednesday; 10 a.m. to 5 p.m., Thursday through Saturday; and 1 to 5 p.m., Sunday. Admission is charged.

OLD MARKET, 11th and Howard Sts., features an array of shops, restaurants, theaters and galleries in the section of town that once served as Omaha's fruit and vegetable market. It is registered as a National Historic District.

MUTUAL OF OMAHA DOME, 33rd and Dodge Sts., Mutual of Omaha Plaza, is a three-story, 19,000 square feet underground addition capped with a massive glass dome. This is one of the

OMAHA'S OLD MARKET PASSAGEWAY—The Old Market, 11th and Howard Sts., features an array of shops and other attractions that once served as Omaha's fruit and vegetable market.

most unique office buildings in the city. The dome is open year-round and tours are available Monday through Friday. Admission is free.

AK-SAR-BEN FIELD AND COLISEUM (Nebraska spelled backward), 63rd and Shirley Sts., Omaha, offers thoroughbred horse racing from May through July each year. One of the largest entertainment/exposition centers of its kind in the world, Ak-Sar-Ben was founded in 1895. A famous racehorse, **Omaha**, is buried at Ak-Sar-Ben. His sire, **Gallant Fox**, was the 1930 winner of the triple crown, and **Omaha** succeeded him to this title in 1935. To win the triple crown in horseracing, a three-year-old must win the Kentucky Derby, Preakness and Belmont Stakes. They are the only father-son combination to achieve this honor.

BELLEVUE

Just south of Omaha is historic Sarpy County and its largest city is BELLEVUE (pop. 21,674), Nebraska's oldest community. It traces its founding to 1822 when the **Missouri Fur Company** established a permanent post here. Well-known to such explorers and trappers as **Stephen Long, John C. Fremont, Kit Carson** and **Jed Smith**, Bellevue was headquarters to **Lucien Fontenelle** the French aristocrat who turned Mountain Man.

Bellevue became an important river port and attracted many

The Asphalt Trail

Interstate 80, completed October 19, 1974, is the major motor route through the "Cornhusker" State, replacing the old "Lincoln Highway," US Highway 30. A brass plaque can be found near Sidney, marking the site of the dedication of the highway.

The interstate begins as one crosses the Missouri River at Omaha and runs south to Lincoln before turning west. At Lincoln I-80 follows the general route of the Nebraska City-Fort Kearny Cut-off.

Just west of Grand Island, I-80 follows the old Oregon Trail and Pony Express route.

STATE'S OLDEST PUBLIC BUILDING—This building at 2212 Main St., Bellevue, is believed to be the oldest commercial public building in Nebraska. It housed the Fontenelle Bank (1856), Sarpy County courthouse (1857), and Bellevue City Hall (1875-1959). It now serves as a museum operated by the Sarpy County Historical Museum.

well-known, early-day travelers. **Prince Maximilian** and **Karl Bodmer** were aboard the *Yellowstone* during one of its calls in 1833. Bodmer's Bellevue landscape is displayed in Omaha's **Joslyn Art Museum**. Other famous artists to chronicle the settlement's activities and personalities included **George Catlin, Alfred Jacob Miller** and **Rudolph Friederick Kurz**. Catlin's portrait of **Chief Big Elk** hangs in the Smithsonian's Museum of Natural History.

Baptist missionaries, **Moses** and **Eliza Merrill**, arrived in Bellevue in 1833 and were followed by Presbyterians **Samuel Allis** and **John Dunbar**. **Father Pierre Jean DeSmet** was a frequent visitor. **Dr. Marcus Whitman**, the famed Oregon missionary-physician, attended Bellevue residents in 1835.

Brigham Young and his Mormons were befriended in this area in 1846 by **Chief Big Elk** and **Peter Sarpy**, fur trader and settlement leader, for whom the county is named. The settlement was a major river crossing for Mormon and Oregon Trail pioneers and the "49-ers."

Permanent settlement by whites came in 1854 with the creation of the Nebraska Territory. **Francis Burt** of Pendleton, South Carolina, was appointed the first territorial governor by **President Franklin Pierce**. He took the oath of office at Mission House, October 16, 1854, and died two days later. Omaha, rather than Bellevue, became the capital of the new territory amid charges of political hanky panky.

The four other Sarpy County communities include GRETNA (pop. 1,606), LAVISTA (pop. 8,756), PAPILLION (pop. 6,377) and SPRINGFIELD (pop. 776). Bellevue served as the county seat of Sarpy County until 1875 when it was moved to Papillion. The county was formed February 7, 1857.

Papillion, meaning butterfly in French, was platted in 1870. Gretna was incorporated in 1889 and LaVista, in 1960. The small community of Springfield suffered a disastrous fire March 19, 1903, when half the town burned as the result of a fire which broke out in the local bowling alley.

Fort Crook, which became headquarters for the U. S. Air Force's **Strategic Air Command** in 1948, was established in 1891. The fort was named to honor the Civil War general and Indian fighter, **George Crook**. It was a recruiting and indoctrination station for troops departing for Cuba and the Philippines during the Spanish-American War and was used to train motor transportation specialists during World War I.

In 1924 a small air facility on the post was dedicated to **1st Lt. Jarvis James Offutt**, Omaha's first World War I air casualty, killed while ferrying an airplane from England to France.

The base continued to be used for various military assignments until World War II when a section served as a prisoner-of-war camp, one of several in Nebraska. These POW camps were used to confine German and Italian soldiers captured in the North African and Italian campaigns and brought to the United States.

EARLY PRESBYTERIAN CHURCH—This Presbyterian Church, 2002 Franklin St., Bellevue, was built in 1856. It is now part of the Sarpy County Historical Museum complex and tours start at the main museum.

The Martin-Nebraska Bomber Co. also leased land and facilities at the fort during the war. They built 1,585 B-26 Marauder and 531 B-29 Superfortress bombers. The *"Enola Gay"* and *"Bock's Car,"* of Hiroshima and Nagaski fame, rolled off the assembly lines at this facility.

The Army Air Corps assumed control of Fort Crook in 1946 and renamed it **Offutt Field**. In 1948 the USAF took control of the base, named it **Offutt Air Force Base** and established SAC headquarters here.

There are many historical points of interest and other attractions for visitors in this area. Among these are:

THE STRATEGIC AIR COMMAND MUSEUM, 2510 Clay St., Bellevue, presents the history of flight with a variety of displays including fighters, bombers, cargo planes, helicopters and missiles of yesterday. Visitors may experience the excitement of a SAC Red Alert through the Alert Center via a multi-media presentation. There are many other exhibits depicting the brief but important history of military flight.

The hours are 8 a.m. to 5 p.m. daily except Thanksgiving Day, Christmas, New Year's Day and Easter. Admission is charged.

HOW TO REACH THE STRATEGIC COMMAND MUSEUM—From I-80 in Omaha, take US 73 and US 75 exit south to N-370, east on N-370 to museum entrance. From I-80 south of Omaha, take N-370 exit east to Bellevue.

SARPY COUNTY HISTORICAL MUSEUM, 2402 Clay St., traces Nebraska's history from 1804 Lewis and Clark exploration and features exhibits of Indian and pioneer living. Admission is charged.

HOW TO REACH THE SARPY COUNTY HISTORICAL MUSEUM—From I-80, see directions to SAC Museum.

FONTANELLE BANK, 2212 Main St., was incorporated as Nebraska's first bank in 1855 and it failed in 1857. The bank building was constructed of handmade bricks in 1856 along the Greek Revival lines. It served as the seat of county government until 1875. It served as the town hall from that time until 1959. This is Nebraska's oldest commercial public building. Historical documents are displayed in the building, listed on the National Register of Historic Places.

THE FIRST PRESBYTERIAN CHURCH, 2002 Franklin St., was built between 1856-58 and is the oldest church building in Nebraska. One of the major exhibits is the handcrafted grand piano brought by steamboat to Bellevue in 1855. The piano had been ordered by **Peter Sarpy**, the fur trader. The building was used for church services for more than a century, until it was replaced by a new church in 1959. The original church building is listed on the National Register of Historic Places. Admission is free.

PIONEER LOG CABIN, 1805 Hancock St., was built of hand-hewn cottonwood in the 1830s and is the state's oldest building. The one and a half story cabin is furnished with period pieces. The cabin is listed on the National Register of Historic Places.

The Strategic Air Command Aerospace Museum is in Bellevue.

HAMILTON HOUSE (a private residence), 2003 Bluff St., was the elegant frontier home built by the Presbyterian missionary, the **Rev. William Hamilton**. The exterior limestone walls are two feet thick and the home is listed on the National Register of Historic Places. Please Note: This house is a private residence and not open to the public.

FONTANELLE FOREST, 1111 Bellevue Blvd. N, is a 1,250-acre natural wilderness where some 40 varieties of trees and 200 species of birds thrive. Naturalists guide tourists along marked trails, to deep ravines, loess ridges, marshes and ancient Indian earth lodges amid splendid arrays of wildflowers and wildlife. Fontanelle Forest is listed as a National Natural History Landmark, National Natural Area, National Environmental Education Landmark and is on the National Register of Historic Places. Admission is charged at the Nature Center.

PIONEER CEMETERY, Lord Blvd. at 13th Ave., provides a sweeping view of the Missouri River Valley. On the highest point, a monument marks the grave of **Big Elk**, the last full-blooded Omaha Indian chief.

MISSION HOUSE MARKER, Warren St. between 18th and 19th Aves., pinpoints the location of the **Presbyterian Indian Mission** that played an important social and civic role in the early days of this frontier settlement.

Other Bellevue Attractions

HAWORTH PARK, N-370 at Payne Dr., offers complete camping facilities, sports complex, picnic areas, fishing pond, river marina and railroad museum.

BELLEVUE MARINA, in Haworth Park, offers complete boating facilities and boarding for the river cruiser, *Belle of Brownville.* The annual raft regatta held on Labor Day draws many visitors.

ST. COLUMBANS MISSION, north end of Calhoun St., serves as the national headquarters for the **Society of St. Columbans**. It is a short walk to Our Lady of Lourdes Grotto. A display of antique oriental art is in the administration building. The chapel contains magnificent stained glass windows.

GIFFORD POINT, east of Camp Gifford Road, is located on a 1,675-acre park, home of a large deer herd. Admission is by annual pass only (available weekdays from Metropolitan Educational Program Agency, 700 Camp Gifford Rd.). Gifford Point is open only on weekends and holidays.

AK-SAR-BEN AQUARIUM—Nine miles southeast of Gretna, on N-31, is the Ak-Sar-Ben Aquarium and Gretna Fish Hatchery Museum, both housed at Schramm Park State Recreation Area.

GRETNA

GRETNA (pop. 1,606), south of Omaha, off I-80, is worth a stop for tourists interested in fish. The **Ak-Sar-Ben Aquarium** is housed at Schramm Park State Recreation Area, nine miles south of Gretna on N-31. This aquarium has been described as "one of a kind" in the midwest. Just south of the aquarium is the **Gretna Fish Hatchery Museum,** on the site of the state's first fish hatchery, which recalls the early days of fish management. Hours are 10 a.m. to 6 p.m. weekends and holidays, and 10 a.m. to 5 p.m. weekdays, Memorial Day to Labor Day. Winter hours are 10 a.m. to 4:30 p.m., Monday and Wednesday. Schramm Park State Recreation Area is open year-round, sunrise to sunset. A State Park Permit ($2 daily, $10 annual) is required. The aquarium is closed Tuesdays, Thanksgiving, Christmas and New Year's Day. To reach the aquarium from I-80, take Exit 432 and go south six miles on N-31.

Two of Nebraska's famous sculpture gardens (there are nine located along I-80) are located west of Gretna at the Platte River eastbound rest area and the Blue River eastbound rest area. *Memorial to the American Bandshell* is at the Platte River eastbound rest area, just south of the Platte River and north of Lincoln. The concept is related to the bandshell, important historical

41

and social aspect of American towns.

Arrival by **Paul Von Ringelheim** is a graceful 35-foot tall sculpture that celebrates the strength and foresight of the pioneers who tamed the Nebraska plains. It's located at the Blue River easthound rest area, just east of the N-15 overpass near Goehner.

LINCOLN—THE STATE CAPITAL

LINCOLN (pop. 171,787), county seat of Lancaster County, became Nebraska's capital city in 1867 when it was a tiny village with only 30 residents. Originally called **Lancaster**, the town was renamed to honor **President Abraham Lincoln**.

Lancaster County was created March 6, 1855 by an act of the Territorial legislature. The town of Lancaster was first settled in 1864. There were large salt deposits in this area which were developed commercially.

It is 59 miles from Omaha to Lincoln via I-80. There are five interchanges from I-80 to Lincoln: Exit 405, 56th St.; Exit 401A, 9th St. (I-180, US 34); Exit 399, Municipal Airport and Cornhusker Highway; Exit 396, West O St. (US 6, N-2); and Exit 395, N.W. 48th St.

The first settler in the county was **John Prey**, who staked out his claim about 12 miles south of present day Lincoln in 1856. A committee was formed in 1859 to select a county seat and they chose a site, now part of Lincoln, and named their new town Lancaster for Lancaster County, Pennsylvania. July 3, 1863, **Elder J. M. Young** arrived, searching for a site for a Methodist colony to establish a female seminary. Young settled in Lancaster.

When Lancaster was selected for the new state capital it was briefly called Capital City. A bill was passed in the state legislature a short time later renaming the town Lincoln.

Lincoln was selected as the capital (Nebraska became the 37th state March 1, 1867) through action of a commission including **Governor David Butler, Auditor John Gillespie** and **Secretary of State Thomas P. Kennard**. The site selection was made July 29, 1867.

John K. Winchell, a Chicago architect, designed three masonry houses in Lincoln for the three commissioners in 1869. Only the **Kennard House** remains and is designated as the **Nebraska Statehood Memorial**.

The first railroad to reach Lincoln was the Burlington & Missouri line from Plattsmouth in 1870. Nebraska's legislature authorized land grants to encourage railroad development in the

THE HISTORIC KENNARD HOUSE—This home at 1627 H St. was built in 1869 for Thomas P. Kennard, one of the three capital commissioners who selected Lincoln as Nebraska's state capital. It has been designated as a statehood memorial and is open to the public.

state in an early session in 1869.

The **University of Nebraska**, home of the Cornhuskers—"The Big Red"—football team, was chartered February 15, 1869 and opened its doors September 7, 1871 with 20 college students and 110 preparatory school pupils.

Among the many famous persons connected with the university was **Gen. John J. "Black Jack" Pershing**, hero of World War I. Pershing taught military science at the university and served as Commandant of Cadets at the university from 1891-95. He was elected to the Nebraska Hall of Fame in 1964.

THE GREAT COMMONER— William Jennings Bryan, three time candidate for the presidency, made his home in Lincoln. A lawyer, Bryan was involved in national politics and liked to be called "The Great Commoner." His home, "Fairview," is one of the historical attractions in the capital city.

The university produced many gifted writers; among them **Willa Cather** (1876-1947), winner of a 1925 Pulitzer Prize for her novel *"One of Ours;"* and **Mari Sandoz** (1896-1966), who achieved fame in 1935 for *"Old Jules,"* the story of her pioneer father who settled in Nebraska's Sandhills.

Other colleges and universities in Lincoln are Nebraska Wesleyan University, founded by the Methodists in 1887; Union College, founded by the Seventh Day Adventists in 1891; and Southeast Community College—Lincoln Campus.

William Jennings Bryan, born in Salem, Illinois, in 1860, arrived in Lincoln in 1887 and entered into the practice of law. He was elected to Congress in 1890. Bryan won the first of three presidential nominations with his "Cross of Gold" speech at the Democratic National Convention in Chicago in 1896. He served two years (1895-96) as editor of the *Omaha World Herald.*

Bryan's home, "Fairview," was built in 1901-02 for over $10,000, money he earned from his publications. Many political personalities of the time visited "Fairview," including **Woodrow Wilson. "The Great Commoner,"** as Bryan liked to be called, served as President Wilson's Secretary of State. Bryan died five years after the highly-publicized Scopes Trial in Tennessee in 1925. He is buried in Arlington National Cemetery. "Fairview" was deeded to the Lincoln Memorial Hospital, now Bryan Memorial Hospital.

Another famous resident was **Charles Gates Dawes** (1865-1951), American statesman and banker. Born in Marietta, Ohio, Dawes became a lawyer in 1886 and practiced law in Lincoln, in offices next to Bryan, until 1894 when he became involved with several major utilities. He worked in **President William McKinley's** presidential campaign in 1896 and served as comptroller of the U.S. Treasury (1897-1901). In 1902 he established himself as a banker with the formation of the Central Trust Company in Illinois. In 1921 he was appointed the first director of the U.S. Bureau of the Budget. In 1923-24, he was head of the reparations committee that advanced the Dawes Plan to help rebuild and stabilize postwar Germany's finances. For his humanitarian work, Dawes was awarded the Nobel Peace Prize in 1925. He served as Vice President under **Calvin Coolidge** and in 1929, President Hoover appointed him ambassador to London. He later served as president of the Reconstruction Finance Corporation.

Another famous Lincolnite was **Nathan Roscoe Pound** (1870-1964), noted botanist and "philosopher of the law." Born in Lincoln, he graduated from the University in 1888 and received his doctorate in 1897. He studied law at Harvard and later served as dean of the University of Nebraska Law College and Harvard Law School (1916-30). In 1962 he was awarded the golden anniversary award of the American Judicature Society, of which he was a founder, for his contributions to legal reform and legal philosophy in the United States. He was the author of numerous books on jurisprudence. Pound was elected to the Nebraska Hall of Fame in 1976.

Don Wilson (1900-1982), who gained national recognition as the radio and TV announcer for the Jack Benny Show, was born in Lincoln.

On April 15, 1922, ground was broken for today's state capitol building designed by **Bertram Grosvenor Goodhue**. The "Tower of the Plains" was completed 10 years later, in 1932. At a cost of $9,800,440.08, the building was built within the budget established and paid for on a "pay-as-you-go" basis. This beautiful building, topped off with a 19-foot bronze statue, the "Sower," by **Lee Lawrie**, can be seen for miles. The pedestal, which is another 13 feet high, is formed of a wheat sheaf topped by a corn stalk. The Sower also acts as a giant lightning rod! The pedestal and statue weigh eight and a half tons.

The Lincoln Monument, on the west side of the capitol lawn, was designed by **Daniel Chester French** in 1912. The original model of this statue is in Lincoln's Tomb in Springfield, Illinois.

One of the largest bank robberies in American history occurred

Wednesday morning, September 17, 1930 when four heavily armed men quietly entered the Lincoln National Bank and Trust Company, 1144 O St., and forced the employees and patrons to lie face down on the floor. In less than 15 minutes the bandits looted the teller's cages and vault and made their getaway in a waiting car. Two men were later sentenced to long prison terms for the crime. A third man, **Gus Winkler**, known to be a member of the **Al Capone** gang, aided authorities in recovering more than a half million dollars in stolen bonds and was freed. Three years later Winkler was shot and killed by underworld gunmen. During that week in 1930, three other Nebraska banks were robbed.

Nebraska's **Unicameral**, adopted in 1935, is the only one-house legislature in the nation. State senators are elected on a non-partisan basis, but all executive offices, including governor and lieutenant governor, are partisan.

The U.S. Army Air Corps established Lincoln Air Base (seen to the west of I-80, adjacent to Lincoln Municipal Airport) as an airfield during World War II. B-47s once operated from this air-base which closed in 1966. The facility is presently used by the Nebraska Air National Guard.

Aviation came early to Lincoln—in 1910 with the opening of the Lincoln Airplane and Flying School, 2415 O St. It was here **Charles A. Lindbergh** took his first flying lessons in 1922.

Today's Lincoln not only serves as the seat of county and state government, but as a manufacturing and distribution center as well. Several insurance companies have their home offices here.

The Nebraska State Historical Society is one of the several historic attractions in the Lincoln area.

NEBRASKA STATE MUSEUM, 15th and P, includes many excellent exhibits.

This is an outstanding museum and is recommended to everyone interested in Nebraska's history. Hours: 9 a.m. to 5 p.m., Monday through Saturday; 1:30 to 5 p.m. Sunday. Closed Veterans Day, Thanksgiving, Christmas and New Year's. Admission is free.

FAIRVIEW, 49th and Sumner Sts., was the home of the famed William Jennings Bryan. Hours: 1:30 to 5 p.m. Saturday and Sunday from Memorial Day through Labor Day. Admission is charged.

FERGUSON MANSION, 700 S. 16th St., was built in 1910 and is filled with furnishings of the period. Open 9 a.m. to noon

THE STATE MUSEUM OF HISTORY, 1500 P St. in Lincoln, houses colorful exhibits of Central Plains history, highlighting early prehistoric times, Indians of the Great Plains and pioneer days. The Nebraska State Historical Society's reference library and the State Archives are located in facilities at 1500 R St. (Below) This display in the Tribal History section of the museum is entitled "The First Nebraskans," a permanent exhibit interpreting 12,000 years of Plains Indian life and culture.

and 1 to 4:30 p.m. Tuesday through Saturday; 1:30 to 5 p.m. Sunday. Closed on Monday. Admission is charged.

STATE CAPITOL, 15th and K Sts., presents paintings and murals to depict the history and culture of the pioneers who settled Nebraska. In the vestibule are three paintings by **James Penney**, reflecting the hard lives of early pioneers. These are titled *"The Homesteader's Campfire," "The First Furrow"* and *"The Houseraising."*

Six mosaics in the Great Hall include *"The United States Survey,"* by **Charles Clement**; *"The Blizzard of 1888"* and *"The Tree Planting,"* by **Jeanne Reynal**; *"The First Railroad,"* by **F. John Miller**, and *"The Spirit of Nebraska"* and *"The Building of a Capitol,"* by **Reinhold Marxhausen**.

The three murals in the Rotunda, by **Kenneth Evett**, are titled *"Labors of the Heart," "Labor of the Hand"* and *"Labor of the Head."*

The tour, which takes approximately 30 minutes, includes a visit to the executive offices, legislative hall and court chambers. The tours start at 9 a.m. and run every half hour (on the hour and half hour) until 4 p.m., weekdays, June through August; 9 a.m. to 4 p.m. (except noon) on the hour, weekdays, September through May; 10 a.m. to 4 p.m. (except noon) on the hour, Saturday and holidays, all year, and 1 to 4 p.m. on the hour Sunday, year-round.

GOVERNOR'S MANSION (just south of the capitol), 1425 H St., features a doll collection of Nebraska's first ladies in their inaugural gowns. It is open 1 to 4 p.m. on Thursdays (except holidays).

THOMAS P. KENNARD HOUSE (Statehood Memorial), 1627 H St., is one of the three structures built in 1869 for the capital commissioners. It is one of the finest remaining examples in the state of Italianate domestic architecture, the leading American style from 1855-75, Nebraska's pioneer period.

Hours: 9 a.m. to 12 and 1:30 to 5 p.m., Tuesday through Saturday; 1:30 to 5 p.m. Sunday. Closed Monday. Arrangements can be made for special tours by calling 471-4764. Admission is charged.

SHELDON MEMORIAL ART GALLERY, 12th and R Sts., houses one of the nation's finest collections of 20th-century American art, including paintings, sculpture, graphics, crafts, and photography. It is open 2 to 9 p.m. Sunday; 10 a.m. to 5 p.m. Tuesday through Saturday (and 7 to 9 p.m. Thursday through

THE TOWER OF THE PLAINS —The Nebraska State Capitol, in Lincoln, is often referred to as the "Tower of the Plains." It took 10 years to build and was constructed on a "pay-as-you-go" basis costing under $10 million.

Saturday). Closed on Mondays.

UNIVERSITY OF NEBRASKA MUSEUM OF NATURAL HISTORY, 14th and U Sts., includes several exhibits of mastodons (also referred to as "mastodonts") and mammoths that once ranged the Great Plains in large numbers. Mastodons are believed to have entered the Great Plains some 10 million years ago while mammoths (true elephants) migrated to this continent over a million years ago. Mastodon and mammoth remains have been discovered in several Nebraska counties. These exhibits, among the finest in the world, are displayed in the museum's "Elephant Hall." The museum is open 9:30 a.m. to 4:30 p.m., Monday through Saturday, and 1:30 to 4:30 p.m. Sunday. The Ralph Mueller Planetarium is also included in this complex. A show in a domed theater setting, is scheduled at 2 and 3 p.m. Saturday and Sunday.There is an admission charge to the planetarium. Admission to the museum is free.

AMERICAN HISTORICAL SOCIETY OF GERMANS FROM RUSSIA MUSEUM, 1139 S. 7th St., is dedicated to preserving the history and culture of this ethnic group. Many interesting items are on display, brought to Nebraska by the emigrants. This also serves as the international headquarters for this group. The museum is open 9 a.m. to noon and 1 to 3:30 p.m. Monday through Friday; 9 a.m. to 2 p.m. Saturday.

The 337 acre South Bottoms Historic District in Lincoln is the largest historic district in Nebraska and recently was added to the National Register of Historic Places. This district is significant for its ethnic history as a home for Germans from Russia, who began arriving in Lincoln in the 1870s. Most homes in this area were designed to resemble small dwellings built by Germans in the Volga region of Russia.

The German-Russian Bottoms are located along Salt Creek, from South St., west of 9th St., across to north of the fairgrounds, west 1st St. to 14th. The area is divided from the South Salt Creek Basin and the North Bottoms by railroad yards and industrial buildings. Originally emigrants settled in one or the other area depending on the families they knew who had settled in the area before they arrived.

Other Area Attractions

FOLSOM CHILDREN'S ZOO, 28th & A St., is considered one of the finest children's zoos in America and features an 1880s village with a children's theater, a miniature steam railroad that circles the grounds, a large variety of birds and animals, includ-

A NOTED AUTHOR—Bess Streeter Aldrich, one of Nebraska's noted authors, made her home in Lincoln for eight years. A native Iowan, she lived most of her life in nearby Elmwood where she is buried.

ing everyone's favorite, Ben, the friendly bear from the Grizzly Adams TV series. It is open 10 a.m. to 5 p.m. Monday through Saturday; 10 a.m. to 6 p.m. Sunday, May to September. On Thursdays it is open to 8 p.m. Admission is charged.

PIONEER PARK AND PRAIRIE INTERPRETIVE CENTER, South Coddington & West Calvert, is a 600-acre park and offers a wide range of outdoor recreation opportunities. Of special interest is the Prairie Interpretive Center that includes animals and prairie grasses native to Nebraska in the 1850s. The park is open from sunrise to midnight daily

ELMWOOD

ELMWOOD (pop. 599), 20 miles east of Lincoln, two miles north of US 34 and N-1, was the home of **Bess Streeter Aldrich**, noted Nebraska novelist. Her best known and most popular book, *"A Lantern in Her Hand,"* was published in 1925.

Her other books, published between 1924 and 1944, include *"Mother Mason"* (1924), *"Rim of the Prairie"* (1924), *"The Cutters"* (1926), *"A White Bird Flying"* (1931), *"Miss Bishop"* (1933), *"Spring Came On Forever"* (1935), *"The Man Who Caught the Weather"* (1936), *"Song of the Years"* (1939), *"The Dream Goes Dead"* (1941), and *"The Lieutenant's Lady"* (1944). Mrs. Aldrich received her first major check as a writer—$175—in 1911 for a short story in a contest sponsored by the *Ladies Home Journal*. The story was titled *"The Little House Next Door."* She published 160 short stories. Most of her stories dealt with family life among pioneers of Iowa and Nebraska, her native and adopted state.

She was born at Cedar Falls, Iowa, February 17, 1881, daughter of **Mr. and Mrs. James W. Streeter**. She graduated from Iowa State Teachers College at Cedar Falls in 1901 and taught school for six years before marrying **Charles S. Aldrich**. A short time later they moved to Elmwood where Charles and a relative purchased the bank. It was at Elmwood Mrs. Aldrich did the bulk of her writing. The Aldriches had four children and Mrs. Aldrich had the responsibility of raising them after her husband's death in 1925. The University of Nebraska awarded her an honorary Doctor of Letters degree in 1934 and she has been inducted in Nebraska's Hall of Fame.

Bess Streeter Aldrich moved to Lincoln in 1946. It was here she died Tuesday, August 2, 1954, in a Lincoln hospital after a month long stay. She was buried in the Elmwood Cemetery. A marker is displayed in Elmwood's City Park.

YORK

YORK (pop. 7,710), 47 miles west of Lincoln on I-80, Exit 353, three miles north on US 81, is the county seat of York County. The town was platted in 1869 and incorporated in 1872. Just east of the I-80 interchange is a westbound rest area which includes a sculpture garden, *"Crossing the Plains,"* by **Bradford Graves**.

In York is the ANNA BEMIS PALMER MUSEUM, 211 East 7th St. It is open the year-round, 9 a.m. to 5 p.m., Monday through Saturday, and 1 to 5 p.m., Sunday, April through November. Admission is free.

AURORA

AURORA (pop. 3,643), county seat of Hamilton County, was founded in 1872 and incorporated in 1877. Hamilton County, organized in 1870, is one of the top grain producing counties in Nebraska. Deep-well irrigation plays an important role in the county's agricultural scene. Aurora is 25 miles west of York.

The Hamilton County courthouse, located in Aurora, was built in 1894. The Civil War statues on the courthouse grounds were erected mainly through the efforts of retired Army **Gen. Develan Bates**, who made his permanent home in Aurora. Bates was awarded the Congressional Medal of Honor during the Civil War while serving as a colonel of the 30th U.S. Colored Troops. He was wounded at the battle of Cemetery Hill, Virginia, July 30, 1864, while leading his troops.

The Bates home is located on the northwest corner of 9th and

J Sts. in Aurora. Only the original iron fence around the home has been removed. This is private property and can only be viewed from the street.

Orville City was selected as Hamilton County's first county seat, May 3, 1870. January 1, 1876 it was moved to Aurora and many of Orville City's buildings were moved to Aurora as a result. Orville City was built around a square, site of the courthouse building, and the community boasted several stores, hotels and saloons. The Hamilton County Poor Farm was located at Orville City until recent times. Orville City was located south of Aurora.

Another small community in the county of some note in the early days was **Farmers Valley**, developed around Farmers Valley mill, built on the Blue River by **John and Asa Martin**. The other business enterprises here were a store, blacksmith shop and postoffice. A large storage building was erected in conjunction with the mill to store wheat and flour. The trade name of flour produced at the mill was *"Nancy Hanks,"* named after a famous race horse. The mill was operated until 1940 and nothing of it remains today.

STOCKHAM (pop. 68) is located south of Aurora on the county line. This small town was the site of the first mill in the county but operated only briefly in the early days.

The **Nebraska City—Fort Kearny Cutoff**, from the Oregon Trail, runs east and west through the county. Along this old trail, used before the days of the railroad, were the **Deepwell Ranch** (1865-67), **Prairie Camp** (1863), **Millspaugh Ranch** (1861-69) and the area's first cemetery (1865). The route of this old trail meanders along I-80, sometimes to the south, other times just to the north, through this region.

The **Ox Bow Trail** ran along the north boundary of Hamilton County, just south of the Platte River.

The Deepwell Ranch was established near the Beaver Creek by **John Harris** and **Alfred Blue** and served as a road ranche along the emigrant-freight trail. Harris and Blue came to the area from a prisoner-of-war camp near Chicago at the end of the Civil War. They had served in the Confederate Army and were captured during the fall of Atlanta. They caught the first wagon train west when they were released from the prison camp and soon after arriving in the area established Deepwell Ranch, so named for its 65-foot water well which quenched the thirst of travelers and their animals on the dusty trail west. The partners built a big sod house and barn to handle the heavy traffic on the trail. The barn, half dug-out and half sod, was capable of handling up to 165 head of horses. The house could accommodate up to 25 persons. Deepwell Ranch was located northeast of Giltner, 11 miles southwest of Aurora (on N-41B Spur).

Prairie Camp, also called "Dirty Shirt Camp," served as a relay station for the Overland Stage line in 1863 on the run between Nebraska City and Fort Kearny. This station included a sod house and a rustic stable partially dug into the river bank to accommodate 20 to 30 head of horses. The trail passed a short distance south of this camp, located east of Aurora.

Briggs Ranch (also called Briggs Fort) was established by **J. T. Briggs** in the early 1860s and a government patent was issued in 1871. Briggs set up the ranch to serve freighters and wagon trains on the Ox Bow Trail or Pike's Peak Trail. This trail was primarily used by the military and freighters for development of the mines in the Pike's Peak area. There was a large barn to accommodate U.S. Cavalry horses. The Ox Bow Trail was used for heavy freighting from 1852-60. Some travel continued on this trail until the arrival of the railroad in 1867-68 when most of the travel on this trail dried up. This is the only point in Hamilton County ever referred to as a fort. It never had any military status and was never used for fighting, other than occasional, unrecorded fisticuffs. The Briggs Ranch site is located north of Aurora, just south of the Platte River.

The first rancher to this area was **Daniel Millspaugh**, who located on Beaver Creek in the summer of 1861. Millspaugh was assisted by his son-in-law, **Jack McClellon**. The **Nebraska City-Fort Kearny Cut-off** was laid out in 1861 by a man hired by **Alexander Majors** of the great freighting firm of Russell, Majors & Waddell. A decent road had already been established to Soltillo, eight miles south of present day Lincoln. The man chosen to lay out the road was **William E. Hill** who started out from Soltillo with his mule teams plowing a line directly west to the Platte Valley. The freight wagons that followed straddled the furrow made by Hill and by the end of the summer of 1861 the new road, a short cut, had been established.

A small community evolved around Millspaugh Ranch, including stores, a blacksmith shop, a saloon and other enterprises to accommodate freighters and other travelers along this trail. Millspaugh Ranch operated as a stop along the trail until 1870. It was located east of present day Aurora.

MURAL DEPICTS RICH HISTORY—The title of this mural is "Overland Trails." It is displayed in Aurora's Plainsman Museum. Several murals in the museum assist the visitor in gaining insights into the area's rich history.

There is an Oregon Trail marker on N-14, three and a half miles south of Aurora. (The term "Oregon Trail" is used very loosely here. The trail actually ran from St. Joseph, Missouri, up into Nebraska further west, near Hastings, and on west.)

Aurora is situated at the intersection of N-14 and US 34, three miles north of the I-80 interchange (Exit 332). A museum houses the historic and educational artifacts of the community and county.

THE PLAINSMAN MUSEUM, 210 16th St., was dedicated July 4, 1976, and its collection includes artifacts from an earlier museum in the community, and the **E. A. Carlson** collection from Hordville, as well as others interested in the preservation of Western heritage and culture.

Through murals, mosaics and exhibits the museum traces the region's history from pre-historic times. They depict the 1540-41 North American expedition of the Spanish explorer **Francisco Vasquez de Coronado** and his search for the mythical "Seven Cities of Cibola" in the land of Quivira. They portray early pioneer days of the area and the present day concerns of the central pivot irrigation system and ground-water depletion.

The museum holds period homes—an original log cabin (1859), a sod house of the plains and turn-of-the-century Victorian homes—as well as a prairie chapel and Main Street, Pioneer Hamilton County. Other exhibits include exceptional doll, clock and china displays; period agricultural implements, early 19th century firearms, antique automobiles and more.

The museum was expanded with the opening of the Agricultural wing dedicated July 4, 1986. This museum houses numerous rural exhibits and displays including vintage farming equipment. In the center of the building is a typical farm scene, including a homestead house, barn and blacksmith shop.

The inventor and developer of the modern day stroboscope, or "strobe," was Nebraskan **Dr. Harold E. Edgerton**. Born in Fremont, Nebraska, in 1903, Harold Edgerton grew up in Aurora, graduated from the local high school and the University of Nebraska. He received his graduate degrees from the Massachusetts Institute of Technology (MIT) and has spent six decades there as a teacher, scientist and inventor. He was one of the founding partners of EG&G, Inc., that employs 23,000 people in 47 divisions around the world. MIT's oceanographic research vessel, *Edgerton*, is named in his honor. He has received numerous honors, among them an Oscar for a film *"Quicker 'n a Wink"* in 1940. He is also the recipient of a Medal of Freedom as well as a medallion of the National Inventors Hall of Fame. He holds more than 40 patents. A featured exhibit in the museum highlights the development of the stroboscope which makes possible high-speed photography of moving objects and "stop motion" analysis of machinery, processes, and other high-speed events.

It is open year-round. Hours: 9 a.m. to noon, 1 to 5 p.m., Monday through Saturday and 1 to 5 p.m. Sunday from April 1 through October 31. Hours: 1 to 5 p.m. daily November 1 through March 31. Closed Thanksgiving, Christmas, New Year's Day and Easter Sunday. Admission is charged.

GRAND ISLAND

GRAND ISLAND (pop. 33,154), 25 miles west of the Aurora Exit (332), is the county seat of Hall County. (There are two exits off I-80 into Grand Island, 381 on N-2 and 312 on US 34 and 281). Grand Island was named for the large island on the Platte River, just south of the city. The name Grand Island came from the French name, "La Grande Island," meaning large or great island. The island is believed to have been discovered and named by French fur traders in the late 1700s. Grand Island or Grand Isle was a well-known landmark for the fur traders in 1810. The name Grand Isle appeared on a French map published in 1821 and on

WORLD-RENOWN ACTOR—
Henry Fonda, who won an
Academy Award for his role in
"On Golden Pond," 1981, was
born and raised in the Grand
Island area. The cottage where
he was born is at the Stuhr Museum. Fonda died August 12,
1982, at the age of 77.

American maps published in 1822 or 1823.

Both the **Stephen H. Long** and **John C. Fremont** expeditions of 1820 and 1842 noted the size of Grand Island and west-bound travelers of the 1830s often mentioned the island in their notes and diaries.

Grand Island and most of north central Nebraska was ceded to the United States government by the Pawnee Indians in 1857. The treaty of 1848 allowed the federal government to establish Fort Kearny military reservation further west. It also was to serve as a buffer zone between the Pawnee and their blood enemies, the Sioux.

The first permanent settlers were colonists, mostly Germans, from Davenport, Iowa, and they arrived here July 5, 1857. The first settlement made by these colonists was in what is now the eastern part of Grand Island. North of the Monfort Packing Plant, on Stuhr Road, is a marker indicating the location of this first settlement. It is interesting how many of the pioneer German family names remain in Grand Island: Stolley Park Road for William Stolley; Stuhr Road, for another German pioneer. **John D. Schuller's** cabin, now located at the Stuhr museum grounds, became the settlement's first postoffice in 1858. William Stolley, born Wilhelm in Schlesweig/Holstein, Germany, in 1831, is credited with having founded Grand Island as a community. He and his family were among the first arrivals in July 1857.

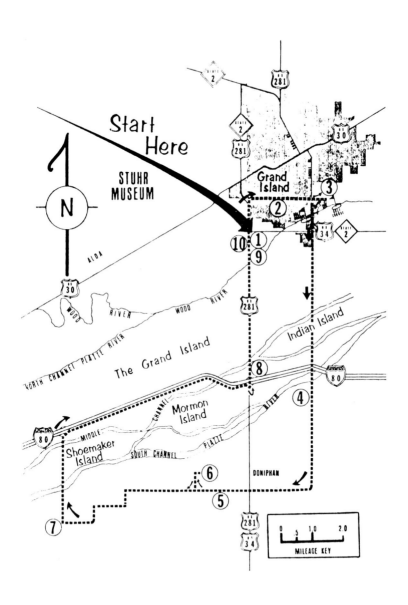

Start
Here

STUHR
MUSEUM

N

Grand
Island

③

②

⑩ ①
⑨

ALDA

WOOD RIVER   WOOD RIVER

281

NORTH CHANNEL PLATTE RIVER

The Grand Island

Indian Island

⑧

80

MIDDLE CHANNEL

Mormon
Island

④

80

Shoemaker
Island

SOUTH CHANNEL   PLATTE RIVER

DONIPHAN

⑥

⑤

⑦

281
34

0   5   10   20
MILEAGE KEY

Key to Sites on Indian Wars Memorial Tour

(1.) Start at STUHR MUSEUM OF THE PRAIRIE PIO-NEER, at US 381 and 34. Museum houses a famed collection of Americana as well as noted art collections. One of the Nebraska's leading attractions.

(2.) STOLLEY PARK, on Stolley Park Rd. at Blaine St., has been placed on the National Register and is on land settled by William Stolley in 1858. The original cabin still stands.

(3.) O.K. STORE, designated by a marker on the Fonner Park grounds at Stuhr and Stolley Park Roads, was opened in 1862, soon after the first settlers arrived.

(4.) Drive south on Locust St. (Old US 281) across the Platte River to the JUNCTIONVILLE RANCHE marker. Site of the one of the area's first trading posts on the Mormon Trail, established in 1864.

(5.) Follow the mapped route to the ANGELA WARREN marker, erected in memory of a pioneer woman shot by an Indian arrow.

(6.) Drive a short distance west and then north to the CAMP-BELL GRAVES, preserved burial sites of a pioneer Hall County family.

(7.) The MARTIN BROTHERS INCIDENT occurred in August 1864 where Nat and Robert Martin were helping their father load hay near their homestead when Indian raiders attacked. The boys, riding double on their mare, started for home but were struck by a single arrow that pinned them together. They tumbled from their horse, were left for dead by the Indians, and lived to tell their story.

(8.) Cross the Platte River again after stop (7), first to Shoe-maker Island and then to THE GRAND ISLAND, or "La Grande Isle" as the French fur traders called it. Stop (8) is at MORMON ISLAND STATE WAYSIDE AREA, just off I-80 on US 281.

(9.) HALL COUNTY PARK is a picturesque, native park, just off US 281, adjacent to Stuhr Museum.

(10.) The OVERLAND TRAIL marker on the west side of US 281 marks the area where the original trail crossed the Nebraska prairie.

Henry A. Koenig and **Fred Wiebe** opened their O.K. Store near the Mormon Trail, running through the area in 1862. Many people do not realize that a major covered wagon trail ran along the north side of the Platte River. This route was followed by explorers and traders for many years. The Mormons, of course, followed the trail in 1846. But the name of the trail varied. It was known as the Council Bluffs Road; it was also the Military Trail or Road—reaching from Omaha to Fort Kearny. It was a major route to the Colorado gold fields in 1858. There are several markers within the city limits of Grand Island tracing the route of this significant western overland trail.

The town of Grand Island was laid out in 1866 by the Union Pacific Railroad and incorporated in 1871.

The streets of Grand Island cut off at angles from the highways as do many other railroad towns, especially those along the Union Pacific line; laid out without any regard for the compass. Railroad towns usually have streets running parallel to and perpendicular to the tracks while most other towns had their streets laid out square with the compass. Grand Island is an extreme example of this kind of railroad town platting.

The Cornhuskers Ordnance Plant, an ammunition loading facility, was established in Grand Island during World War II. The plant was closed after the Korean War and reopened during the Vietnam conflict.

Several famous people were born and raised in Grand Island. Among the notables are **Henry Fonda**, the actor; **Sandy Dennis**, actress; **Sharon Kay Ritchie**, Miss America 1956 (although in this contest she represented the state of Colorado where she was a student); **Bobby Reynolds**, All-American football player; **Hal Haloun**, the artist; **Joe Feeney**, tenor on the Lawrence Welk Show, and **Angela Brumbaugh**, who models under the professional name of Angelique Evans.

Grace Abbott, social reformer and social worker, was born in Grand Island in 1878. Her social work drew national attention and she was appointed director of the Child Labor Division of the U.S. Children's Bureau, a position she held from 1921-34. She wrote several books, the most important being *"The Child and the State"* (two volumes), published in 1938. She died in 1939. Grace Abbott was elected to the Nebraska Hall of Fame in 1976.

There are numerous historic spots in the Grand Island and surrounding area. To the south on Locust St. (Old US 281), across the Platte River, is the **Junctionville Ranche** marker. This is the site of one of the area's first trading posts on the Mormon Trail, established in 1864. This well-remembered Junctionville Ranche stood at the junction of two trails, both used by overland freighting outfits. The Ox-Bow Trail and the Nebraska Cut-Off created a junction at this point.

Further south, and west of Doniphan a little more than two miles, is the **Angela Warren** marker, erected in memory of a pioneer woman shot by an Indian arrow. Just beyond and to the north are the **Campbell Graves**, preserved burial sites of a pioneer Hall County family. Five miles west is the site of the **Martin Brothers Incident**.

A step beyond the ordinary is the **Stuhr Museum of the Prairie Pioneer**, located in Grand Island. This museum honors **Leo B. Stuhr** (1878-1961), whose father, Peter, founded the museum. Leo Stuhr was a graduate of the University of Nebraska as a chemist. His estate provided funds for the formation of the museum as it is seen today.

STUHR MUSEUM OF THE PRAIRIE PIONEER, 3133 W. Highway 34, is a 200-acre complex which propels the visitor back into yesteryear. There are six major elements of the museum.

The main building was designed by the late **Edward Durell Stone**, one of the foremost architects in the modern world. It contains an art gallery, 100-seat auditorium where visitors may view a short orientation film on the museum's attractions, "Land of the Prairie Pioneer," narrated by the late **Henry Fonda**, and a wide range of exhibits relative to pioneer life in Nebraska. The building is open year-round and takes approximately one hour to view the exhibits and see the film.

The Gus Fonner Memorial Rotunda, south of the main building, houses Indian and Old West memorabilia of a noted collector. The rotunda is designed like a giant wagon wheel, with exhibit wings as "spokes" and an Indian sculpture grouping as the "hub." Gus Fonner (1873-1959) was the son of German immigrant, John, who operated a livery stable in Grand Island. John spent two seasons with the "Buffalo Bill" Wild West Show. The Fonner collection of artifacts from his lifetime formed the basis of the museum. The Fonner Rotunda is open year-round and it takes approximately 45 minutes to view the exhibits.

A Log Cabin Farm, with eight structures, is located east of the main building. The farm interprets the period of 1857-67 and the main buildings date from 1857, constructed with either round or squared cottonwood logs. Open May through September, it takes approximately 45 minutes to visit.

Railroad Town, southeast of the main building, is an authentically re-created town of the 1860s, set along a railroad right-of-way. Sixty original buildings were moved to the site with a business district consisting of a bank, general store, postoffice, hotel, barbershop, shoe shop and newspaper office. There is a depot, blacksmith shop, school house, country church, early-day farmstead and homes, including the cottage where Academy Award winner ("On Golden Pond," 1981) actor **Henry Fonda** was born. All buildings are furnished to the era. Summer craftspeople ply their trades throughout Railroad Town. Included are woodworkers, spinners, blacksmith and stained glass artist. Open May through September, the sightseeing tour of Railroad Town takes approximately one hour.

The Antique Auto and Farm Machinery Exhibit is located on the east grounds. The 200-piece exhibit includes an 1880 thresher, 1890s steam engines, early kerosene, distillate and gasoline tractors as well as many examples of horse and tractor-drawn farm implements. Also included in the exhibit are 15 antique automobiles; among these are a 1903 American, 1909 Model T Ford and 1913 Overland. It is open May through September.

The Nebraska Midland Railroad, Nebraska's only authentic, operating steam train, operates across the museum's 200-acres. The 13-unit train includes a 1908 Baldwin steam locomotive and 1897 coach. The train may be boarded at two locations—Railroad Town and Buffalo Junction. The train runs continuously Sunday afternoon starting at 1 p.m. and from 10:30 a.m. to 4:30 p.m. Monday through Friday. A fare is charged. It operates May through September. The train trip around the museum takes approximately 30 minutes.

The summer schedule, May through September, 9 a.m. to 6 p.m., Monday through Saturday; 1 to 5 p.m. Sunday. Admission is charged for adults and children over the age of seven; children under seven are free. (Extra charge for train rides). Fall, winter and spring schedule (only Main Building and Fonner Rotunda open) 9 a.m. to 5 p.m., Monday through Saturday; 1 to 5 p.m. Sunday, admission half rate.

HOW TO REACH STUHR MUSEUM OF THE PRAIRIE PIONEER—From I-80 Grand Island exit (Exit 312), north on US 34 and 281 to US 34 East, turn east to museum entrance. From east Grand Island exit (Exit 318), north on US 34, turn west on US 34, 6.5 miles to museum entrance.

The Stuhr Museum of the Prairie Pioneer is in Grand Island.

THE O.K. STORE, built on a site in front of the stadium at Fonner Park, Grand Island, was opened in 1862 by **Henry Koenig** and **Fred Wiebe** and not only served as the area's first store but also first telegraph station. When the Union Pacific arrived at what is known as **Grand Island Station**—and the new town was platted—the store building was moved to the downtown area of the new town.

During the Indian uprisings in the Platte Valley in 1864-65, Grand Island settlers did not leave for safer areas but gathered instead at the O.K. Store, hastily threw up a sod stockade and fortified what became known as **"Fort O.K."** This makeshift fort accommodated 68 men and 100 women and appeared to the Indians strong enough to withstand an assault. **William Stolley**, another settler, established **"Fort Independence"** about two miles west to accommodate another 35 persons.

Maj. Gen. Samuel R. Curtis, commanding general, Department of Missouri, visited Grand Island in 1864 and was impressed by the defenses of "Fort O.K." Curtis left a six-pounder artillery piece to bolster the fort. This cannon has been placed on the Hall County courthouse grounds, 1st and Locust Sts. The site of the O.K. Store is commemorated by a marker.

HOW TO REACH THE O.K. STORE SITE—From I-80, see directions to Fonner Park.

PIONEER PARK, 1st St. W and Cleburn St. S, was the site of the first Hall County courthouse, completed June 28, 1873. The two-story structure was built at a cost of $16,500. The park has been preserved as a memorial to the county's pioneers. A marker in the park tells the story of its history.

HOW TO REACH PIONEER PARK—From I-80, exit US 281 (Exit 312), north to US 30, east to Cleburn St. S, south on Cleburn three blocks.

CAMPBELL MONUMENT, approximately three miles west of Doniphan just off Platte River Dr. at the end of Amick Ave., is a granite stone serving as a gravestone and a memorial of the Indian raid July 24, 1867 on the **Peter Campbell Ranch**. Sioux raiders swept down on the area and killed **Mrs. Thurston Warren** and her infant son and wounded her 14-year old son. Campbell and his 14-year old son, John, were helping a neighbor, six miles away, with his harvest when they received word of the raid. Campbell and his son found Mrs. Warren lying dead in the doorway of her cabin, about a quarter mile from his own homestead. When he reached his ranch he found his home robbed and de-

THE MARTIN BROTHERS INCIDENT—This marker, 11 miles southwest of Grand Island, describes the story of Nathaniel and Robert Martin who were pinned together by a Sioux arrow during an 1864 Indian raid.

stroyed and four of his children missing—two girls and two boys. The children were recovered from the Indians later that September in North Platte.

The Martin Brothers Incident

During the Indian rampage along 400 miles of the Oregon Trail in early August 1864 an unusual and dramatic event occurred about 11 miles southwest of Grand Island when Indians struck the farmstead of **George Martin**. Martin had settled in the region in 1862 and began farming. He and his two young sons, Nathaniel and Robert, were loading hay near their homestead when they were attacked by a small band of Sioux raiders. Martin picked up his repeating rifle and fought to hold off the marauders. In the meantime his boys jumped on their mare and, riding double, headed for home.

As they fled the Indians gave chase, filling the air with arrows. An arrow hit Nathaniel in the back, passed through his body, and lodged in Robert's back. Pinned together by the arrow, the boys tumbled from their pony. The Indians thought they were nearly dead and did not bother to finish them off or scalp them. The boys survived and lived to tell their grandchildren their unusual story. Robert never fully recovered from his back injury, however.

A MARKER AT THE I-80 WEST ALDA REST AREA, approximately five miles west of Grand Island, describes this incident. A monument, three miles south of the Alda exit (Exit 305) from I-80, marks the area.

STOLLEY STATE PARK, off Stolley Park Rd., between Blaine St. and Park Dr., is the home of one of the area's most important settlers, **William Stolley**. The Stolley home has been restored and is open to the public. Visitors in this area, who are interested in history, should plan to see all of the historical markers in the park.

HALL COUNTY COURTHOUSE, Locust and First St., Grand Island, noted for its striking architectural design, is listed on the National Register of Historic Places.

A MOBILE MUSEUM, operated by the Nebraska State Historical Society, is placed in the westbound Rest Area on I-80, just east of Grand Island. It tells the history of the surrounding area and is open 8 a.m. to 7 p.m. daily, Memorial Day through Labor Day.

HASTINGS

Sixteen miles south of I-80 interchange at Grand Island, Exit 312 on US 281, is HASTINGS (pop. 23,019), county seat of Adams County. It was founded in 1872 as a railroad town (Burlington Railroad) and incorporated in 1874. It was named for a railroad construction engineer, **Thomas D. Hastings**, and became the county seat in 1878. Adams county was organized December 12, 1871.

The famous **Print Olive-Fred Fisher** murder trial was held in Hastings in the spring of 1879. Olive and nine others were tried

HOUSE OF YESTERYEAR—The Hastings Museum is a museum of natural science, pioneer history, Indian lore and astronomy. When it originally opened it was called the "House of Yesterday."

for the murder of homesteaders **Luther Mitchell** and **Ami Ketchum** the night of December 10, 1878. The homesteaders were killed to avenge the death of **Bob Olive**, Print's brother, in a bizarre feud between Texas cattlemen and the sod-busting homesteaders in Custer County.

The feud came to a head in the summer of 1878 when Olive cattle trampled the Mitchell-Ketchum corn crop and they retaliated by killing some of the cattlemen's steers and selling the beef in Kearney. **Print Olive** finally convinced the sheriff in Kearney, **David "Cap" Anderson**, who scandalously misused his office, to issue arrest warrants for Mitchell and Ketchum. Anderson deputized Bob Olive to bring them in. Bob Olive's small posse of five men, backed by his brother, Print, and another small posse, descended on the Mitchell-Ketchum homestead November 27. In the ensuing gunfight Mitchell mortally wounded Bob Olive and Ketchum wounded one of the possemen before driving them off.

Mitchell and Ketchum fled to Central City and on advice of a friendly judge surrendered to **Merrick County Sheriff Bill Letcher** December 5. Letcher returned the pair to Kearney for safekeeping. Print Olive bribed Sheriff Anderson to turn Mitchell and Ketchum over to him, and the night of December 10 Olive and Fisher and some cronies strung the homesteaders up. Just before jerking the wagon out from under them, Print shot Mitchell in the back at point-blank range, setting his overcoat on fire. The bodies were found by a search party the next day and the grotesque corpses, burned and frozen, were photographed by **H. M. Hatch**, which created headlines in newspapers from coast to coast.

After a brief investigation, Print Olive and Fred Fisher, along with the eight others, were arrested for the murders. They were jailed in Kearney because it was rumored the cattlemen and their cowboys would break them out of jail. Olive and Fisher were moved to the jail in Clay County as a further precaution and still later moved to the state penitentiary in Lincoln for safekeeping. A decision was made to hold the trial in Hastings and the presiding judge was **William A. Gaslin, Jr.**, of the 5th Judicial District. Gaslin was known for being a stern frontier judge and usually held a .45 caliber pistol in his lap during any unusual trial. One of the accused turned state's evidence and April 17, 1878, Olive and Fisher were found guilty of second degree murder and given life sentences in the Nebraska penitentiary. The others were found innocent.

The trial drew large crowds and there was a constant fear there would be an attempt to free the accused. **Gov. Albinus Nance** called on **Brig. Gen. George Crook**, commandant of Fort Omaha, for troop support to keep the peace. Thirty-five men from Company H, 9th US Infantry, were sent to Hastings to keep guard over the court proceedings for several days.

Two years later the Nebraska Supreme Court ordered a new trial for Olive and Fisher, ruling the trial should have been held in Custer County where the murders took place. The two men were freed and never retried. The legal battle cost Print Olive most of his money and other cattlemen-homesteader feuds in the state soon abated and the two factions lived relatively at peace in Nebraska from that day on.

Hastings College, 7th and Turner, was opened in 1882 and is an accredited private church-related (Presbyterian) co-educational liberal arts college.

Cigar making was a major industry in the town from 1880 into the 1920s. Several local brands appeared in the area tobacco shops.

There are several historic points of interest in Hastings.

FISHER RAINBOW FOUNTAIN—This fountain, named in honor of Hasting's Mayor Jacob Fisher, was dedicated in 1933. The electric fountain was one of the displays exhibited at the 1932 Adams County Fair and was part of an electrical exposition to show off Hastings as one of the largest municipally-owned electric plants in the country.

HASTINGS MUSEUM, US 281 at 14th St., is a museum of natural science, pioneer history, Indian lore and astronomy. The museum also houses the Adams County Historical Society. **The J. M. McDonald Planetarium**, a gift to the city from the **J. M. McDonald Foundation**, is housed in the museum. The planetarium presents regularly scheduled sky shows Monday through Sunday. The museum is open 9 a.m. to 5 p.m., Monday through Saturday; 1 to 5 p.m., Sunday and holidays. Closed New Year's, Thanksgiving and Christmas. Admission is charged.

CROSIER MONASTERY AND MUSEUM, 14th and Pine, features a collection of wood carvings and artifacts of the primitive Asmat people of New Guinea. Tours arranged by appointment.

HIGHLAND PARK CEMETERY, 13th and Burlington, was Hasting's first cemetery and contains a sculpture commemorating the Oregon Trail travelers who passed through Adams County.

OREGON TRAIL MARKERS are placed in several spots in the county with the most prominent found on West US 6. In a few spots tourists can view wagon ruts from Oregon Trail days. It is suggested contact be made with Adams County Historical Society for directions to these various places.

Other Area Attractions

ERMA'S DESIRE, Grand Island eastbound rest area, just south of the Platte River, is perhaps the best known sculpture garden along I-80. Its spires point to the skies and are reflected in the nearby lake.

NAVAL AMMUNITION DEPOT, east on US 6, Hastings, was a mammoth Naval ammunition facility built during World War II. Ten miles of bunkers are still visible in what is now an industrial park.

WOOD RIVER

WOOD RIVER (pop. 1,318) is 15 miles west of Grand Island; Exit 300 from I-80, four miles north on N-11 to US 30. The town was founded in 1882. It was given its name by **Joseph Johnson**, publisher of the *Huntsman Echo*.

There is a Mennonite monument 12 miles north of I-80 on N-11. This was the site of a Mennonite church and small community.

Wheat, corn, milo and soybeans are the crops raised in this agricultural area.

HOMETOWN HERO—Dick Cavett, noted TV personality, was born in Gibbon November 19, 1936. The family lived at 14 May Avenue for about five years after their son was born. He attended high school in Lincoln.

SHELTON

SHELTON (pop. 1,044) is 24 miles west of Grand Island; Exit 219 from I-80; north four miles to US 30. Shelton was founded in 1851 as **Wood River Center**. The name was changed to honor a Union Pacific executive by **Postmaster Patrick Walsch**.

The oldest newspaper, west of Omaha, is the *Huntsman Echo,* founded in 1854. This newspaper was well-known to many emigrants along the Mormon Trail.

Shelton is a farm community and corn and beans are the main crops. There is an alfalfa mill at Shelton.

GIBBON

GIBBON (pop. 1,531) is 30 miles west of Grand Island; Exit 285 from I-80, north four miles to US 30. The town originated as **Gibbon Siding**, named for **Bvt. Maj. Gen. John Gibbon**, a Pennsylvanian, who was cited five times for heroism during the Civil War. He participated in a number of Indian campaigns after the war. As a colonel of the 36th Infantry Regiment, Gibbon served as commanding officer of **Fort Kearny**, December 4, 1866 to May 1867.

The Union Pacific reached this point in July 1866. **Col. John Thorp's Soldier's Free Homestead Colony**, made up of 80 families, arrived at Gibbon. At the time Gibbon consisted of a small railroad section house. The colonists took up temporary quarters in railroad box cars. Another 49 families arrived later as members of the colony. The town was incorporated in 1872.

Dick Cavett, the well-known and popular TV personality, was born in Gibbon, November 19, 1936. The family lived at 14 May Ave. for four or five years after their son was born.

Today, Gibbon's economy centers on agriculture and the railroad. Two major farm industries are turkey growing and beef packing.

The story of Gibbon is on a historical marker at **Windmill Wayside Park**, N-10C, 3.5 miles south of town. A park entry permit is required. The Gibbon Heritage Center was opened in the former Baptist Church in Gibbon in 1978 and is open on Sundays, 1 to 4 p.m. or by appointment.

KEARNEY

KEARNEY (pop. 21,149), county seat of Buffalo County, was founded in 1871 and incorporated in 1873 with a population of 250. It is 40 miles west of Grand Island. The name Kearney was taken from nearby Fort Kearny, named for **Brig. Gen. Stephen W. Kearny**. Fort Kearny was the first Army post established on the Oregon Trail. (The spelling error, adding the second "e," is not explained.)

A small settlement, called **Kearney City**, but also known as **Dobytown**, sprang up south of the Platte River on the Oregon Trail, a mile and a half west of the fort in the 1850s. The stage line established a "home" station in this settlement and **Russell, Majors & Waddell** operated a major freight operation from this point. Dobytown had the reputation of being a haven for outlaws, gamblers and prostitutes and many emigrants passing through complained of price gouging as well as other forms of cheating.

With the coming of the railroad, traffic dried up on the Oregon Trail. When Fort Kearny was abandoned in 1871 so was Kearney City. Some of the folks picked up and moved the three miles north to the railroad line where others had started to locate.

By 1890 Kearney was a boom town as the population swelled to more than 10,000. There was a move, spearheaded by **Moses H. Sydenham**, a former postmaster at Fort Kearny, to have the nation's capital moved here. A quarter million dollars was raised to build a large cotton mill. The Boy's Training Home (initially called the State Reform School) was established in Kearney in 1879.

George W. Frank, from Corning, Iowa, arrived in Kearney during this period and formed the G. W. Frank Improvement Company. In addition to land speculating, Frank took control of

Fort Kearny State Historical Park is six miles southeast of Kearney.

the Kearney Canal Company, established the cotton mill, built the power house and organized the Kearney Electric Company. He and his wife built the city's most elegant and fashionable home in 1889 for the grand sum of $40,000.

In the early 1890s Kearney's economy collapsed. Industries closed, real estate values tumbled and many people left the city. In 1900 the population stood at 5,634. The cotton mill finally closed in 1902. The property was later used for an amusement park which was destroyed by fire March 18, 1922. It was located on US 30, west of Kearney.

Nebraska State Normal School (a two-year teachers college), later to become **Kearney State College**, was founded in 1905 and currently has an annual enrollment of approximately 9,000 students.

In 1912 a state tuberculosis hospital was located in Kearney and operated until 1972.

The U.S. Army Air Corps established an airbase at Kearney during World War II and kept it operational until 1949.

Several historic sites and attractions are located in this area.

FORT KEARNY STATE HISTORICAL PARK, six miles southeast of Kearney, is the site of Fort Kearny, established in the spring of 1848 by **Lt. Col. Ludwell E. Powell** and his regiment of Missouri Mounted Volunteers. The site was selected and construction was directed by Army engineer, **1st Lt. Daniel Woodbury**.

Woodbury named the post Fort Childs, in honor of his father-in-law, **Brig. Gen. Thomas Childs**, a hero of the Mexican War. On December 30, 1848, the War Department officially named the new fort, Fort Kearny, in honor of **Brig. Gen. Stephen Watt Kearny**, a noted frontier soldier and hero of the Mexican War, who had died a year earlier.

Fort Kearny's mission was to guard the emigrant roads, the Oregon Trail, running along the south side of the Platte River, and the Mormon Trail, running along the north side of the river, from Indian threats and outlaw bands. Its troops also protected the commercial transportation lines utilizing the roads, the stage lines, freighters, and, briefly the **Pony Express**.

Many of the Army's young officers, who would gain fame during the Civil War as generals, were stationed at the fort. Among these were **1st Lt. James E. B. Stuart**, 1st U.S. Cavalry; **Capt. Alfred Sully**, 2nd U.S. Infantry; **Capt. Frederick Steele**, 2nd U.S. Infantry; and **1st Lt. Henry Heth**, 6th U.S. Infantry.

74

CALLED TO DEFEND AGAINST INDIANS—One of the many military units assigned to or operating from Fort Kearny was the 2nd Nebraska Cavalry, commanded by Col. Robert W. Furnas, seated at the far left. He is shown here with his staff officers in 1862-63. The regiment was called to defend the frontier against Indian attacks during the Civil War.

Dr. George L. Miller, one of the founders of the *Omaha World-Herald* newspaper, served as the sutler at Fort Kearny from 1861 to 1864.

One of the post-Civil War commanding officers (briefly in 1866) was **Capt. Arthur MacArthur, Jr.**, 3rd U.S. Infantry. MacArthur, awarded the Congressional Medal of Honor for bravery in the battle of Missionary Ridge, Tennessee, November 1863, became a career officer and held the rank of lieutenant general when he retired in 1909. He was the father of another famous Army general, **Douglas MacArthur**, who was awarded the Congressional Medal of Honor, April 1, 1942, for his leadership in the defense of Bataan in the Philippine Islands.

Billy Cody (later to become the famous Buffalo Bill) was about 11 or 12 years old when he first appeared at the fort in January 1857 while working as a messenger boy in one of Majors & Russell's wagon trains hauling freight between Fort Leavenworth and Fort Kearny.

There were several Pony Express and stage stations in the area of Fort Kearny. To the west about five miles was **Craig's Stage Station** which served as a Pony Express stop in 1860-61 and as an Overland Stage station. **Dobytown**, just to the west of the fort, served in similar capacities. Further west, about 13 miles (six miles southeast of Elm Creek and 18 miles west of Kearney) was another Pony Express and Overland Stage station called **Garden** or **Platte Stage Station**. To the east about 10 miles from the fort was the small station called **Hook's** or **Dogtown**.

In the pre-Civil War period (1848-61) the various regiments assigned to the fort included the Missouri Mounted Volunteers, Mounted Riflemen, 6th U.S. Infantry, 1st Dragoons, 2nd Dragoons, 4th U.S. Artillery and 2nd U.S. Infantry.

During the Civil War (1861-65) the regiments represented were the 1st U.S. Cavalry, 4th U.S. Cavalry, 10th U.S. Infantry, 2nd Nebraska Volunteer Cavalry, 7th Iowa Volunteer Cavalry, 1st Nebraska Veteran Volunteer Cavalry, 1st Nebraska Militia, Pawnee Scouts, Omaha Scouts and the 3rd, 5th and 6th U.S. Volunteers (the galvanized Yankees).

Post-war Fort Kearny (1865-71) accommodated units of the 1st Nebraska Veteran Volunteer Cavalry, 7th Iowa Volunteer Cavalry, Pawnee Scouts, Omaha Scouts, the three regiments of the U.S. Volunteers, 2nd U.S. Cavalry, 18th U.S. Infantry, 36th U.S. Infantry, 30th U.S. Infantry, 3rd U.S. Artillery, 27th U.S. Infantry and 9th U.S. Infantry.

The development of the transcontinental railroad brought an end to the need for wagon trains, stage lines, freighters and also Fort Kearny. The fort was abandoned May 22, 1871 through General Order No. 87. The stores and materials at the fort were transferred to Fort McPherson. The military reservation lands were open to homesteaders in 1877.

An Army veteran, **Sgt. John Holland**, settled on 160-acres of the land and began to improve his quarter section where the fort had stood. He sold his interests to **William O. Dungan** and Dungan gained full title October 8, 1880. He kept the area in its original condition and it became a favorite camping spot for local residents.

The Fort Kearny Memorial Association was formed September 5, 1922 after The Fort Kearny National Park Association, formed in 1906, was dissolved in 1910. The Memorial Association gained title to 40 acres of the quarter section in May 1928. The deed to this site was turned over to the State of Nebraska for a state historical park December 13, 1929.

Fort Kearny State Historical Park features a visitor's center with an exhibit of period artifacts. A slide presentation shown in the center's theater graphically depicts the Fort Kearny story. Open daily from 8 a.m. to 8 p.m. A State Park Entry Permit ($2 daily, $10 annual) is required.

HOW TO REACH FORT KEARNY STATE HISTORICAL PARK—From I 80, take Kearney exit (US 44) south two miles, turn east on N-Spur 50A for approximately four miles. From I-80 (seven miles east of Kearney), take exit 279 (N-10) south three miles to N-Spur 50A, turn west on N-Spur 50A and drive for approximately three miles.

DOBYTOWN, the name given to Kearney City on the Oregon Trail, was located 1.5 miles west of the Fort Kearny military reservation. This was a tiny, raw frontier settlement where a parched emigrant or a bored soldier could slake his thirst with cheap whiskey and while away a few hours in a card game or consort with "soiled doves" for female companionship. A historical marker on N-Spur 50A commemorates the place.

TRAILS AND RAILS MUSEUM, 710 West 11th St., Kearney, is operated by the Buffalo County Historical Society. The museum building is the 1898 Union Pacific depot moved from Shelton, Nebraska. The baggage room has been converted into an exhibit room for the history of transportation through this region. The museum also houses rare photos, diaries, letters and other memorabilia. Just outside the depot, set on tracks, is Union Pacific Engine No. 481. Also on the museum grounds are two other historical buildings. One is an 1884 house that served as an overnight stopover for freighters and the other is a country schoolhouse built in 1871. Both have been restored and furnished in late 19th century style.

Open daily, April 1 through October 31 or by appointment. Admission is free.

HOW TO REACH TRAILS AND RAILS MUSEUM—From I-80, exit north on 2nd Ave. (N-44) to 11th St., turn west on 11th to 7th Ave.

THE FRANK HOME NATIONAL HISTORIC SITE, West

US 30, Kearney, was the palatial home of **George W. Frank**, an early day Kearney entrepeneur. It is built of Colorado limestone which was cut on the premises and includes a Tiffany window from New York, hand carved woodwork and six fireplaces. The original tile roof imported from Holland has been replaced.

Hours: 2 to 4:30 p.m. daily except Mondays during the summer months and by appointment for group tours the rest of the year. For information contact Marian Johnson, Frank House, West US 30, Kearney, (308) 237-3446 or the Public Information Office, Kearney State College (308) 236-9082. Admission is a $2 donation.

HOW TO REACH THE FRANK HOME NATIONAL HISTORIC SITE—From I-80, take Kearney exit north on N-10 and 44, north to US 30, turn west on US 30.

FORT KEARNEY MUSEUM, 131 Central Ave., Kearney, houses a private collection of over 10,000 historical items, including artifacts from Egypt, China and the American frontier. Admission is charged.

HOW TO REACH THE FORT KEARNEY MUSEUM—from I-80, take Kearney exit north on 2nd Ave. (N-44) to 4th St., east on 4th St. to Central Ave., north on Central Ave. to the museum.

<h2 style="text-align:center">MINDEN</h2>

Twenty miles south of Kearney is the town of MINDEN (pop. 2,896), county seat of Kearney County. Minden has become known as the "Christmas City" for its elaborate Christmas pageant held the first two Sundays in December each year. The pageant cast consists of 115 local citizens and is performed on the courthouse square. The pageant begins 7 p.m. for each of its two performances. Admission is free.

The town was settled by Danish, Swedish and German emigrants over 100 years ago. The idea of the formation of the town originated with five men who worked together in a broomcorn field in 1875. Each man bought a quarter section of land (160 acres) at the center of the county. Town lots were sold in 1876 and in 1878 the county seat was moved from Lowell to the new town. The town was named for Minden, Germany, home of the town's first postmaster.

One of the early day "hot spots" in Minden was the **Prairie Home Restaurant**, located on the east side of the town square. It was a favorite haunt for cowboys and settlers alike and was the scene of many gunfights and brawls. The old bullet-scarred

THE HIGHLY PUBLICIZED PIONEER VILLAGE—Pioneer Village, a private museum in Minden, is one of the most publicized in Nebraska. The complex contains 25 buildings housing thousands of objects dating back to the 1830s.

frame building was torn down for a new postoffice several years ago.

The main attraction here is **Harold Warp's Pioneer Village**.

PIONEER VILLAGE, on US 6 and 34, Minden, was designed by its founder "to show man's development since 1830." Its 25 buildings house thousands of objects ranging from depression glass to the first jet airplane, machinery displays, hundreds of antique automobiles and kitchens from every decade.

Pioneer Village features a sod house, one room country school, a frontier stockade, a pioneer church, a railroad depot and much more. Craft demonstrations of weaving, spinning, broom-making and printing are popular attractions. There are more than 50,000 historic items displayed chronologically and arranged in such a way so the visitor wastes little time walking. Strongly recommended for all ages, it is open daily year-round. Admission is charged.

Other Area Attractions

NEBRASKA WIND SCULPTURE, located on a lagoon to the north of I-80, three miles west of Kearney, was created by California artist **George Baker**. Kinetic, and made of stainless steel, the sculpture stands 16 feet high and is 25 feet long and weighs 7,200 pounds. It floats on pontoon-like structures anchored to underwater concrete piers.

The SANDHILL CRANE MIGRATION is a spectacular sight for motorists along I-80 between mid-February and mid-April when thousands of these birds are on their annual trip north. This area is part of the natural flyway for these and other migratory birds.

ODESSA

ODESSA is 11 miles west of Kearney (Exit 263 from I-80), two miles north to US 30. There were three important places on the Oregon Trail, between Kearney and Odessa, along the south bank of the Platte River. These were **Keeler's Ranch**, a well-known trading post; two miles further west, **Craig's Stage Station**, serving the Overland Stage line; and **McClain's and Russell's Ranche**, another trading post serving travelers along the trail. In 1860-61, Craig's Station also served as a Pony Express and contract mail station.

ELM CREEK

ELM CREEK (pop. 861) is 18 miles west of Kearney (Exit 257 from I-80), two miles north on US 183 to US 30. This is also the exit for CHEVYLAND MUSEUM. The museum is open seven days a week from June 1 to September 1, 8 a.m. to 8 p.m. Admission is charged.

The town was founded in 1866-67 as a Union Pacific Railroad station about a mile west of the present site and near the east bank of Elm Creek from which it derived its name, **Elm Creek Station**. It was settled by ex-soldiers under the Homestead Act and timber claim preemptions. The village was moved to its present site in 1883 when it became Elm Creek. It was incorporated as a village in 1887. A wooden bridge was built over the Platte River in the 1890s (replaced by the concrete structure in more modern times). This wooden structure was one mile in length and had three turnouts. Before irrigation the Platte River was said to be "a mile wide and an inch deep." It was considered a dangerous river to cross because of ever shifting quick sand.

It serves as a farm center and has a pork buying station and several alfalfa mills. Corn is the principle crop. Many bald eagles nest here during the winter months.

MASSACRE SITE NEAR LEXINGTON—This historical marker locates the Plum Creek Massacre, southeast of Lexington, August 7, 1864. Indians swooped down on a wagon train and killed 11 men and captured a small boy and young woman.

OVERTON
OVERTON (pop. 633) is 13 miles west of the Elm Creek Exit 257; Exit 248 from I-80, north on N-24B Link to US 30. This is also an exit for the Plum Creek Cemetery where victims of the **1864 Plum Creek Massacre** were buried (see Lexington listing for the story). The cemetery can be reached from Exit 248 by driving south on N-24B Link to the deadend. Turn west four miles or so to the cemetery, just north of the road. It is well marked.

The town was founded in 1873 and named for a railroader.

Overton is also known as the flyway route for Sandhill cranes. Each spring, hundreds of these interesting and beautiful birds make the fields south of Overton a rest stop on their long flights.

LEXINGTON
LEXINGTON (pop. 6,889), county seat of Dawson County, was laid out in 1872 along the railroad and named Plum Creek, to commemorate the settlement to the south that had been known by the same name by emigrants on the Oregon Trail for well over a decade. Lexington is 20 miles west of Kearney.

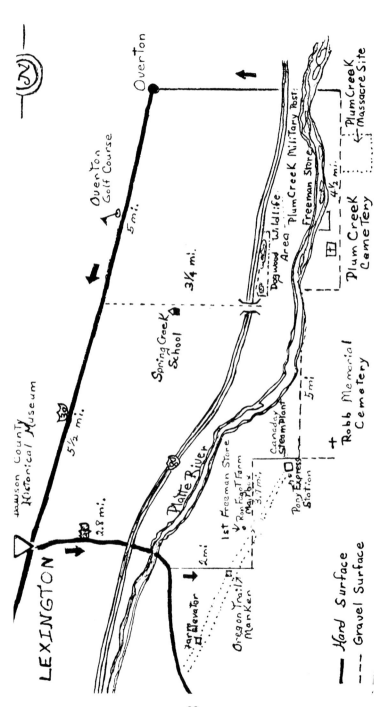

LEXINGTON

Dawson County Historical Museum

Overton

Overton Golf Course

5 mi.

5½ mi.

2.8 mi.

¾ mi.

Spring Creek School

Platte River

1st Freeman Store ↓Ron Figot Farm Mailbox

Farm Elevator

Oregon Trail Marker

2 mi.

3.7 mi.

Pony Express Station

Canaday Steam Plant

Robb Memorial Cemetery

5 mi.

Dogwood Wildlife Area

Plum Creek Military Post

Freeman Store

4½ mi.

Plum Creek Cemetery

Plum Creek Massacre Site

── Hard Surface
-- Gravel Surface

82

A small Army post was established at Plum Creek, about 10 miles southeast of today's Lexington, in 1864 as trouble with the Indians began brewing that spring. A Pony Express station had been constructed near the post site in 1860. **Daniel Freeman** and his wife, Louisa, with their three young children, established a trading post about the same time to serve the traffic on the Oregon Trail.

There were several Indian raids in the area and two are listed in several published local histories as the **Plum Creek Massacre** (1864) and the **Plum Creek Massacre** or **Turkey Leg Raid** (1867).

The town of Plum Creek was renamed Lexington in 1889.

In August 1864 the plains exploded as the Sioux and Cheyenne Indians went on a full-scale campaign against the whites, raiding along 400 miles of the Oregon Trail, in a desperate attempt to halt the white invasion of their Great Plains hunting lands.

THE PLUM CREEK MASSACRE occurred the morning of August 7, 1864 as a train made up of 11 wagons started to move westward along the Oregon Trail from their campsite just south of the Platte River and the Plum Creek Military Post. The wagon train, including 11 men, a woman and young boy, was bound for Denver. At 6 a.m. the wagons were ready and the trip began. On one of the wagon seats was 19-year old **Nancy Morton**, who was handling the reins for her husband's team as he lay asleep inside after a late night of guard duty.

The wagon train was on the trail for only a half hour when Oglala Sioux raiders struck the train in full fury. The men in the party were killed and Mrs. Morton was wounded with two arrows in her side. Among the dead were Mrs. Morton's husband, Tom; her brother, Will; and their cousin, John. The father of the young boy in the train was also a victim. The boy, **Danny Marble**, was unharmed and he and Mrs. Morton were taken captive.

1st Lt. Joseph Bone, commanding a small detachment of Company G, 7th Iowa Volunteer Cavalry, at the Plum Creek Station, sent this terse telegram to his superior, **Col. Samuel Summers**, commanding officer at Fort Kearny, 35 miles to the east:

"Send company of men here as quick as God can send them. One hundred Indians in sight firing on ox train."

The Indians escaped with Danny and Mrs. Morton while the troops at Plum Creek went to the massacre site and quickly buried the dead in the event the Indians returned to mutilate their bodies. The cemetery is about 1.5 miles west of the actual massacre site.

Danny Marble, along with three other white captives, was turned over to **Maj. Edward Wynkoop**, commander of Fort Lyon, in the Colorado Territory, September 11, 1864. He was taken to Denver and died there a few weeks later from the injuries he had sustained at the hands of his Indian captors.

Mrs. Morton was released in January 1865 near Fort Laramie. After recuperating she returned to her hometown of Sidney, Iowa, and November 19, 1865 married **George W. Stevens**. They had three children. **Nancy Morton Stevens** died near Jefferson, Iowa, August 12, 1912, 48 years after her harrowing experience in the **Plum Creek Massacre**.

HOW TO REACH THE PLUM CREEK MASSACRE SITE —From I-80, take (Exit 237) US 283 exit south two miles to the Canaday Steam Plant Road. Travel about 1.5 miles south to the Oregon Trail marker (a grey monument on the west side of the road), continue south to intersection, turn east (left) and stop briefly about 100 yards east of Ron Fargot's mailbox to see where Daniel Freeman operated his first store along the Oregon Trail (site in the field to the north, next to a small stand of trees). Continue to the Canaday Steam Plant, turn east and continue down the road for about five miles, winding and angling to the east, to the Plum Creek Cemetery. To the far north, about a half mile, is the site of Daniel Freeman's Plum Creek store and just to the east was the location of the Plum Creek Military Post. Site may be reached from the Overton exit (Exit 248) by driving south on N-24B link to east west road, turn west on this road to the Plum Creek Cemetery. (Please sign the guest register in the mailbox at the cemetery). Drive another 1.5 miles east of the cemetery to the site of the Plum Creek Massacre (south side of the road).

PLUM CREEK MASSACRE or TURKEY LEG RAID occurred August 6, 1867 when a Cheyenne raiding party, led by **Chief Turkey Leg**, derailed a train west of Plum Creek (Lexington). The engineer and fireman, **L. L. Hills** and **Percy Browne**, were killed when the train struck a barricade the Indians had set up across the tracks. A lineman, **William Thompson**, and crew of five section hands were sent out to repair the line but were attacked by the raiders. Thompson was scalped and the section hands were killed.

Thompson's nightmare continued during the night as he watched still another train crash against the barricade. The Indians attacked the eastbound train and the engineer, attempting to outrun his attackers, didn't see the barricade in time to keep his train from being derailed. Thompson's life was probably spared because the second train was carrying a cargo of liquor destined for the work camps and the Indians went on a drunken spree.

Maj. Frank North and his **Pawnee Scouts** were dispatched to the scene and gave chase to the Indians. North and his men defeated **Turkey Leg** in this running fight. Seventeen raiders were killed and a woman and boy were captured along with 35 head of stock belonging to the raiders.

In the meantime, Bill Thompson found his scalp and soaked it in a bucket of salt water during his trip to Omaha where he hoped doctors could sew the scalp back on. The attempt failed and his scalp today hangs in the Union Pacific Museum in Omaha. Bill Thompson returned to England where he died in 1911.

HOW TO REACH THE PLUM CREEK MASSACRE or TURKEY LEG RAID SITE—From I-80, take Lexington Exit 237, US 283 north two miles to US 30, turn west on US 30 and drive about three miles to the marker.

DAWSON COUNTY HISTORICAL SOCIETY MUSEUM, 805 North Taft, Lexington, has an excellent collection of historical artifacts contributed by relatives of pioneer families. Exhibits and detailed information about early Indians and pioneer activities in the area are featured. Furnished log cabin, antique household appliances, antique farm machinery, steam locomotive and a unique locally built airplane are included in the museum's exhibits.

The airplane was built in 1917 by 21-year old **Ira E. McCabe**, a Lexington resident. McCabe eventually went to Chicago where he became a successful inventor with 133 patents to his credit, including the mercury switch.

The museum is open the year-round. Winter hours: November 1 through March 31, 1 to 5 p.m., Tuesday through Thursday. Summer hours: April 1 through October 31, 1 to 5 p.m., Tuesday through Sunday. It is closed Mondays.

HOW TO REACH THE DAWSON COUNTY HISTORICAL SOCIETY MUSEUM—From I—80, take (Exit 237) Lexington exit (US 283) north to 8th St., east on 8th St., to Taft St., just north on Taft St.

COZAD

COZAD (pop. 4,452) is located on the 100th meridian, the

100th longitudinal line west of Greenwich, England. The 100th meridian is the natural demarcation line between the humid east and the arid west. A large sign in downtown Cozad reads: "The 100th Meridian, 247 miles west of Omaha," replacing a sign that stood for years along the Union Pacific Railroad's right-of-way.

The Union Pacific railhead reached this point, considered an important goal in the construction of the transcontinental railroad, October 5, 1866. Three weeks later, October 26, more than 250 railroad and territorial officials arrived to celebrate the U.P.'s achievement to that date.

John Jackson Cozad, a land speculator from Cincinnati, Ohio, arrived in the area in 1872. He had attempted to establish a community near Cincinnati, a town he called Cozaddale.

Cozad became a Nebraska town in 1874 and for several years **John Cozad** worked hard to locate settlers in the area in spite of prairie fires, drought, blizzards and grasshopper infestations. A professional gambler, as well as a land speculator, Cozad also had many enemies. He became involved in a shooting scrape and the man he shot eventually died from the wound he sustained. Cozad fled the country and settled in the east under an assumed name where he lived out the rest of his life.

John J.'s youngest son was **Robert Henry**, who spent several of his boyhood years in Cozad. Robert became a world famous painter and art teacher as **Robert Henri.**

Robert Henri taught his art students to record life directly and spontaneously which clashed with the "art for art's sake" doctrine that prevailed. He was joined by seven other artists and the group became known as **The Eight** or **Ashcan School**. Henri taught in New York City from 1903 until his death in 1929. He was the author of the book *"The Art Spirit,"* published in 1923. (There is an excellent book, *"Son of a Gamblin' Man,"* about Henri, written by Nebraska author, **Mari Sandoz**.)

Cozad is a farm center with hay as its principle crop.

PONY EXPRESS & STAGE STATION, Ave. E and 9th St., was moved to Cozad in 1938 from south of the Platte River near Darr Road. The station, located in City Park, is a small cabin built in 1849 as a trading post that was called **Willow Island Station** when it was utilized as a Pony Express and Overland Stage station in the 1860s. The station also served as a military outpost during the Indian raids of 1864-65. The cabin was acquired by the Dawson County American Legion Post 77 and moved to Cozad for use by the Boy Scouts. It was rebuilt and

86

dedicated in 1938. Three plaques on the site and building give a brief history of the building. It is not open for public viewing.

HOW TO REACH THE PONY EXPRESS & STAGE STATION—From I-80 (Exit 222), north on N-21; one block north of stoplight.

The Hendee Hotel, 220 East 8th St., was built in 1879 by **John Cozad** and is historically significant to Cozad as a social and commercial focus in the growing community and for its association with several prominent early settlers. **Robert Cozad**, John's youngest son, lived in this hotel as a youth. **Stephen A. Hendee**, a prominent local merchant, purchased the property from Cozad and owned it for 27 years. The Hendee Hotel is listed on the National Register of Historic Places.

THE ROBERT HENRI MUSEUM, opened in 1986, is located in this historic building. It relates to the background of this unique American artist and his early days in Nebraska. Hours are 9 a.m. to 5 p.m. daily and 1 to 5 p.m. Sunday and holidays. Admission is charged.

GOTHENBERG

GOTHENBURG (pop. 3,476), center of a major alfalfa growing area, was incorporated as a village in 1885. Over 100,000 acres of alfalfa annually produce over 450,000 tons of dehydrated meal and pellets.

The Swedish influence is prevalent in Gothenburg and is symbolized in the spirit of **"Febold Feboldson,"** the Swedish pioneer who could spin taller tales and outdo the legendary Paul Bunyan. "Feboldson" is said to have hitched a team of buffalo to his snowplow and accidentally dug the Platte River. This is just one story depicting the "greatness of the man."

Gothenburg has two historic attractions including an original Pony Express station and Swedish markers in a pioneer cemetery.

ORIGINAL PONY EXPRESS STATION, located in downtown Gothenburg, is one of two remaining such stations in this area. The building was erected in 1854 on the Oregon Trail, four miles east of Fort McPherson, Lincoln County, and was used as a fur trading post and ranch house. The structure was used by **Russell, Majors & Waddell** as a station for their ill-fated **Pony Express** from early 1860 to late 1861.

For the next several years, after 1861, it was used as an Overland Stage Company station. When the stage line went out of business the building was used as a bunk house and storage fa-

ORIGINAL PONY EXPRESS STATION—This building, in Gothenburg's Ehmen Park, is one of two remaining Pony Express stations in
this area. This station was built in 1854 on the Oregon Trail, four
miles east of Fort McPherson (a National Cemetery today). A fur trading post and ranch house were the original uses of the structure. In
1860-61 it became a station for the Pony Express and later as a station for the Overland Stage Company. Some 50,000 persons annually
visit this historic building.

cility on the Williams Upper "96" Ranch. In 1931, **Mrs. C. A.
Williams** recognized the historic significance of the building and
donated it to the Gothenburg American Legion. The building
was moved to Gothenburg's city park and refurbished. Dedication of the building to the memory of the Pony Express Riders
and Pioneers of the Old West occurred October 2, 1931. The
American Legion turned the building over to the City of Gothenburg at the same time.

The site of the station moved to Gothenburg is marked with a
plaque by the Oregon Trail Memorial Association.

"One of the best eating places on the Platte" was the reputation of **Midway Station**, Pony Express and Overland Stage station, located three miles south of Gothenburg on the Lower "96"
Ranch. Five miles further west on the Overland Trail was **Dan
Smith's Ranche** which served as a stage station and military
outpost during the Indian raids of 1864-65. Eight miles due west
of Gothenburg was **Gilman's Station**, another Pony Express

and stage station and military outpost during the Indian problems. The old **Midway Station** is part of a ranch building built in 1897. It is located on private property and is not available to the public.

Gilman's Ranch came under heavy attack in the spring of 1865. **Pvt. Francis W. Lohnes**, Company H, 1st Nebraska Cavalry, was awarded the **Congressional Medal of Honor** for his "gallantry in defending government property against Indians" at the ranch May 12, 1865. He was wounded in this attack and temporarily relieved of duty. The native New Yorker received his medal July 24 and corporal stripes August 1. Corporal Lohnes deserted December 24.

Gothenburg's Pony Express Station is open 8 a.m. to sundown daily during the summer months and is open for tours at other times by special request. About 50,000 tourists annually visit this historic exhibit. Admission is free.

HOW TO REACH THE ORIGINAL PONY EXPRESS STATION—From I-80 (Exit 211) at Gothenburg, north on Lake Ave. to 15th St., just east on 15th St. in Ehmen Park.

SWEDISH MARKERS AT PIONEER CEMETERY—Three Crosses, marking the graves of three little children who died in 1885, were made by their Swedish grandfather, a blacksmith, of Swedish steel.

HOW TO REACH THE PIONEER CEMETERY—From 15th St., north on Lake Ave. two miles, then two miles west. Cemetery is on the south side of the road.

BRADY

BRADY (pop. 374) is 13 miles west of Gothenburg; Exit 199 from I-80, north two miles to US 30. *"Nebraskan Gateway"* by **Anthony Padovano** is another part of Nebraska's sculpture garden. Nestled in a grove of giant cottonwoods, *"Nebraskan Gateway"* is made of 100,000 pounds of granite. It's located at the Brady westbound rest area. Jeffrey Reservoir is 14 miles south of Brady.

MAXWELL

MAXWELL (pop. 410) is 11 miles west of the Brady exit (199); Exit 190 from I-80, north two miles on N-56A Spur to US 30. Two miles south on N-56A Spur, from I-80, is **Fort McPherson National Cemetery** and site of **Fort McPherson** (1863-1880). (For details about Fort McPherson see North Platte listing.)

NORTH PLATTE

NORTH PLATTE (pop. 24,475), county seat of Lincoln County, was laid out in 1866 with the coming of the Union Pacific Railroad and was incorporated in 1871. It serves an irrigated farm region. North Platte is 60 miles west of Gothenburg.

The Platte River splits just east of town to become the **North Platte River** and the Mormon Trail continued to run along the north bank of this branch in the early days and the **South Platte River** and the old Oregon Trail ran along the south bank of this branch. Originally the Oregon Trail followed the South Platte for about 60 miles, then crossed the river and swung northeast 25 miles or so to the south side of the North Platte River. Later the Oregon Trail followed the South Platte River to Julesburg, Colorado, then turned northwest to the North Platte River to a point south of present-day Bridgeport, Nebraska.

"The Greatest Enterprise..."

Hailed as "The Greatest Enterprise of Modern Times," the Pony Express, used to demonstrate the overland route across the center of the continent was superior to the southern route, was launched April 3, 1860 by Russell, Majors & Waddell.

The 2,000-mile, 10-day trip started at St. Joseph, Missouri, in the east and followed a route through Marysville, Kansas, up to Fort Kearny, across to Chimney Rock, on the South Pass, down to Salt Lake City, over to Carson City, through the Sierras and into Sacramento before the last lap to San Francisco. There were many Pony Express stations in the Nebraska Territory.

The Pony Express was a short-lived venture. Completion of the telegraph across the country by October 24, 1861 brought an end to the need for the "Pony". The last run of the Pony Express, already in bankruptcy, was November 20, 1861.

CODY'S HEADQUARTERS AND HOME—This 18-room mansion was headquarters for Col. William F. "Buffalo Bill" Cody at his Scouts Rest Ranch in North Platte. It was here the great showman entertained visitors from all walks of life, including military leaders, statesmen and European royalty.

North Platte was home to the legendary **William Frederick "Buffalo Bill" Cody** (1846-1917). His home and retreat, **Scouts Rest Ranch**, was built in 1878.

SCOUTS REST RANCH, in northwest North Platte, houses mementoes of Cody's colorful career as an Army scout, Indian fighter, Pony Express rider, buffalo hunter and Wild West pro-

GREAT SHOWMAN—While still serving as a scout and guide "Buffalo Bill" Cody put together his Wild West Show that traveled all over the country and Europe. He built a beautiful home in North Platte and was visited by many dignitaries. In 1967-68 he was placed in the Nebraska's Hall of Fame.

BUFFALO BILL'S WILD WEST SHOW POSTER—"Buffalo Bill's" famed Wild West Show and Congress of Rough Riders of the World originated in North Platte where Cody had established his Scouts Rest Ranch.

moter in a luxurious 18-room mansion and colorful show barn. The ranch is now a 65-acre State Historic Park.

In 1867 the Kansas Pacific railroad was being built west through Kansas and the **Goddard Brothers**, who had the contract for feeding the 1,200 labor force, were looking for a hunter to provide the mainstay for the track crews' fare—buffalo meat. The job was first offered to the celebrated **"Wild Bill" Hickok**, but he declined and recommended young **Bill Cody** for the job, already somewhat famous as an Indian fighter and scout. Cody accepted the job for $500 per month to provide the hindquarters and humps of 12 buffalo daily. He worked for Goddard Brothers less than 18 months and during this time killed 4,280 buffalo and gained the sobriquet of **"Buffalo Bill."**

In 1868, Cody's title as the greatest buffalo hunter was challenged by Army officers stationed at Fort Wallace, Kansas. Their own chief of scouts, **Billy Comstock**, also had a reputation as a great buffalo hunter. They pitted Comstock against Cody in a match held east of Sheridan, Kansas, with a $500 wager riding on the outcome. The two men were to hunt eight hours one day from 8 a.m. to 4 p.m. Each kill had to be made from horseback. When the time was up, Cody had killed 69 of the shaggy beasts; Comstock, only 46.

Buffalo Bill organized a bronc riding contest in North Platte between cowboys from local ranches to help celebrate Independence Day in 1882. This show was such a success he decided to take it on the road as part of his **"Buffalo Bill's Wild West Show and Congress of Rough Riders of the World,"** and thus, the rodeo was born. **The North Platte Nitely Rodeo** is the only rodeo running seven nights a week in the summer and sanctioned by the Professional Rodeo Cowboys Association. RODEO 100, the 100th anniversary of the origination of the rodeo in North Platte, was celebrated during the 1982 edition of NEBRASKALAND DAYS and the Buffalo Bill Rodeo.

Scouts Rest Ranch is open 10 a.m. to 8 p.m., daily, from Memorial Day to Labor Day. The Cody Home is also open 8 a.m. to noon and 1 to 5 p.m. the rest of the year. A State Park Entry Permit ($2 daily, $10 annual) is required.

HOW TO REACH SCOUTS REST RANCH—From I-80 (Exit 177), north on US 83 (Jeffers St.) to Rodeo Rd., west on Rodeo Rd. (West US 30) to Buffalo Bill Ave., then north on Buffalo Ave. to Scouts Rest Ranch. The distance is approximately six miles.

WESTERN HERITAGE CENTER MUSEUM, just off Buffalo Bill Ave. (see directions to Scouts Rest Ranch, above), preserves over 100 years of history. The museum, operated by the Lincoln County Historical Society, has thousands of items on display showing the kinds of tools, equipment and weapons used by early day settlers. The following buildings are open with appropriate displays: Union Pacific Railroad Depot, Original Fort McPherson Log Cabin Headquarters Building, Log Cabin Pony Express Blacksmith Shop, 1895 Lutheran Church, Country School, Hay Barn and Main Building. It is open 9 a.m. to 8 p.m. every day from Memorial Day through Labor Day. It is closed in winter but special tours are available through the caretaker who lives on the grounds. Admission is free.

CODY PARK, just off North Jeffers Ave., reviews the railroad's past and present through displays of giant steam engines and exhibits in the old restored railroad depot.

FORT McPHERSON NATIONAL CEMETERY, 15 miles east of North Platte and 15 miles west of Gothenburg, just off I-80, is the site of Fort McPherson, which once guarded the Oregon Trail and settlers against Indian raiders. The original five-company Army post was established in September 1863 by a detachment of Company G, 7th Iowa Volunteer Cavalry, commanded by **Maj. George M. O'Brien**, and was named **Cantonment McKean**, in honor of **Gen. Thomas J. McKean**, Commanding General, District of Nebraska, Department of Missouri.

The post was renamed **Fort Cottonwood**, after the nearest settlement, Cottonwood Springs, in 1864 and finally renamed again in 1866 in honor of the Union Army's **Maj. Gen. James Birdseye McPherson**, killed in the Battle of Atlanta, July 22, 1864.

During the height of the Indian uprising in August and September, 1864, a disastrous event occurred at Fort Cottonwood. It seems that scurvy had broken out at the fort and seven of the stricken men were sent out to gather fresh fruit and wild plums, in the canyons some seven miles south of the post. This occurred September 20 with a captain, a corporal and an orderly in charge of the ambulance carrying the patients. They met two other troopers in the area, detailed to round up some stray mules, who joined their party. While the soldiers were busy picking plums they were attacked by Indian raiders.

The captain got his men back in the ambulance and they made a mad dash for the fort. In the running fight the Indians killed

94

MARKS OLD FORT'S PARADE GROUND—This statue of a 7th Iowa Cavalryman, along the road about a mile east of Fort McPherson National Cemetery, marks the site of the old fort's parade grounds and headquarter's flag pole.

the two soldiers who tried to retreat on horseback. The ambulance driver lost control of his team and the corporal and captain were thrown out of the wagon. The Indians spotted the corporal and killed him after a brief fight while the captain watched from his hiding place.

The main body of Indians chased the ambulance and finally overtook it. They killed the orderly and seven patients. The captain returned to the fort that night and related the story of what has become known as the **Cottonwood Massacre**. Eleven soldiers were killed while nine Indians met their death in the fight.

Cottonwood Station, also called **McDonald's Station or Ranch**, was one of the best known of the Pony Express and Overland Stage stations. It was located just west of the Fort McPherson military reservation.

Eleven miles west of **Cottonwood Station** was **Jack Morrow's Ranche**, one of the most famous stations in the Platte Valley. Jack Morrow was a prominent frontier businessman and was one of the characters of the Plains. He was an accomplished scout and well-known Indian trader.

Due south of North Platte was a Pony Express and stage station called **Cold Springs** or **Cold Springs Ranche and Stage Station**.

About halfway between North Platte and Hershey, to the west, was **Fremont Station**, another stage station. Eight miles further west, opposite Hershey, was another home station for the Pony Express and Overland Stage Co., **Fremont Springs** or **Buffalo Ranch**.

All of these stations were important posts and gathering places for settlers during the Indian uprisings.

The regular routine at Fort McPherson was enlivened on June 10, 1867, with the arrival of the 7th U.S. Cavalry, under the command of **Lt. Col. (Bvt. Maj. Gen.) George Armstrong Custer**, who was, within less than a decade, to receive immortal fame in his last stand on the Little Big Horn, June 25, 1876. Custer and his six companies of cavalry remained at the fort for five days before continuing their campaign southwest against the elusive Sioux and Cheyenne Indians.

Maj. (Bvt. Maj. Gen.) Eugene A. Carr, commanding the 5th U.S. Cavalry, assumed command of Fort McPherson May 20, 1869 and less than three weeks later (June 9th) led an expedition against the Cheyennes along the Republican River to the south and west. After a march of nearly 300 miles, Carr and his troops surprised the Indians at Summit Springs, northwest Colorado Territory. In the **Battle of Summit Springs**, 52 Indians were slain, and 15 women and children taken captive. The entire village of 84 lodges was completely destroyed. Also participating in this expedition were the **Pawnee Scouts**.

That fall two companies of the 5th U.S. Cavalry, with **Bill Cody** serving as scout, were dispatched from Fort McPherson to investigate the disappearance of a 12-man survey party, led by **Nelson Buck**, at a spot on the Beaver Creek (just west and south of the unincorporated village of Marion, approximately 19 miles south and east of McCook). The troops found surveying instruments and flags, an ambulance belonging to the surveyors, a blood-splattered carbine, and three dead Indians. No trace of the surveyors was ever found. An Oglala Sioux, **Pawnee Killer**, is believed to have been responsible for the massacre of these 12 men.

The **Grand Duke Alexis of Russia** arrived in the United States in January 1872 as a guest of our country. **Gen. Philip N. Sheridan** was assigned as the official host representing the U.S. government. Alexis expressed an interest in participating in a buffalo hunt out west so plans were made for a trip to Nebraska for this purpose. The Washington party arrived January 12 by special train and were outfitted from Fort McPherson. In the party with the Duke were **General Sheridan, Lt. Col. George A. Custer, "Buffalo Bill" Cody** and **J. B. "Texas Jack" Omohundro** with troops from Companies E and K, 2nd U.S. Cavalry, from Fort McPherson. The hunt took place some 60 miles southwest of the fort and was proclaimed a great success by Alexis.

Fort McPherson was officially abandoned June 5, 1880. Many Army units were stationed at the fort during its almost 17-year existence including the 7th Iowa Volunteer Cavalry, 1st Nebraska Veteran Volunteer Cavalry, 6th West Virginia Veteran Volunteer Cavalry, 6th U.S. Volunteer Infantry, 2nd U.S. Cavalry, 18th U.S. Infantry, 3rd U.S. Artillery, 5th U.S. Cavalry, 9th U.S. Cavalry, 3rd U.S. Cavalry, 9th U.S. Infantry and the famed **Pawnee Scouts**, led by the fearless **Maj. Frank North**. **"Buffalo Bill" Cody** served periodically as a guide and scout for the fort. His daughter, Orra, was born at Fort McPherson 3 p.m., August 13, 1872. **James B. "Wild Bill" Hickok** spent several weeks at the fort in the spring of 1868 serving as an Army scout and buffalo hunter.

Fort McPherson National Cemetery was established October 13, 1873 by the War Department on a site on the military reservation. The cemetery contains the dead of 21 abandoned frontier military posts and forts as well as servicemen from all other wars since the Civil War. More than 500 of the early grave markers simply read: "U.S. Soldier, Unknown." Gates open from 8 a.m. to 5 p.m. daily year-round.

HOW TO REACH FORT McPHERSON NATIONAL CEMETERY—From I-80 (Exit 190), two miles south on N-56A Spur. One mile southeast of the cemetery, continuing on the

EXPELLED INDIANS—Major Eugene A. Carr, commanding the 5th U.S. Cavalry, was responsible for driving the Indians out of Nebraska's Republican Valley in 1869 in a campaign that culminated at the Battle of Summit Springs.

same road, is a statue of a 7th Iowa Cavalryman, marking the site of the parade ground and headquarter's flag pole at Fort McPherson. This statue is located on the south side of the road.

SIOUX LOOKOUT, about a mile south of I-80 on US 83, is one of Lincoln county's highest points and was an observation post used by Sioux Indians to watch the movements of soldiers and emigrants along the "Great Medicine Road of the Whites" (the Oregon Trail). A monument of an Indian scouting the valley is perched atop this bluff in commemoration. A historical marker about Sioux Lookout can be found at the Mid-Plains Community College and State Farm Rd. intersection.

HERSHEY

HERSHEY (pop. 633) is 13 miles west of North Platte; Exit 164 two miles north to US 30. The town was platted in 1891 by **Annie S. Guthrie**, widow of a railroad engineer. It was incorporated in 1909. The town was named for Pennsylvanian **J. H. Hershey**, a partner in the Paxton & Hershey Land & Cattle Company.

Between North Platte and Hershey, along the south bank of the South Platte River, was the location of **Fremont Station** (also called **Bishop's Station**), serving the stage lines as well as the Pony Express as a home station. Two miles west of this station, on the Overland Trail, was **O'Fallon's Bluff Station and Military Post**. During the hostilities with the Indians in 1864-

65, this station served as a small military outpost, manned by a small detachment of cavalry troops. This was the general area also of the **Lower California Crossing** used by some of the emigrants to cross the South Platte River to reach the south bank of the North Platte River to continue their trip west on this trail.

This is farm country where corn, wheat, alfalfa and cattle are raised.

SUTHERLAND

SUTHERLAND (pop. 1,241) is six miles west of the Hershey exit (164); Exit 158 from I-80, north one mile on N-25 to US 30. The town was platted in 1891 and incorporated in 1905. The town was named for **George Sutherland**, an officer of the Union Pacific Railroad.

Opposite Sutherland on the Overland Trail was **Bob William's Ranche**, often attacked by Indian marauders in the mid-1860s. Three miles west was **Moore's Ranche**, attacked and destroyed by Indians twice within an 18-month period during the Civil War. Two miles west of Moore's was **Dorseys** or **Elk Horn Stage Station** and still five miles further west (not far from today's Paxton) was the desolate **Alkali Station, Telegraph Office and Military Post**. This was a lonely and dreary place and soldiers assigned duty here often deserted.

Cattle ranching is the mainstay of this area's economy.

The coal powered **Gerald Gentlemen Power Plant**, three miles south of town, was completed in 1981.

PAXTON

PAXTON (pop. 572) is 12 miles west of Sutherland Exit 158; Exit 145, a mile north of US 30. Paxton serves as a small farm center.

Somewhere between Paxton and Ogallala to the west was the **Middle Crossing** where emigrants crossed the South Platte River to reach the North Platte River route west.

OGALLALA

OGALLALA (pop. 5,264) earned its title as "Cowboy Capital" of Nebraska back in the 1870s when the town was the end of the **Old Texas Trail Drive**. The town, founded in 1868, was named for the Oglala ("scatter one's town") band of Teton Sioux Indians. It was incorporated in 1884. It is the county seat of Keith County and is 50 miles west of the North Platte.

Three men, the **Lonergan brothers** and **Louis Aufdengarten**, arrived in the area during the spring of 1868 to change the destiny of the dusty crossroads shipping point. Others soon

OGALLALA BOASTED A "BOOT HILL"—This old Western cemetery in the north section of Ogallala gained its name because many of
the men buried here "died with their boots on." Many were said to
have been killed in gunfights.

joined them in developing a town.

Cattlemen used Ogallala as a shipping point until 1886. Often a
dozen or more herds of 2,500 or more each were held on the south
side of the Platte River waiting for room at the railroad's loading
chutes. After the long, dusty trail drive, the cowboys liked to
whoop it up in saloons with such names as "The Cowboy's Rest"
and the "Crystal Palace," all fronting on Railroad Street, the
main road. The last building on the street was the "Ogallala
House;" the dining room was acclaimed for its excellent meals. It
was operated by **S. S. Gast**. Louis Aufdengarten was the proprie-
tor of the town's general store.

By 1880, Ogallala consisted of a courthouse, school, hotel, two
dwelling places and a population of 25 permanent residents.

During the period of 1882-84, settlers and farmers reached
Ogallala to buy up cheap railroad land which had come on the
market.

A serious epidemic of Texas fever swept over Nebraska in the
summer of 1884. The disease quickly spread and caused heavy

losses to Nebraska herds. Texas cattle were banned from Nebraska for a time.

Today Ogallala serves as a trading center for a large agricultural area.

The city has several historical attractions.

BOOT HILL CEMETERY, five blocks west of Main St. between 10th and 11th Sts., was the early day burial place for settlers, cowboys, and emigrants. The first burials were in 1875 and among the first funerals were those of **Mrs. Sarah Miller**, who died in childbirth, and her infant.

It seems her body and that of her child were exhumed several years later to be reburied in the regular Ogallala cemetery which had been established. Mrs. Miller's body was petrified and she appeared almost as she had in life, even with the skin on her face. At the same time the infant's body was not petrified. Supposedly this was one of the first cases of human petrification to be discovered on the North American continent. The story, kept secret for many years, claimed Mrs. Miller's body was so heavy it was necessary to use a derrick to remove and lift the body from the grave. The authority for this story came from **Mans Sheffield**, a 50-year resident of Ogallala.

Another early day burial on Boot Hill was that of **"Rattlesnake " Ed Worley**, who was killed over a $9 bet in a "monte" game in **Bill Tucker's** "Cowboy's Rest" saloon.

Many cowboys were buried in Boot Hill. They were buried with their boots on, thus the name "Boot Hill." The bodies were buried in canvas bags and laid on several boards and dirt was shoveled in to fill the grave. Each grave was initially marked with a wooden marker. It is said that many a good story is buried with the dead on "Boot Hill."

THE MANSION ON THE HILL, located at the top of North Spruce St., along US 26 and N-61, is the oldest brick landmark in the area. It currently serves as a museum, operated by the Keith County Historical Society. The elegant old home was built in 1887 for **L. A. Brandhoefer**, a banker.

The house was built of brick kilned in Ogallala and has walls 18 inches thick. The front entrance features a stone carriage step to assist the ladies entering a buggy or other conveyance.

The house and museum are open to the public daily from 2 to 8 p.m. from Memorial Day to Labor Day.

FRONT STREET, just off US 30, recreates the 1875-95 era when Ogallala was the end of the Texas Cattle Trail. Here is

FRONT STREET WHERE COWBOYS REVELED—This famous street in Ogallala, "Nebraska's Cowboy Capital," is a re-creation of Ogallala in the 1860s when it was the end of the Texas Trail. Great herds of Texas longhorns were driven to Ogallala to be loaded on railroad cars to be shipped to eastern markets.

where trail-weary cowboys could let off steam.

Other Area Attractions

THE KEYSTONE CHURCH, in the tiny little town of Keystone, a few miles northeast of Ogallala, was the only combined Roman Catholic and Protestant Church in America. Erected in 1908, the frame church has reversible pews with a Catholic altar on one end of the building and a Protestant altar at the other. The little church no longer is in use but is open to the public every Sunday afternoon during the summer months. Keystone is located on the north bank of the North Platte River.

PIONEER SOD HOUSE, in Paxton (Exit 145 from I-80) 19 miles east of Ogallala on US 30, features a collection of the prized possessions of the early Nebraska settler.

Up/Over, in the Ogallala westbound rest area just east of Ogallala exit, is another installment of I-80's unique sculpture garden. An interesting arrangement of I-beams has resulted in this dynamic representation of the importance of both the land and sky in Nebraska.

BRULE

BRULE (pop) 438), was named for the Brule ("burned") tribe of the Teton Sioux Indians and is located on US 30, nine miles west of Ogallala. From I-80, Brule can be reached by taking Exit 117.

Opposite and less than a mile west of Brule is the identified site of the Pony Express and Overland Stage home station in the 1860s called **Diamond Springs**. Three miles further west was the famous pre-1859 **Upper Crossing** or **Old California Crossing** and the identified site of the famous **Beauvais Ranche.**

Beauvais was an old French trader who established an Indian trading post here several years before the Civil War. During the Indian uprisings of 1864-65, a small military garrison was established here to guard the trail and telegraph lines.

This area was hard hit by Indian raiders in the mid-1860s as the Cheyenne and Sioux tried desperately to head off further invasion of their hunting lands by white emigrants and settlers.

BIG SPRINGS

BIG SPRINGS (pop. 505), 10 miles west of Brule Exit, was the scene of the first and greatest robbery of a Union Pacific train. The legendary **Sam Bass** and five other outlaws halted UP express train No. 4 the night of September 18, 1877 and took $60,000 in gold and currency from the express car. The bandits also took several thousands of dollars and other valuables from passengers on No. 4.

The Bass gang captured **John Barnhart**, the stationmaster and destroyed the telegraph so no alarm could be sent. They then forced the train to stop and robbed it.

The loot was split up under the Lone Tree, on the north side of the Platte River, and the robbers paired off and made good their escape.

Sam Bass returned to Texas and formed another gang and they robbed four trains within the next few months. The "Robin Hood of Texas," as Bass became known, was mortally wounded Friday evening, July 19, 1878 in Round Rock, Texas, 15 or 20 miles from Austin.

Sam Bass died Sunday, July 21, on his 27th birthday. He was buried in Round Rock and his sister placed a headstone on the grave with an epitaph that read: *"The Brave Man Reposes in Death Here. Why Was He Not True?"*

Sam Bass was born July 21, 1851 near Mitchell, Indiana, and left home when he was 17 years old to become a cowboy. He "turned bad" before he reached his 21st birthday and gained notoriety as a road agent and train robber in Texas over a six year period. He spent a brief period at his "trade" in Deadwood, Dakota Territory. A marker commemorating the Big Springs train robbery has been placed in the city park.

One of the first buildings in Big Springs was the **Phelps Hotel**, built in 1885 by **Mrs. Sarah Phelps**. This building is listed on the National Register of Historical Places. Big Springs can be reached by taking Exit 107 from I-80.

JULESBURG, COLORADO

Just west of Big Springs, in Colorado, is the small community of JULESBURG, established and reestablished several times in the early days.

The original Julesburg, two miles east of the present town, served as a Pony Express and Overland Stage station in the early 1860s and was called **Fronz** or **Elbow Station**. (It is erroneously marked as **Butte Station**, according to Historian Merrill J. Mattes.) This settlement was born in 1859 as a trading post owned by **Jules Beni**, later killed by the notorious **Jack Slade**.

In the fall of 1864, during the Indian uprisings, a company of 7th Iowa Cavalry, commanded by **Capt. Nicholas O'Brien**, established an Army post nearby. This post was originally called **Camp Rankin**, then designated **Fort Rankin**, and a few months later officially became **Fort Sedgwick**. This fort was attacked by Cheyenne and Sioux warriors January 6, 1865 to avenge their heavy losses at the infamous **Sand Creek Massacre** which had occurred just a few weeks earlier. Fourteen soldiers of Company F, 7th Iowa Cavalry, were killed in this attack.

Although the attack on the fort failed, the Indian raiders returned February 2nd to burn and sack the Julesburg settlement.

The Pony Express and southern route of the Oregon Trail split at Julesburg with these two trails following Lodgepole Creek northwest to a point three miles east of present day Sidney, then north past Mud Springs to Court House Rock and back along the North Platte River, almost paralleling US 385 for almost 75 miles west and north. The South Platte trail from Julesburg led to Denver.

There is an excellent local museum, operated by the Sedgwick County Historical Society, located in the old Union Pacific depot in Julesburg. This area is rich in early Western history.

CHAPPELL

CHAPPELL (pop. 1,086), 19 miles west of the junctions of I-80

FORT SIDNEY GUARDED BLACK HILLS TRAIL—The Post Commander's Home at old Fort Sidney has been restored and is open to the public. Fort Sidney was established in 1867 and closed in 1894.

and I-76, just off I-80 (Exit 85), is the county seat of Deuel County.

Serving as a wheat-growing area, Chappell was platted in 1884. The town was named for **John Chappell**, an official of the Union Pacific Railroad.

The Oregon Trail, Pony Express trail, Overland Stage road and Western Union line from Julesburg ran just south of the site of Chappell. **Nine Mile Station**, a Pony Express and stage station, was located two miles southeast of present day Chappell.

There is a historical section in the Chappell Memorial Library, 289 Babcock Ave. This library was a gift to the city from **Mrs. John Chappell**. It is open Tuesday, Thursday and Saturday afternoons and evenings.

An unusual Indian and art collection are exhibited in the **Elfreda Gross House**, 1066 Fifth St. Guided tours are by appointment only. Call (308) 874-2959.

SIDNEY

SIDNEY (pop. 5,996), 16 miles west of Chappell, is the county seat of Cheyenne County and was named for **Sidney Dillon**, New York solicitor for the Union Pacific Railroad. It was incorporated in 1885 as a village.

The town developed around **Fort Sidney** and grew rapidly because it was nearer the Black Hills than any other railroad point of consequence at the time of the 1876-77 gold rush to the Dakotas. The fort, initially a sub-post to **Fort Sedgwick** at Julesburg, was called **Sidney Barracks** until October 1870 when it became an independent Army post. **1st Lt. James Burns**, of the 5th Cavalry, was the fort's first commander. It was established in 1867 to protect railroad construction crews on the Union Pacific's portion of the transcontinental railroad. Troops from Fort Sidney participated in the **Battle of Wounded Knee** in December, 1890. The post was officially deactivated and abandoned June 1, 1894.

Initially the fort served as a two company post but by 1885 had been expanded to accommodate five companies of the 21st Infantry. Cavalry units were not stationed at Fort Sidney after 1883. When the fort was fully developed, it contained 14 buildings set around a large parade ground. A marker on a bluff just north of town indicates the location of a lookout post used by the fort during the problems with Indian raiders in the area. Troops at the fort were called upon for a variety of assignments—to escort emigrant and supply trains, for cattle herds for various agencies and garrisons, for paymasters traveling from one post to another, for scouting expeditions, mail carriers and to guard wagon work crews and stock herds for the posts. They also were called upon to construct and maintain roads, repair telegraph lines and provide hospital service to the area.

During the first Indian raid on the town there were no troops at the Barracks. Residents had to take refuge in the railroad roundhouse and fought the Indians from this position. Troops arrived by train the next day to drive the Indians off. **Mrs. William T. Allen**, an expectant mother, was in the midst of labor pains when the Indians attacked. She gave birth in the roundhouse without the aid of a doctor or midwife.

Today, all that remains at the fort is the Post Commander's Home and some of the officers' quarters. A plaque is also located on US 30 on the eastern outskirts of town.

Although gold was discovered in the Black Hills in 1874, it was another two years before prospectors began pouring into the region because of treaties with the Indians in the Dakotas. Finally the Army would not enforce these treaties any longer and whites descended on the Indian lands.

Early day Black Hills prospectors usually arrived in Sidney by train and purchased their equipment and supplies here. It was a wild and wide-open town in those days with dance halls, gambling parlors and saloons that never closed their doors. According to at least one story about Sidney, there were 23 saloons in a single block at one time.

Shootings were regular occurrences and drew little attention. A man was shot and killed during a dance one evening and instead of stopping the festivities, the corpse was dragged to a corner and propped up against the wall and the dance continued. During the evening another man was killed and his body was dragged across the floor and propped up against the first corpse. It was not until the third man was killed during the evening that the dance came to an end.

There were several lynchings during this hey-day period in the life of Sidney. One such lynching occurred in May 1879 and involved **Charles Reed** living with **Mollie Wardner**. One morning, a friend of Reed's, **Henry Loomis**, with two other friends, walked by Mollie's house and she called out inviting Loomis and his friends in. Loomis rebuked her for her remarks and when Reed heard about this he immediately looked Loomis up and severely wounded him with a pistol shot. Reed was jailed and Loomis died shortly after. Sympathy for Loomis created a public outcry and soon a lynch mob was formed. **Charles Reed** was dragged from his cell and carried to the nearest telegraph pole.

The Omaha Scouts

The Pawnee Scouts, led by Major Frank North and his brother, Luther, gained fame for their exploits in fighting other Indians for the white man's causes.

Another company, the Omaha Scouts, also served with distinction on the frontier during the period when hostile Indian bands were making a last-ditch effort to stop the invasion of their hunting lands by the onslaught of white settlers. This company, serving as a cavalry unit, was organized and commanded by Captain Edwin R. Nash.

The Pawnee Scouts were organized in 1864 and served on the frontier for several years after the Civil War. The Omaha Scouts were organized in 1865 and served only briefly.

Supposedly, Reed made a grand gesture at this point. He called out to the mob "I'll jump off, gentlemen, and show you how a brave man can die. Goodbye, gentlemen, one and all." His body hung on the pole for two days before it was buried.

For six years—from 1875-81—the 267 mile trail north from Sidney to the mining town of Deadwood and Custer was the principle route used to and from the gold fields. Gold was hauled down the **Sidney-Black Hills Trail** to be shipped by rail to other parts of the country for processing. Many of these shipments were valued at $200,000 each.

The **Sidney-Black Hills Trail** became obsolete with the completion of rail service to Pierre, Dakota Territory, in October, 1880. A marker on US 30 at the western outskirts of Sidney tells the story of this important trail.

Sidney has remained an important railroad town and trading center for a wide agricultural area.

The **Sioux Ordnance Depot** was established 10 miles northwest of Sidney at the outbreak of World War II. During the peak of the war the depot employed 1,400 civilian and military personnel. This Army munitions depot operated during the Korean and Vietnam wars. It was deactivated June 30, 1967. German and Italian prisoners-of-war were brought here to work on the railroad during World War II when there was a shortage of manpower.

Oil was discovered in Cheyenne County August 9, 1949, when the **Ohio Oil Company** brought in Mary Egging No. 1, the first of many discoveries in the Denver-Julesburg Basin. This first oil well, producing 225 barrels a day, is located about 10 miles northeast of Sidney. A marker is located three miles south of Gurley on US 385 indicating the location of Mary Egging No. 1.

There are four other incorporated communities in Cheyenne County, including DALTON (pop. 344), incorporated July 1, 1901, and GURLEY (pop. 213), incorporated May 1, 1917, both north of Sidney on US 385; LODGEPOLE (pop. 413), west of Chappell on US 30, and POTTER (pop. 370), incorporated April 4, 1912, west on US 30.

Lodgepole is home of LODGEPOLE MUSEUM, a block north of US 30. It contains railroad and agricultural displays. It is open by appointment. Information is available at the site.

Sidney has preserved much of its history through two facilities —the original **Fort Sidney Post Commander's House** and **Officers' Quarters** (double-set) housing the Cheyenne County

REMOTE MUD SPRINGS STATION—All that is left of the old Mud Springs Pony Express, stage and telegraph station is this historical marker on the site near Dalton. A large force of Indians attacked this tiny station February 4, 1865 and were held at bay by 19 men, just long enough to be rescued by the 11th Ohio Cavalry from Fort Laramie.

Museum.

FORT SIDNEY POST COMMANDER'S HOUSE, 544 Jackson St., is a complete restoration. The living quarters are just as the Post Commander left them in 1894. Open 1 to 5 p.m. daily in warm weather.

FORT SIDNEY OFFICERS' QUARTERS MUSEUM, 544 Jackson St., is also a complete restoration housing artifacts and displays that relate the history of Cheyenne County. Open 1 to 5 p.m. daily; 1 to 4 p.m. daily in the winter.

Both houses are listed on the National Register of Historic Places and are maintained by the Cheyenne County Historical Association.

CHRIST EPISCOPAL CHURCH, in Sidney, was built around 1886 and has been used as a place of worship by frontiersmen and Indians. It is still in use today.

The *"Roadway Confluence,"* is located in the Sidney westbound rest area just east of the Sidney exit. This 35 foot tall aluminum sculpture takes the eye upward in commemoration of the major role of Nebraska in the development of transcontinental transportation.

WESTERN NEBRASKA TECHNICAL COLLEGE MUSEUM, features military artifacts. It is open 8 a.m. to 4:30 p.m. daily, May through August. WNTC campus is located on the old Sioux Ordnance Depot grounds. It can be reached by driving eight miles west on US 30 then two miles north on Spur S17A.

Other Area Attractions

PRAIRIE SCHOONER MUSEUM, Dalton, features exhibits on local and area history. It is open 1 to 5 p.m. weekends, Memorial Day to Labor Day.

MUD SPRINGS PONY EXPRESS, STAGE & TELEGRAPH STATION was located about seven miles north, west off US 385, from present day Dalton or about 23 miles north of Sidney. In 1865 this station served the Overland Stage Company and Western Union Telegraph Company and was guarded by nine soldiers and manned by 10 civilians. February 4, 1865 a large force of Indians attacked the tiny station in the mid-afternoon. A telegram was sent to **Lt. Col. William O. Collins**, commanding officer at Fort Laramie, 105 miles northwest of the beleaguered outpost. Collins commanded the 11th Ohio Cavalry and quickly gathered a force to ride to Mud Springs. He also dispatched **Lt. William Ellsworth**, commanding Company H, 11th Ohio Cavalry, at **Camp Mitchell**, only 55 miles northwest of Mud Springs, to the scene of the fighting which continued through February 8th. The rescuers arrived in time to save Mud Springs in story book fashion. A plaque and flag pole mark the site of Mud Springs Station and there is a small museum in the same area. This museum, located in an old stone schoolhouse building, is operated by the Nebraska State Historical Society. It is open 9 a.m. to 5 p.m., Monday through Saturday and 1 to 6 p.m., Sunday, during the months of June, July and August. The museum and memorial site are 5.3 miles north and 1.8 miles west of Dalton.

POTTER (pop. 369), about 20 miles west of Sidney on US 30, has a museum depicting the rich heritage of the area.

KIMBALL

KIMBALL (pop. 3,113), 39 miles west of Sidney, is the county seat of Kimball County. The railroad came to Kimball in 1868 when the town was known as **Antelopeville**, renamed Kimball in 1886 for **Thomas L. Kimball**, a general manager of the Union Pacific Railroad. A postoffice was established at Antelopeville in

"Museum Without Walls"

Nebraska's sculpture garden stretches across the state on Interstate 80 at nine rest areas.

Once called "a museum without walls...created in the midst of our prairie landscape," the project was created from the ideas of Thomas A. Yates and Norman Geske, who proposed the project in August 1973 to the Nebraska American Revolution Bicentennial Commission. The commission endorsed the effort with a $100,000 grant. The Nebraska Arts Council, Nebraska Art Association and the National Endowment for the Arts also helped support the garden.

No tax money was used in constructing the lasting art experience. Nebraska business firms raised the major share of the $500,000 needed to establish the garden.

Traveling west across Nebraska from Omaha, the sculptures are:

Memorial to the American Bandshell, Platte River eastbound rest area.

Arrival, Blue River eastbound rest area.

Crossing the Plains, York westbound rest area.

Erma's Desire, Grand Island eastbound rest area.

Nebraska Wind Sculpture, Kearney westbound rest area.

Nebraskan Gateway, Brady westbound rest area.

Up/Over, Ogallala westbound rest area.

Roadway Confluence, Sidney westbound rest area.

Seed of Nebraska, Kimball eastbound rest area.

1877 with **John J. McIntosh**, serving as the postmaster. Kimball County was established in 1888.

Kimball is the center of the largest complex of Intercontinental Ballistics Missiles in the world. Two hundred **Minutemen III** ICBMs are harbored in silos in the immediate tri-state area. A giant **Titan I** missile (now obsolete) stands 100 feet tall in Gotte Park, nine blocks east of the intersections of N-71 and US 30. The town claims the title of **Missile Center, USA.** (Free overnight camper parking is permitted in Gotte Park.)

In the early 1950s oil was discovered in the area and today Kimball County boasts over 1,300 producing wells. Kimball is proud of its title as **Oil Capital of Nebraska.**

Agriculture has always been the mainstay of the area's economy, with wheat and cattle as the major commodities. The town of Kimball is 29 miles from the Wyoming state line.

At Kimball Municipal Airport, in 1964, a one-time, international record was established for the world's longest free flight in a solo glider.

PLAINS HISTORICAL MUSEUM, 2nd and Chestnut Sts., in downtown Kimball, features exhibits relating to area history. It is open 1 to 4 p.m. Monday, Wednesday and Friday during the summer months or by appointment.

"Seed of Nebraska," at the end of the sculpture garden, is located at the Kimball eastbound rest area. The concrete T-beams rise 45 feet from the ground, and steel and ceramic spheres reflect Nebraska and the importance of growth to this state.

There are only two other small communities in Kimball County—DIX (pop. 275), eight miles east on US 30, and BUSHNELL (pop. 186), 12 miles west on US 30.

Dix began as a postoffice March 4, 1887 on land owned by **Margaret Robinson**, originally from Dixon, Illinois (later hometown of **President Ronald Reagan**). The name Dixon, in this case, was shortened to Dix.

Bushnell originated as Orkney when a postoffice was established September 22, 1886. The town was organized in 1892 and the name changed to Bushnell May 18, 1895.

Banner County to the North

Twenty nine miles north of Kimball (25 miles north on N-71 and four miles west on N-4A) is HARRISBURG, county seat of Banner County, which has a population of 1,000 persons. Harrisburg, with some 250 inhabitants, is the only community in the county. The town and county were founded in 1889. **Charles A.**

NEBRASKA'S MISSILE CENTER—Kimball, in the southwest corner of Nebraska's panhandle, is the center of the largest complex of Intercontinental Ballistics in the world. This display is located in the city's Gotte Park.

Schooley, from Harrisburg, Pennsylvania, was one of the first settlers and donated land for the town site. The new town was first called Randall, then Centroplus. Finally Schooley, who also built the county courthouse, named it Harrisburg for his Pennsylvania hometown.

Scattered throughout Banner County are Minutemen missile silos, under control of Warren AFB, Cheyenne, Wyoming.

Harrisburg is the home of BANNER COUNTY HISTORICAL MUSEUM complex with several historical buildings as well as numerous historical displays and exhibits in the 40' x 100' museum building.

NEBRASKA'S SCULPTURE GARDEN—This is one of the sculptures in Nebraska's Sculpture Garden, located in nine of the rest areas along Interstate 80. This sculpture appears in the westbound rest area just east of Sidney.

Section 3

*Until the late 1850s the Oregon Trail followed the South
Platte River after leaving present day North Platte while
the Mormon Trail continued to follow along the north bank
of the North Platte River. The Oregon Trail followed the
South Platte for some miles before crossing back to the
south bank of the North Platte. There were three crossings
usually taken by the emigrants—the nearest was Lower
Crossing from a point near present day Sutherland, where
it was only two miles to the North Platte; Middle Crossing,
just a few miles east of present day Ogallala where it was
about nine miles to the North Platte, and Upper Crossing,
a few miles west of present day Brule, some 20 miles
north to the North Platte.*

*From these points the Oregon Trail followed the North
Platte River to present day Wyoming. Today this route
begins at Ogallala as US 26 and runs northwesterly
into Wyoming.*

*Today's US 26 actually follows the old Mormon Trail
from Lewellen to Bridgeport, a distance of 56 miles before
crossing to the south bank where it parallels the Oregon
Trail for a dozen miles before crossing the river again to run
along the north bank following the general route of the
Mormon Trail.*

*These two trails—the Oregon Trail and the Mormon
Trail—were heavily traveled for nearly two decades. It was
along these trails emigrants noted some of the great
landmarks along their westward route—Courthouse
Rock, Jail Rock and, of course, the spectacular
Chimney Rock and Scott's Bluff. While Indians seldom
attacked or bothered travelers along this part of the
route, many died here as a result of diseases contracted
earlier along the trails. Many graves marked the trail
along this 160 mile stretch.*

*This route offers some of the most picturesque and
historic sights in western Nebraska.*

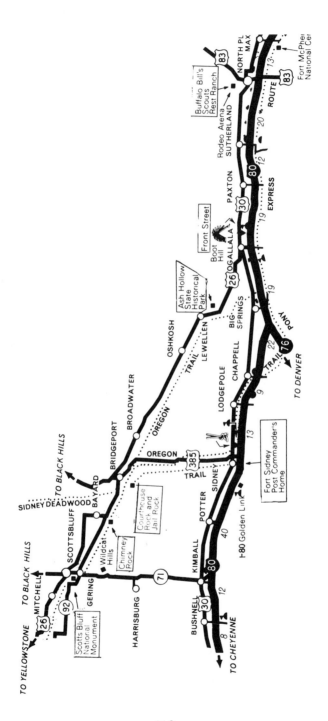

NORTH PL
MAX

Fort McPhers
National Cer

83

ROUTE 83

13

Buffalo Bill's
Scouts
Rest Ranch

Rodeo Arena
SUTHERLAND

20

PAXTON

80

12

EXPRESS

30

19

Front Street

Boot
Hill

OGALLALA

GALLALA

26

BIG-
SPRINGS

19

Ash Hollow
State
Historical
Park

OSHKOSH

LEWELLEN

OREGON

TRAIL

BROADWATER

CHAPPELL

PONY

22

76

TRAIL

LODGEPOLE

9

TO DENVER

BRIDGEPORT

OREGON

385

TRAIL

13

Fort Sidney
Post Commander's
Home

BAYARD

TO BLACK HILLS

SIDNEY DEADWOOD

SIDNEY

Courthouse
Rock and
Jail Rock

I-80 Golden Link

SCOTTSBLUFF

POTTER

40

Wildcat
Hills

Chimney
Rock

TO BLACK HILLS

MITCHELL

GERING

71

KIMBALL

80

92

HARRISBURG

BUSHNELL

30

12

26

Scotts Bluff
National
Monument

8

TO YELLOWSTONE

TO BLACK HILLS

TO CHEYENNE

116

WHAT THE PIONEERS SAW—Famous Chimney Rock was just one of the many landmarks along the Oregon Trail in this part of Nebraska. The Oregon Trail Wagon Train, Bayard, offers trips along the old trail in this area.

OGALLALA TO THE WYOMING STATE LINE
Via U.S. Highway 26

Ogallala is Nebraska's "Cowboy Capital" and is the starting point for this picturesque drive to the Wyoming state line. (See listing in Section 2).

LEWELLEN

LEWELLEN (pop. 368), 30 miles west, is just west of Lake McConaughy and north of the North Platte River on one of the earliest trails west, the **Mormon Trail**. Lewellen was laid out in 1906 and the railroad arrived the next year. The town was incorporated in 1920. Just south and east of Lewellen is **Ash Hollow**, famous on the **Oregon Trail** which paralleled the Mormon Trail along the south side of the North Platte River.

ASH HOLLOW STATE HISTORICAL PARK, located ½

mile east and three miles south of Lewellen on US 26, was not only a noted spot on the Oregon Trail but an important prehistoric site also. Fossils, pre-dating the Ice Age, have been found here including camels, rhinoceroses and long-jawed mastodons. Archaeological excavations in Ash Hollow indicate that early man used the area as much as 8,000 years ago. **E. D. Cope** gathered a collection of fossils here in 1879. An interpretive center in the park provides information about these scientific discoveries as well as the early day history of the American emigrants on their move westward.

The first wagons traveling through Ash Hollow are believed to have been those of **Capt. Benjamin L. E. Bonneville** and his trading expedition in 1832. The first women to enter Ash Hollow were two missionary wives, **Myra Eells** and **Mary Walker**, who traveled West in 1838. The first emigrant train to travel the valley was the **Bidwell-Bartleson Party** which passed through Ash Hollow in 1841.

WINDLASS HILL is part of the park, located 2¼ miles south on US 26. This hill on the Oregon Trail was difficult to descend and time consuming. Wagons had to be lowered down the steep slope by ropes. Men, animals and wagons were endangered in this intricate maneuver although only two accidents were actually reported by travelers here. Once the wagons made it to the bottom of the hill the emigrants spent a few days resting themselves and their animals and repairing equipment. An abandoned trapper's cabin, built in 1846, served as an unofficial postoffice where mail was deposited to be picked up and taken to the "states" by eastbound travelers.

There were as many as four trading posts in the canyon at different times during the 1840s and 1850s. Archaeological research has located the site of one of these posts along the trail. Here, emigrants could trade for supplies and Indians could barter skins for beads, ornaments and supplies. This may have been the trading post and U.S. mail station burned by the Indians in the spring of 1855. Nearby is a restored schoolhouse built in 1903 of native stone.

An interpretive center has been built over the entrance of the Ash Hollow Cave and a visitors' center opened on the bluffs overlooking the mouth of the canyon. Once in the park, in the Windlass Hill section, one can view deep wagon ruts created by the heavy travel over a century ago. The Visitors Center is open 8 a.m. to 6 p.m. daily, the year-round. A Park Entry Permit is re-

Court House and Jail Rocks were famous landmarks on the Oregon Trail.

quired ($2 daily, $10 annual).

A number of pioneer graves may be found in a cemetery on a grassy slope in Ash Hollow. Among those buried here are **Rachel Pattison**, a young girl who died of cholera in 1849. **Dennis B. Clary** and **W. H. Gilliard**, both ministers, were the earliest settlers. Clary was the first permanent settler in Ash Hollow. He and Gilliard were responsible for the establishment of the Ash Hollow community cemetery.

The **Battle of Ash Hollow**, also known as the **Battle of Blue Water**, occurred September 3, 1855 on Blue Water Creek, north of Lewellen, when **Gen. William S. Harney**, with some 600 troops, attacked a band of some 250 Brules, led by **Little Thunder**, to punish them for the **Grattan Massacre** of 1854. That massacre occurred August 19, 1854, a few miles east of Fort Laramie, when **Lt. John L. Grattan**, 28 soldiers and an interpreter were killed by a party of Brule Sioux Indians in a dispute over a lame cow belonging to a Mormon emigrant.

In the Battle of Ash Hollow Harney's forces sustained light casualties—five killed, seven wounded and one missing. The Indians, on the other hand, had 86 killed, six wounded and 70 women and children taken captive. The prisoners were taken to Fort Kearny where they were held briefly. **Spotted Tail**, a subchief involved in the Grattan Massacre and the Battle of Ash Hollow, surrendered to authorities at Fort Laramie a short time later for his part in these actions. He was wounded at Ash Hollow—twice by pistol fire and twice by saber slashes.

The Army established a temporary fort—**Fort Grattan** just south of the Platte River in 1855-56 as a show of force to the Indians. General Harney used Fort Kearny as headquarters while gathering forces for this campaign against the Indians.

OSHKOSH

OSHKOSH (pop. 1,060), 12 miles west of Lewellen, is the county seat of Garden County. Five men established the **Oshkosh Land and Cattle Company** in 1885. (Two of the men were from Oshkosh, Wisconsin, thus the name for their company.) A general store and postoffice were opened in 1889. The town was platted in 1905 and the railroad arrived in 1908. Oshkosh became the county seat in 1909.

There are two small museums in Oshkosh. One is the original ROCK HOUSE SCHOOL MUSEUM with interesting displays of local historical significance and the THEATRE MUSEUM with bird displays from the **Miles Maryott** collection. The Thea-

Three National Monuments

There are three U.S. National Monuments in Nebraska.

Agate Fossil Beds National Monument, which became famous for its deposits of animal fossils, is located in Sioux County in the Panhandle.

The Homestead National Monument of America, site of one of the first pieces of land claimed under the Homestead Act of 1862 by Daniel Freeman, is located near Beatrice.

Scotts Bluff National Monument, a landmark site on the Oregon Trail, is located near Gering in the Panhandle.

tre Museum occupies the old rock Opera House built in 1908. Both museums are open daily from Memorial Day to Labor Day and by appointment. Donations are accepted.

South of Oshkosh on N-27, at the end of the bridge, is a marker for the **John Hollman** gravesite. The grave is two miles west of this point. Hollman, one of the early day emigrants, died here on the Oregon Trail. Hundreds of emigrants along the western trails died annually from disease, injuries and gunshot wounds. A few were killed by Indians raiders.

Crescent Lake National Wildlife Refuge is located 25 miles north of Oshkosh. This area north is part of Nebraska's famed Sandhills region, some of the nation's best cattle raising country. There are several very large cattle ranches to the north.

LISCO, 16 miles west, was founded by **Reuben Lisco** in 1909. The Union Pacific Railroad arrived in 1908. It remains an unincorporated farm town.

BROADWATER (pop. 161), 14 miles west, is located on the old Mormon Trail. N-92 crosses the North Platte River here and continues northwest following the river. About 14 miles west on N-92 is the site of the **Amanda Laman** grave along the old Oregon Trail. She died of cholera and was buried here June 23, 1850. Her husband returned to St. Louis to purchase a tombstone for her grave and returned with it in a later emigrant train. Amanda Laman was one of the thousands of emigrants to fall victim to cholera.

121

Between Broadwater and Bridgeport are the **Ancient Bluff Ruins**, a curious set of formations along the Mormon Trail. It was a resting place along the trail.

BRIDGEPORT

BRIDGEPORT (pop. 1,685), 16 miles west, offers a spectacular view of **Courthouse Rock** and **Jail Rock**, rising abruptly from the level plain. These famous landmarks are located six miles south of Bridgeport. Courthouse Rock was named by some of the earliest day travelers from St. Louis on the Oregon Trail who believed the largest landmark resembled the courthouse building back home. Another story claims the butte was named after an outlaw band of 12 desperadoes that had been tried, convicted and executed on the summit for their vicious crimes. There are many other old tales about these landmarks and how they came to be.

Bridgeport is the county seat of Morrill County, a farm trade center.

Bridgeport was an important site on the **Sidney-Black Hills Trail**. It was here the trail crossed the North Platte River over the 2,000 foot wooden toll bridge, **Clarke's Bridge**, constructed in 1876. This bridge was built by **Henry T. Clarke** of Omaha and was used until 1900. Several buildings were constructed at the southern end of the bridge, including a postoffice, general store, stage barn and other miscellaneous buildings, all destroyed by a raging prairie fire in 1910. A toll of $1 was charged for a team using the bridge; an individual was charged 50 cents. At times soldiers were called upon to guard the span from Indian attacks. A Pony Express relay station was established near Courthouse Rock. Remains of **Courthouse Rock Station** have been identified five miles south and one mile west of Bridgeport.

PIONEER TRAILS MUSEUM, south on US 385 across from the Burlington Northern depot, Bridgeport, offers exhibits and displays relating to area history. It features one of the most complete displays of a barbed wire collection as well as many other items. It is open 10 a.m. to 6 p.m. Monday through Saturday and 1 to 6 p.m. Sunday, Memorial Day through Labor Day.

BAYARD

BAYARD (pop. 1,448), 15 miles west, was named for Bayard, Iowa, in 1887. Three and a half miles southwest of Bayard is famous **Chimney Rock**, believed to have been named by **Joshua Pilcher**, employed by the Missouri Fur Company, in 1827. The tall spire could be seen by emigrants on the trail for three or four days before they reached the site. A historical marker is located

A PICTURESQUE SIGHT—Chimney Rock, south of Bayard, was a familiar landmark to pioneers on the Oregon Trail. This National Historic Site is located south of Bayard.

on US 26 and N-92, 1.5 miles from Bayard. Chimney Rock was designated a National Historic Site August 9, 1956.

From Bayard US 26 intersects N-92 at a point about 1½ miles northeast of this historic site. A county road off N-92 runs to within a ¼ mile of Chimney Rock. Travel from this point is by foot only. There are no services at this site and the National Park Service warns that the terrain is rough and it is essential hikers wear good boots and hiking clothes. Hikers are especially warned to watch for rattlesnakes. This side trip is well worth the time and effort. The Nebraska Historical Society operates a Mobile Museum, just off the highway, telling the history of this area, between Memorial Day and Labor Day. The museum is open daily from 8 a.m. to 7 p.m. during these summer months.

The **Chimney Rock Pony Express Relay Station** was located between the landmark and the North Platte River about 300 yards off the Oregon Trail. The site was located in 1980 and the foundations of the building are still visible. Persons wishing to visit this site should contact The Oregon Trail Wagon Train, Bayard.

McGREW (pop. 109), on N-92 five miles west of the turn off to Bayard, was incorporated in 1911. It serves as a small farm town.

MELBETA (pop. 151), eight miles on N-92, is only a mile east of the site of **Ficklin's Spring Station**, which served as a Pony Express and stage station, along the Oregon Trail. This station was named for **Benjamin F. Ficklin**, general superintendent for the Pony Express field operations. A marker indicates the location of this important station. The town was incorporated in 1914.

The Oregon Trail route splits near present day Melbeta, with one route going around the southern edge of Scotts Bluff (referring to the range of bluffs here rather than the single, large bluff in today's National Monument). After 1851 the main route went through the pass at Scotts Bluff. Both of these routes came together again at Horse Creek, about 25 miles west.

MINATARE (pop. 968), two miles north of Melbeta on US 26, was named for the Minnetaree, a Sioux Indian tribe. Minatare was incorporated in 1906.

SCOTTSBLUFF/GERING

Scottsbluff/Gering have joined together to promote the area they share.

GERING (pop. 7,511), founded in 1887 and incorporated in 1890, is the county seat of Scotts Bluff County. SCOTTSBLUFF (pop. 14,130) was settled after 1885, laid out in 1899 and incorporated in 1900. Scottsbluff is located on the north side of the North Platte River, just across from Gering. Both serve an extensive irrigated farm region.

Scotts Bluff County was originally part of Cheyenne County but as the population grew in 1886-87, many felt the county was too large. As a result, an election was held the following year to create four new counties—Banner, Deuel, Kimball and Scotts

SITE OF PONY EXPRESS STATION—This monument, a mile west of Melbeta, marks the site of Ficklin's Springs Station which served the Pony Express. In the early 1870s it was used as the cattle ranch headquarters for Mark Coad.

Bluff—sharply reducing the size of Cheyenne County.

Gering was founded as **Vendome** April 27, 1887 but was renamed shortly after for **Martin Gering**, the town's first banker. Gering became the county seat with the creation of Scotts Bluff County.

Scottsbluff was named for **Hiram Scott**, the trapper who died in 1828 near the bluffs which today bears his name after being deserted by his companions. The story is told that Scott was with a party of trappers when he was wounded. Two companions were to accompany Scott by boat down the North Platte River to a point near the Bluffs. On this river trip, the boat capsized and their supplies were lost. The two companions soon realized that the main trapping party had passed and having no supplies, abandoned Scott. His skeleton was found near the bluffs a considerable distance from where his companions say he died.

The town was laid out by the Lincoln Land Company, a subsidiary of the Burlington Railroad, which arrived in February 1900.

During World War II, the U.S. Army Air Corps operated a

training facility at the county airport, just east of Scottsbluff. A World War II prisoner-of-war camp was located east of the airport.

TERRYTOWN (pop. 726), at the northwest corner of Gering city limits, was incorporated January 24, 1949.

There are many historic attractions in the area.

THE NORTH PLATTE VALLEY MUSEUM, 10th and J St., Gering, contains many exhibits and displays on regional history. It is one of the finer small museums and through its presentation does an excellent job of portraying life in this area. Hours: 8:30 a.m. to 5 p.m., Monday through Saturday, 1 to 5 p.m. Sunday.

REBECCA WINTERS GRAVE SITE, 1.5 miles east of Scottsbluff on US 26, marks the grave of a 50-year old Mormon woman who died August 15, 1852, a victim of cholera. She was born in New York in 1802 and was a pioneer of the Church of Jesus Christ of Latter Day Saints. In June 1852, Rebecca, with her husband, Hiram, joined others of their faith in the great journey to Utah. Cholera struck their wagon train when it arrived in Nebraska's Platte Valley and many died. Rebecca fell ill and died suddenly. She was buried in a prairie grave with a simple ceremony. A friend chiseled her name and the year on an iron wagon tire to mark the grave. The Burlington Railroad found the grave marker in 1902 and changed their right-of-way to save and protect the grave. Rebecca's descendants later erected a monument at the grave.

SCOTTS BLUFF NATIONAL MONUMENT, three miles west of Gering on N-92, was created by an Act of Congress in 1919 and the OREGON TRAIL MUSEUM was established under a provision of the Act. The National Park Service acquired the 3,000 acre tract December 12, 1919. In 1949 the William H. Jackson Memorial Wing was opened at the museum. Jackson, a noted pioneer artist-photographer, worked as a bullwhacker on a wagon train passing this area in 1866. Many of his paintings are on exhibit in the museum.

Jackson, at the age of 95, pointed out his 1866 campsite to members of the Oregon Trail Memorial Association during a visit to the National Monument in 1938.

Programs held in the park during the summer tell the story of the struggle of the pioneers who traveled the American West. These film showings start at 9 p.m., weather permitting. Museum summer hours (starting June 1): 8 a.m. to 8 p.m. daily. A $3 a day charge is made for taking vehicles up the summit of Scotts Bluff

A PROMINENT TRAIL SITE—Scotts Bluff National Monument, near Scottsbluff, was named for an early-day trapper who died at its base. This massive formation is one of the most prominent sties on the road West.

and hours are from 8 a.m. to 7:30 p.m. There are also hiking trails to be enjoyed. Visitors may walk less than a mile from the museum to a point where ruts from wagons crossing Mitchell Pass on the Oregon Trail are still visible. These wagon ruts can also be seen from the Bluff's summit. Also from this summit one can see Chimney Rock to the east and Laramie Peak, over 100 miles to the west.

Dome Rock, just to the south of Scotts Bluff, received its name from early day trappers. Between these two bluffs is **Mitchell Pass** which eventually became the route of the Pony Express, freighters, stage coaches and telegraph lines. This pass, unnamed until 1864, became an important part of the Oregon Trail in 1852. Originally Mitchell Pass was called several names by the emigrants, the Devil's Gap, Marshall Gap, and simply the pass through Scotts Bluff or The Gap.

A Pony Express "home station" was established at **Andrew Drips'** trading post at Scotts Bluff. This station was halfway between Mud Springs and Fort Laramie, both designated as home stations for the Pony Express. In the late 1850s, **John M. Hock-**

aday, a mail contractor, operated **U.S. Mail Station No. 23** at this point. Later, in the 1860s, it served the Overland Stage lines and Pacific Telegraph (later Western Union) as an operating station.

Pierre Chouteau, Jr. & Company (formerly the American Fur Company) established a trading post, called **Fort John** (the original Fort John was at Fort Laramie), at Scotts Bluff (near the site of the later Fort Mitchell) in late 1849. **Andrew S. Drips**, a well-known fur trapper and trader for nearly 30 years, was in charge of this trading operation. Their competitors and rivals were the Robidouxs and to confuse them, Drips moved his post from Scotts Bluff to a location in **Helvas Canyon**, not far south of Robidoux Pass. The canyon was due south of the pass through Scotts Bluff. Drips moved Fort John again during the winter of 1851-52—back to Scotts Bluff to take advantage of redirected travel through the Gap.

Two and a half miles northwest of the pass, just off US 26, is the site of **Fort Mitchell**, constructed in the fall of 1864 to guard the trails after the Indian uprisings on the Plains that summer. **Capt. Jacob S. Shuman**, commanding officer, Company H, 11th Ohio Cavalry, was ordered to build the fort and during the construction period, which started around the first of September, the sub-post of Fort Laramie was called **Camp Shuman**. The named was changed to **Camp Mitchell**, then **Fort Mitchell**, to honor **Brig. Gen. Robert B. Mitchell**, commanding general, District of Nebraska, responsible for the safety of all who traveled the emigrant and overland trails. The fort was abandoned in 1867.

Robidoux Pass, the original pass, lies eight miles southwest of Gering in the Wildcat Hills. This pass was used as a section of the route of the Oregon Trail through 1851. As in Mitchell Pass, wagon ruts are still visible in Robidoux Pass, possibly named for **Basil Robidoux**, an early day French fur trader. The old trail went through Gering Valley and at the west end of the pass Robidoux established a trading post in 1848 to serve the heavily traveled trail. This post was destroyed by Indians in a raid in 1852. Robidoux Pass was used from 1843 to 1851 when the trail was changed to a more northerly route, closer to the North Platte River, through Mitchell Pass. There are several pioneer graves in the Robidoux Pass area. Among these is the grave of **F. Dunn**, 26, from Illinois, who died of cholera about 10 p.m., June 13, 1849. (His grave was recorded by U.S. government surveyors in 1878.) Pioneer diarists noted many fresh graves along the trail. This general area has been the site of successful archaeological digs over the years sponsored by the Smithsonian Institute and University of Nebraska Museum. The University has found some unusual artifacts and bones at a site northwest of Signal Butte, southwest of Robidoux Pass.

Other Area Attractions

WILDCAT HILLS AND GAME RESERVE, eight miles south of Scottsbluff on N-71, is a scenic spot where one can see buffalo, elk and deer. There are a number of foot trails for hikers in the Reserve, as well as picnic facilities with clear running water. Stage Hill, on the old stage route from Kimball to Gering, is in the Reserve.

MITCHELL

MITCHELL (pop. 1,984), eight miles west of Scottsbluff on US 26, was incorporated in 1902. It was named in honor of **Brig. Gen. Robert Mitchell**, the general who led troops against the Indians in 1864-65.

Thirty-four miles north of Mitchell, on US 29, is AGATE FOSSIL BEDS NATIONAL MONUMENT, administered by the National Park Service since 1965. The Agate Fossil Beds contain deposits dating from 25 to 13 million years ago, during the Miocene Epoch. Among the ancient life found is the **Diceratherium**, a small fleet-footed, two-horned rhinoceros that once roamed the Great Plains in large numbers; the **Moropus**, with a head like a horse, body of tapir, with front legs like a rhinoceros with claws used for defense and to dig up roots for food, and the **Dinohyus**, a gigantic pig-like mammal with a large head with tusks, also referred to as the "Terrible Pig."

The first to discover fossil bones at Agate Fossil Beds was **Capt. James H. Cook**, about 1878. Fossils found at this site have been exhibited throughout the world. Cook acquired Agate Springs Ranch in 1887 from his father-in-law, **Dr. E. B. Graham**, who had established the ranch a few years earlier. Captain Cook opened his ranch to paleontologists and there have been many scientific excavations over the years.

Monument headquarters and visitors' center is three miles east of Agate Springs Ranch, between the Niobrara River and the county road. The Monument occupies some 1,970 acres of land.

MORRILL (pop. 1,138), six miles west of Mitchell, was incorporated in 1907.

HENRY (pop. 155), seven miles west of Morrill, was originally in Wyoming. The town was moved into Nebraska so residents could enjoy better railroad freight rates. The town was incorporated in 1916.

LYMAN

LYMAN (pop. 549), six miles south of Henry on N-79C Link, was incorporated in 1922. Two historical events are recorded for this area. The **Horse Creek Treaty** was signed here in 1851 and the **Battle of Horse Creek** fought nearby in 1865.

The largest assembly of Indians in American history—some 10,000—including Arapahoes, Arikari, Assiniboin, Blackfeet, Cheyenne, Crow, Gros Ventre, Mandan and Sioux, gathered near the junction of the North Platte River and Horse Creek to sign the **First Treaty of Fort Laramie**, more commonly called the **Horse Creek Treaty** September 8, 1851. Purpose of this treaty was to put an end to intertribal warfare and provided for safe passage of emigrant trains along the Platte. It was broken almost immediately after being signed.

A Pony Express relay station, **Horse Creek Station**, was located on the west bank of Horse Creek, about two miles northeast of Lyman, in 1860-61.

The Battle of Horse Creek occurred June 14, 1865. A military contingent, commanded by **Capt. William D. Fouts**, commanding officer of Company D, 7th Iowa Cavalry, was escorting 1,500 Sioux Indians, including warriors, women and children, from Fort Laramie to Fort Kearny to break up the growing number of Indians gathering around Fort Laramie. Other officers in the party were **Capt. John Wilcox**, commanding a detachment of Company B; **1st Lt. Jeremiah Triggs** and **2nd Lt. Dudley Haywood**, both of Company D, and **1st Lt. James G. Smith**, Company A. Fouts and Triggs had their families with them on this expedition.

The trip started June 11 and two days out of Fort Laramie the Indians began quarreling among themselves as many believed the Army was taking them on a "death march." As the expedition was breaking camp the morning of June 14, the Indians balked. When Captain Fouts and a small escort went to investigate the Indians opened fire instantly killing the captain and four of his enlisted men. Four other troopers were wounded. Captain Wilcox assumed command and in the ensuing fight the Indians escaped north.

Lyman is one mile east of the state line via N-92. Henry, six miles north on US 26, is adjacent to the state line.

Section 4

In southwest Nebraska, two major highways, US 6 and 34, are the major arteries east to Hastings. The last town on US 6 in Colorado, before entering Nebraska, is Holyoke, about 12 miles from the state line. US 34 runs through Wray and Laird, Colorado, before entering Nebraska.

US 34 runs through Republican Valley wheat and corn land until it joins US 6 near Culbertson, some 75 miles east. In the 1870s and '80s, this area was the scene of major Texas cattle drives heading for the railhead at Ogallala.

Near Trenton, in Hitchcock County, in the summer of 1873, the Pawnee Indians suffered heavy casualties in a one-sided battle against the Sioux. The Pawnees may have been wiped out had not a cavalry troop come to their aid.

US 6, to the north, follows along the general route of the Frenchman River and the major historic attraction is Champion Mill State Historical Park.

After the two highways join, the first major town is McCook, home of Nebraska's U.S. Senator George W. Norris, father of the Tennessee Valley Authority.

Further east, and south on N-89, is Hendley, hometown of Edwin Perkins, who concocted Kool-Aid, and seven miles east on N-89 is Beaver City, hometown of Dr. Frank Brewster, the "flying doctor" of the 1920s and '30s.

Back on US 6 and 34 are the towns of Holdrege, home of the Phelps County Museum; Minden, home of the nationally-known Pioneer Village, and Hastings, home of Hastings College and the Hastings Museum.

This route runs through both dryland and irrigated farm country. Wheat, corn, milo and alfalfa are the principal farm crops. This is also cattle country.

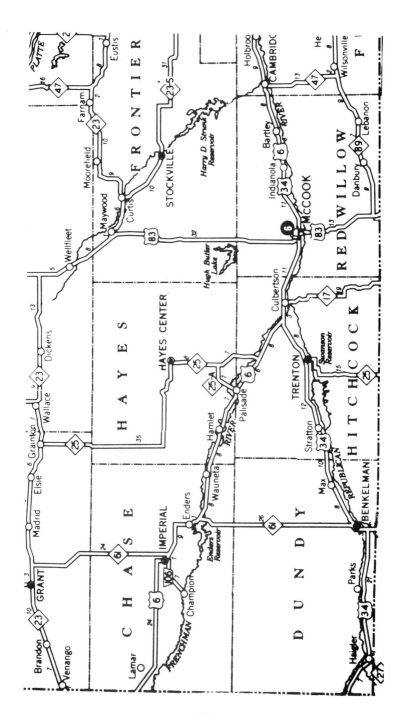

LONELY PRAIRIE SENTINEL—Windmills are still used to pump water for livestock in many of the large pastures in western Nebraska. Scenes like this are frequent sights in the ranching areas.

THE STATE LINE TO HASTINGS
East via US 6 and 34

The trip from the Colorado-Nebraska state line to Hastings, via US 6 and 34, is 188 miles. The highways, about 25 miles apart as they enter Nebraska, merge 70 miles into the state and continue as one to Hastings where they split again. This section is devoted to the 188 mile trip from the state line to Hastings.

Entering Nebraska on US 6, the traveler passes LAMAR (pop. 60), just north and six miles from the Colorado state line. Lamar was named to honor **Lucius Q. C. Lamar**, Secretary of Interior in **President Grover Cleveland's** first cabinet and an Associate Justice of the U.S. Supreme Court.

Twenty-four miles east of the state line is IMPERIAL (pop. 1,941), county seat of Chase County, named for **Champion S. Chase**, a one-time mayor of Omaha and Nebraska's first Attorney General. The county was organized in 1886. The postoffice of Imperial was established December 14, 1885 and the name, Imperial, was provided by **Thomas Mercier**, a French Canadian who settled in the area.

CHAMPION

Seven miles southwest of Imperial, on N-15A Spur, is CHAMPION, site of Champion Mill State Historical Park. Originally called **Hamilton**, the town of Champion was renamed for Champion S. Chase in 1887. The town is the site of the **Champion Mill**, on the banks of Frenchman River, the only water-powered mill still operable in Nebraska. The mill was built in 1886-88. It burned in the early 1890s but was immediately rebuilt. The mill was turned over to the Nebraska Game and Parks Commission as a state historical park in a ceremony held September 25, 1969. A State Park Permit ($2 daily, $10 annual) is required.

CHASE COUNTY HISTORICAL SOCIETY MUSEUM is located in Champion. It houses an extensive Indian artifacts collection, together with pioneer memorabilia and some machinery and tools.

Nine miles east of Imperial is the tiny village of ENDERS, serving Enders Reservoir.

WAUNETA

Seventeen miles east of Imperial is WAUNETA (pop. 740) which some say was named for the song, *"Juanita."* The town was founded in 1887 by **W. S. Fisher.** A waterfall on Frenchman Creek, a block from Main Street, served as a hiding place for several women and children during one of the first Indian raids in this area.

Driving east is the tiny village of HAMLET (pop. 60), in the southwest corner of Hayes County, and eight miles further is PALISADE (pop. 401), just across the county line in Hitchcock County. Founded in 1879, Palisade was named for the bluff along the nearby river. The town was incorporated in 1894. Oil was discovered in this area in the 1960-70s and there are many producing wells in the region.

ESTELLE POST OFFICE was located in the vicinity of Hamlet. Begun in 1878 by John Daniels, it was finished in 1881. It was constructed as a rectangular building of native stone with a flat roof.

HAYES CENTER (pop. 231), county seat of Hayes County, named for **President Rutherford B. Hayes**, lies 14 miles north of Palisade on N-25A. Ten miles from Hayes Center, on Red Willow Creek, is the site of the **Grand Duke Alexis** camp of 1872 when the Russian duke, 22 year old brother of the Czar, came to

OLD MILL STILL OPERABLE—Champion Mill, located on the banks of Frenchman Creek at Champion, is the only water-powered mill still operable in Nebraska. The old mill, a state historical park, was built in 1886-88 and burned in 1890 only to be immediately rebuilt.

the area for a buffalo hunt. **"Buffalo Bill" Cody** led the party hosted by **Gen. Phil Sheridan** and an Army contingent from Fort McPherson up on the Platte. **Spotted Tail** and a large band of his Sioux warriors were camped in the area during the duke's hunt and they were induced by Cody to participate in the hunt and perform a war dance for the royal guest. (See listing for North Platte.)

Fourteen miles east of Palisade US 6 meets with US 34, three miles west of Culbertson.

ENTERING NEBRASKA ON US 34

Crossing into Nebraska on US 34, the traveler first arrives in HAIGLER (pop. 224), established on the site of the Three Bar Ranch owned by Jake Haigler, the first postmaster. Four miles east of Haigler a marker locates the **Texas Trail Canyon**, a major cattle trail north after 1880. In 1883-84 a checkpoint was set up in the canyon where Texas cattle could be checked for brands and disease. The trail drives ended in 1886. The notorious

INDIAN WAR CHIEF—Pawnee Killer led the band of Sioux warriors in an attack on units of the 7th U.S. Cavalry while they were camped near Benkelman June 24, 1867. He also was involved in the Nelson Buck survey party massacre on Beaver Creek in 1869.

Olives—Print and **Ira**—used this canyon as part of their range in 1876. One of the early deaths here occurred when Ira Olive killed a cowboy in a gunfight.

BENKELMAN

Eleven miles east is PARKS, on the north side of the highway and approximately 13 miles further east is BENKELMAN (pop. 1,228), county seat of Dundy County. The town, founded in 1886 as **Collinsville**, is situated at the forks of the Republican and Arikaree Rivers. Near here was the **Leavenworth and Pike's Express Company's Station 18**. Dundy County was formed May 8, 1884.

Oil has been developed in the county during the early 1980s. Corn and wheat are the principle crops.

Lt. Col. George A. Custer, commanding six companies of the 7th Cavalry, camped at the southern outskirts of present day Benkelman June 22-30, 1867. As dawn broke June 24 Custer's camp was attacked by a band of Sioux Indians led by **Pawnee Killer**. The raiders wounded a sentry, parlayed with Custer and his officers and rode away. A short time later Pawnee Killer's raiders ambushed a captain and his troop of 40 men seven miles northwest of Custer's camp. Two Indians were killed in this brief encounter.

SITE OF HISTORIC INDIAN BATTLE—A marker and monument (seen on the left), just outside of Trenton, commemorates the last battle between the Sioux and Pawnee Indians. A party of Sioux warriors attacked a band of Pawnee buffalo hunters in the valley below August 5, 1873 killing between 60 and 75 Pawnees.

From Benkelman, US 34 runs through the Republican Valley to MAX, eight miles east and on 10 miles further to STRATTON (pop. 496), one of the many towns devastated by the Republican River flood of May 1935. Stratton was founded as **Frontier** in 1879 and was incorporated as the town of Stratton in 1881.

TRENTON (pop. 797), 12 miles east of Stratton, is the county seat of Hitchcock County. The town, which served the great Texas trail herds being driven to the Ogallala railhead, was first called **Trail City**. The town was laid out by the Lincoln Land Company when the Burlington Railroad line was extended to

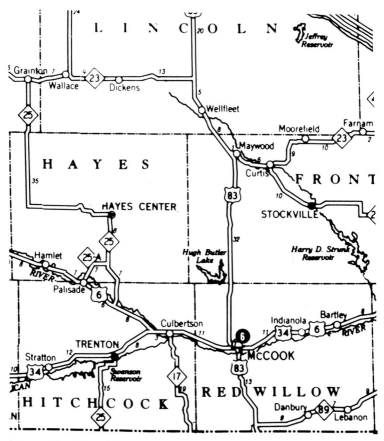

Denver in 1882. The town was moved in 1885 and renamed Trenton, for Trenton, New Jersey. Hitchcock County was organized August 30, 1873 and was named for **U.S. Senator Phineas W. Hitchcock**. Trenton became the county seat in 1893.

Just east of Trenton, on US 34, is **Massacre Canyon** where **Sky Chief** and 700 Pawnees, on a buffalo hunt, were surprised and attacked by a well-armed Sioux war party on August 5, 1873. These two Indian tribes had been fierce enemies for centuries and the Sioux believed the Pawnees had trespassed into their territory. In the one-sided battle somewhere between 60-75 Pawnees were killed and more than 100 were wounded or captured.

Cavalry units stationed at Fort McPherson, near North Platte, were in camp on Blackwood Creek, now Culbertson. They were summoned by a handful of settlers who were being harassed by Sioux Indians camped along the Frenchman River near Palisade.

In the battle the Pawnees were broken and fled to the Republican River south of the canyon and then east along the river to Culbertson. They continued to their village on the Loup River. A short time after their return, they were moved to a reservation in Oklahoma (then Indian Territory).

A monument and marker are located along the highway to commemorate this tragedy, the last battle between these Indian tribes. The faces of **John Grass** (Sioux) and **Ruling-His-Sun** (Pawnee) are carved in the 35-foot granite monument.

THE CARMODY SITE is located on a ridge a quarter of a mile below Trenton Dam. Glass beads and other evidence suggests the Pawnees also visited this site.

US HIGHWAYS 6 AND 34 ARE JOINED

Seven miles east of Trenton US 34 and US 6 converge and for the next 130 miles (to Hastings) these highways are joined.

CULBERTON

Three miles east of the junction is CULBERTSON (pop. 767), Hitchcock's first county seat (1873-1893). The town was founded as a trading post during the summer of 1873 by **W. Z. Taylor**. For the first two years Taylor's store, J. E. Kleven's blacksmith shop and postoffice made up the town named for **Maj. Alexander Culbertson**, a noted early day fur trader who was living in Orleans, Nebraska, at the time.

In 1875, Texas cattle by the thousands were brought into this area. Ranchers ranged their cattle during the spring, summer and fall months and moved into Culbertson during the winter months. The railroad arrived in 1881 to bring homesteaders to the county and the town became a pioneer irrigation center. A marker in Culbertson's city park, a block south of the highway at the small tower, briefly describes Culbertson's early day history.

STONE CHURCH is located along Driftwood Creek, seven miles south of Culbertson. It is a one-story, native-stone structure with a steep gable roof.

McCOOK— HOMETOWN OF SENATOR NORRIS

McCOOK (pop. 8,404), located at the crossroads of US 6 and 34 (east-west) and US 83, (north-south), was established as a frontier outpost and cattlemen's trading center on the Republican River in 1879 on land belonging to the **Rider Sheep Ranch**. **Alexander Campbell**, division superintendent for the Burlington & Missouri Railroad, chose **Fairview** for his division point with the help of Rider and others. The building of a roundhouse, railroad shops and other structures drew an influx of railroad

FRANK LLOYD WRIGHT DESIGN—This home, at 602 Norris Ave., McCook, is the only structure in Nebraska designed by the famed Frank Lloyd Wright.

workers and the town grew. Fairview became the town of McCook with the filing of the original plat in 1882. The city was named for **Brig. Gen. Alexander McDowell McCook** (1831-1903), one of a family of which eight brothers and their father all served as officers in the Union Army during the Civil War.

McCook became the county seat of Red Willow County in 1896. The county was founded in the spring of 1873 with Indianola selected as the county seat.

A United States land office opened in 1883. Settlers continued to take up the farmland by homestead, preemption or under timber claim laws. Some of the early day ranchers got their start with calves left behind on the Texas cattle drives heading north to the Ogallala railhead passing west of McCook, in the vicinity of Culbertson.

Harold Sutton, a McCook jeweler, had his new home on Norris Avenue, designed by **Frank Lloyd Wright** (1867-1957), one of American's most influential architects, in 1905. It is the only Frank Lloyd Wright structure in Nebraska. There are three houses of similar design in the midwest—one in Chicago, one in LaGrange, Illinois, and one in South Bend, Indiana. Wright's first distinctive buildings were homes he designed in his famous "prairie style," which took open spaces inside the home and expanded these outdoors through porches and terraces. The Suttons lived in the home from 1905 to 1959 when they sold it to a local physician who used the house as a clinic until 1978 when it was sold to a private party. It was listed on the National Register of Historic Places in 1978. The residence, at 602 Norris Ave., is not open to the public but may be viewed by driving or walking by.

In 1926 McCook Junior College, the first junior college in the state, started in the upper level of the old YMCA on Norris Ave. downtown. It expanded to a campus of its own in 1935. In 1973, it became McCook Community College, a part of the statewide system of technical community colleges. **Senator Perlee W. Scott**, of McCook, introduced the bill in the state legislature in 1925 to establish a junior college system in Nebraska.

In late May 1935 a flood destroyed millions of dollars of property and took over 100 lives in the Republican Valley. McCook was one of the hard hit communities in this disaster Under the direction of the Bureau of Reclamation and the U.S. Corps of Engineers, four large dams and lakes were built in the McCook area. These include the 1,628 acre **Hugh Butler Lake**, 12 miles north off US 83; 4,974 acre **Swanson Reservoir**, 30 miles west off US 34; 1,707 acre **Enders Reservoir**, 35 miles northwest off US 6; and 1,768 acre **Harry Strunk Lake**, 35 miles east off US 6.

There have been other natural disasters in this area. A June 11, 1928 storm hit the west part of town destroying 115 homes, but, miraculously there were no fatalities. A flash flood struck July 18, 1928 and washed out extensive railroad trackage and bridges as well as part of the highway east of McCook. The dust storms in the '30s are still the topic of conversation when folks talk about "the good old days." Some of these storms were so severe lights had to be turned on by 3 o'clock in the afternoons. Many people suffered from dust pneumonia.

Harry Strunk, founder and publisher of the *McCook Daily Gazette,* was one of the leaders and a driving force behind the efforts to harness the rivers in Southwest Nebraska and Northwest Kansas. He is honored for his untiring efforts of more than 30 years in this work by having the lake behind Medicine Creek dam, north of Cambridge, named for him. The **Harry D. Strunk Rest Area**, two miles east of McCook, also honors him. Strunk, who died in 1960, was an imaginative newspaper publisher as well

141

as a crusading editor. In 1929 he purchased a Curtiss Robin airplane, dubbed it the "Newsboy" and used the plane to fly some 389 miles daily to deliver his newspapers to 46 farm communities. A depressed economy and a wind storm that damaged the "Newsboy" ended this delivery system. Today the "Newsboy" hangs from the ceiling of the Space Museum in Seattle, Washington.

The U.S. Army Air Corps Air Training Command established an airbase northwest of McCook in February 1943. Heavy bomber crews received advance training here before being assigned to overseas duty during World War II. Probably the most colorful commanding officer at McCook Airbase was **Col. John R. "Killer" Kane**, who was awarded the Congressional Medal of Honor for leading a daring air raid over the Polesti, Rumania, oil refineries August 1, 1943, as a member of the 9th Air Force. The airbase was closed shortly after the war. Many of Hollywood's celebrities, including the incomparable **Bob Hope**, performed for the airmen at McCook airbase.

Oil was discovered in the county in the 1950s with the largest oil field in the state, the **Sleepy Hollow field**, discovered in the fall of 1960. This field is located 1.5 miles southwest of Bartley and runs six miles long and three miles wide. McCook became a center for oil drilling companies.

Two of Nebraska's governors were one-time residents of McCook. Democrat **Ralph G. Brooks**, who served several years as McCook's Superintendent of Schools, served as governor from January 1959 to September 9, 1960. He died while serving in office and was succeeded by **Lt. Gov. Dwight Burney**. His widow, **Darleene Brooks**, served briefly as McCook's postmaster. Democrat **Frank B. Morrison**, who practiced law in McCook for many years, served as governor 1961-67. **Ray McCarl**, controller of U. S. Currency, was born and raised in McCook.

Senator George William Norris (1861-1944) lived in McCook for many years.

GEORGE W. NORRIS HOME, 709 Norris Ave., has been restored and is a state and national historic site. Senator Norris, a liberal Republican, served 10 years (1903-13) in the U.S. House of Representatives. He was elected to the U.S. Senate in 1912 and served with distinction for 30 years. The Senator fathered bills which created the **Tennessee Valley Authority** (1933) and **Rural Electrification Administration** (1935). He was the sponsor of the 1932 **20th Amendment** to the Constitution

142

HOME OF THE FIGHTING LIBERAL—Senator George W. Norris made his home at 709 Main St. (now Norris Ave.) in McCook. This has been a branch museum of the Nebraska State Historical Society since 1969.

("**Lame Duck**" **Amendment** which abolished the "lame duck" session of Congress and changed the date of the presidential inauguration). He helped author the Nebraska constitutional amendment that established a unicameral (one house) legislature (1935). He was read out of the Republican Party in 1936 and became an Independent.

The Norris Home is open 8 a.m. to 5 p.m., Monday through Saturday, and 1 to 5 p.m., Sunday. Admission is free.

HOW TO REACH THE GEORGE W. NORRIS HOME—US 6 and 34 (2nd St. in McCook) to the center of town, turn north on Norris Ave. for seven blocks. The home is on the left side (west) of Norris Ave.

HIGH PLAINS MUSEUM, 423 Norris Ave., contains regional

HIGH PLAINS MUSEUM—This regional museum is located at 423 Norris Ave. in McCook. It is open to the public every afternoon.

pioneer materials and features a small library with a historic photo collection and a collection of historic books. It is open every afternoon 1:30 to 4:30 p.m. daily.

FITCH HOUSE, located three miles southwest of McCook on Driftwood Creek, was built during 1873-76 as a home and frontier trading post.

Other Historic Happenings in the Area

Fifteen miles south of McCook on US 83 and east on N-89 is the Beaver Valley. In early September 1878, **Chief Dull Knife** and a band of 300 Northern Cheyennes broke from their reservation in Oklahoma and staged an epic flight across Kansas and Nebraska. Dull Knife and his warriors, in search of horses, guns and supplies, raided along the Beaver Creek between the small communities of **Danbury** and **Marion**, along N-89, September 30 from an attack on Oberlin, Kansas, some 15 miles to the south. Fourteen settlers were killed in this general raid and the raiders torched everything that would burn— homes, hayfields, stacked grain and straw and wooden farm equipment. The fires set the prairie aflame and confused and terrorized the populace. **Dull Knife** and his band were captured a short time later and taken to Fort Robinson in the northwestern part of the state.

A mystery surrounds the disappearance of **Nelson Buck** and a government surveying party he headed in 1869. Buck's party was surveying along Beaver Creek, in the area of Marion, about 3

144

ONE OF THE SMALLEST COUNTY SEATS—This tiny, frame court-house in Stockville, with only 45 residents, serves as the county seat of Frontier County.

miles east of US 83 junction, when they were believed to be at-tacked by a Sioux hunting party led by **"Pawnee Killer."** The 12 men were never found and later "Pawnee Killer" during an in-terview on the reservation, admitted his men had killed eight of the surveyors and he believed the remaining four were killed by other Indians. A historical marker has been established just west of Marion on the south side of N-89 to commemorate this event.

Forty nine miles north of McCook on N-23 Spur, via US 83, is the small town of STOCKVILLE (pop. 45), county seat of Fron-tier County. Several sensational murder trials have been held in the small, wooden frame courthouse here. The county was organ-ized in 1872 and Stockville, trading center for area ranchers, be-came the seat of government. It was 10 years later that home-steaders began to arrive and the small trading center emerged as a town. Once hostile Sioux Indians, members of the Whistler band of Cut-off Oglala, settled in the area in 1870 and lived at peace with white settlers for many years.

The little town is located near Medicine Creek which became a route through the area used by soldiers at Fort McPherson, charged with guarding the frontier. Regular visitors to the area were **"Buffalo Bill" Cody** and **"Texas Jack" Omohundro**, who served as guides for eastern sportsmen who came west to hunt buffalo.

INDIANOLA

INDIANOLA (pop. 855), 11 miles east, was platted in 1872 and named after Indianola, Iowa, home of **Isaac Starbuck**, one of the founders. Indianola was the original county seat of Red Willow County, officially selected May 27, 1873. The first courthouse was in a multi-purpose building that also served as a church and community meeting hall. A new courthouse was dedicated December 23, 1881. In 1896 the county seat was moved to McCook.

The body of an Indian woman, who died of wounds suffered in the Massacre Canyon fight between the Sioux and Pawnee August 5, 1873, is buried in Indianola's city park. The story told is that the young squaw's baby had been killed and she herself had been left for dead on the battlefield. Seriously wounded, she crawled to the trail where she was picked up by a hunter who brought her to Indianola. She was unwilling to enter the home of **George A. Hunter** who wanted to help her and she died under a wagon near the homestead several days later.

Twenty-three persons were killed in a tragic railroad crash a quarter of a mile west of Indianola May 29, 1911. Early that cold, foggy morning the westbound Burlington's "Flier" passenger train collided with an eastbound local passenger train as it was about to enter a siding. Among the dead were the engineers and firemen on both trains. Most of the deaths resulted from the scalding steam which spewed from the two wrecked engines. Twelve cars were derailed.

Indianola was one of the many towns along the Republican River to suffer damage during the rampaging May 1935 flood. Property damage was immense but no lives were lost.

A Prisoner-of-War camp was established one mile north of Indianola in September 1943 to house captured German soldiers of **Field Marshall Erwin "The Desert Fox" Rommel's Afrika Korps** in World War II. The camp was set up in five compounds, each with 1,000 capacity, and guarded by 300 military personnel and 89 civilians under the command of **Col. Frederick Whitten**. The POWs were allowed to work outside the camp with most being assigned to area farms where they earned 80 cents per day for their labors. Others worked in McCook, the county seat 11 miles west, as auto mechanics. Each evening, after their work as-

President Opposed Statehood

President Andrew Johnson vetoed the act passed by Congress admitting Nebraska into the Union in early 1867. Congress, in passing the act for statehood, had required certain changes in its constitution. Johnson believed this action violated the U.S. Constitution.

Johnson also opposed statehood for Nebraska because the territory had elected two Republicans to become Senators when statehood was granted. At the time the Republicans were trying to impeach Johnson and he feared the two new Senators might be just enough to convict him.

Congress overode the president's veto and Nebraska was admitted as the 37th state March 1, 1867. Republican David Butler was elected the state's first governor.

signments, they were returned to their compounds. Those not allowed out of camp could earn money by working as janitors and maintenance personnel in the camp. Only eight prisoners attempted to escape and they were captured shortly after leaving the camp.

A story is told that one prisoner caught a train out of Indianola to Lincoln, and there hopped another train that brought him right back to Indianola and the camp.

The camp was equipped with a soccer field, a favorite sport of the Germans. Prisoners had access to a camp theater and post exchange. Not more than 3,500 prisoners were held at a time at Indianola. The camp closed in September 1945.

BARTLEY

BARTLEY (pop. 342), six miles east, was founded in June 1886 on land owned by a Methodist minister, **Rev. Allen Bartley**, who had been sent here by Bishop Mallalieu to establish a university. The site had been chosen a year earlier by the bishop. By the summer of 1886, 27 buildings had already been constructed in the new town. **Mallalieu University**, named for the founding bishop, opened in September 1886 and graduated its first class in

1888. A short time later the school closed because of economic conditions brought on, in part, by severe droughts in the area.

Many bank robberies occurred during the Great Depression of the 1930s and Bartley was the scene of one of these crimes. Two men held up the Bartley State Bank at gunpoint Friday, May 3, 1935, and escaped with $4,921.65. Max Soncksen and Arley Johnson were captured a few days later and charged with the robbery. Within weeks the pair was tried, found guilty and sentenced to 15 years in the state penitentiary.

CAMBRIDGE

CAMBRIDGE (pop. 1,209), eight miles east, was founded in 1874 and was first called **Scratchpost**, then **Pickleville** and then **Northwood**. The town was almost wiped out by a prairie fire and then a diphtheria epidemic. It suffered heavily in the great Republican River flood of 1935 and again in 1947 by a flash flood of Medicine Creek.

Three and a half miles west of Cambridge, half mile north of the highway, is the site of an early-day disaster. A 17-person party of Bohemian emigrants were nearing Richmond Canyon when a cloudburst sent a 15-foot wall of water rushing down the canyon and into their path. Several were swept away, their bodies never recovered. Five bodies were found and buried in the Cambridge Cemetery.

Twenty three miles southeast of Cambridge on N-89, via N-47, is the tiny farm community of HENDLEY (pop. 39). It was here **Edwin Elijah Perkins**, who developed **Kool Aid**, began his entrepreneurial career at the age of 11. The youngster read an ad which said, "Be a manufacturer. . .Mixer's Guide tells how. . . Write today." He wrote for the book and soon was concocting his own perfumes, flavorings and medicines in the family kitchen. The need to make money to finance these experiments led him to act on another advertisement which read, "Start a print shop in your home. . .Make money." He sent away for the press and soon was printing calling cards and labels for his perfumes. He sold his cards and perfumes through magazine advertisements and student agents. The development of **Nix-O-Tine Tobacco Remedy** launched Perkins into his successful mail order business, the **Perkins Products Company**.

When he was 42 years old Perkins and his wife, Kitty, moved to Hastings where he continued to expand his business to include 125 kinds of flavorings, spices, toiletries, medicinal and house products which were sold under the **"Onor Maid"** label. It was in

Cornhusker Topography

Nebraska's elevation rises from about 840 feet above sea level in the southeast corner to approximately 5,424 feet above sea level at the western border.

The Platte River drains approximately 53 percent of the state while the extreme northern area is drained by the Niobrara River which empties into the Missouri River. The southern section of the state is drained by the Republican River. Nebraska is the only state entirely in the Missouri River Basin.

Hastings Perkins developed Kool Aid's predecessor, **"Fruit Smack,"** a liquid, fruit-flavored soda drink concentrate. Popular though it was, the glass "Fruit Smack" bottles often broke and spilled, leading Perkins to develop the powdered soft drink concentrate we know as **Kool Aid**.

In 1931 Perkins moved Kool Aid to Chicago and served as its president until 1956 when he sold his company to General Foods.

Perkins was born in Lewis, Iowa, January 8, 1889, and moved to Nebraska at an early age. He died at Rochester, Minnesota, July 3, 1961.

Cambridge was one of the communities to benefit from the Perkins Foundation founded by Edwin and Kitty Perkins. It donated generously to the Cambridge Memorial Hospital and the Perkins Building at the hospital provides care for the elderly. The foundation has provided funds for several projects in Hastings including Good Samaritan Village, Villa Grace, Perkins Auditorium Concert Hall and Perkins Library on the Hastings College Campus and Mary Lanning Memorial Hospital. Funds have also been made available to Doane College. Among the displays in the library at Hastings College is an Onor Maid sample

NORRIS HOME IN BEAVER CITY—This was the Beaver City home of young George W. Norris who became famous as a U.S. Senator.

case, Fruit Smack bottle and early Kool Aid packages and Perkin's original printing press.

HOLBROOK

HOLBROOK (pop. 293), nine miles east, began inauspiciously as **Burton's Bend** for Burton's Bend Trading Post founded in 1870 by **Isaac "Ben" Burton** and his partner, **H. Dice**. After the Civil War, hostile Cheyenne and Sioux Indians roamed this region which was a great buffalo range. Burton and Dice supplied buffalo hide hunters until the great herds dwindled. **Maj. Eugene A. Carr's Republican Valley Expedition of 1869**, from Fort McPherson, cleared the Indians from the area. The town developed around the trading post and was renamed Holbrook with the coming of the railroad in the late 1880s.

Northwest of Holbrook, on Deer Creek Lutheran Church grounds, a handful of settlers organized **Deer Creek Evangelical Lutheran Congregation** in 1877. The congregation met in homes of its members until 1888 when they began building a small church on land contributed by **A. E. Phillipson**, a charter member. The church was completed in 1889 and used until the present church was dedicated May 1904. A historical marker identifies the site of the original **Norwegian Lutheran Church**.

ARAPAHOE (pop. 1,104), six miles east, is at the crossroads of

150

THE FLYING DOCTOR—Dr. Frank Brewster (left) stands beside his Curtiss-Wright biplane with his pilot, Wade Stevens, in 1919. Dr. Brewster made his sick calls out in the rural areas with his small airplane.

US 6 and 34 and US 283. Twelve miles south on US 283 and three miles east on N-83 is the county seat.

BEAVER CITY-HOMETOWN OF THE FLYING DOCTOR

BEAVER CITY (pop. 777) is located 12 miles south of Arapahoe on US 283 and three miles east on N-89. Settled in 1872, Beaver City is the county seat of Furnas County.

Two men were important in Beaver City's past.

George W. Norris, who became a power in the United States Senate, practiced law in Beaver City starting in 1885. Born in Sandusky, Ohio, in 1861, he passed his bar examination in 1883. From 1895-1902 Norris served as a district court judge. He entered national politics in 1903 when he was elected to the U.S. House of Representatives. (For more details see the McCook listing.)

The second man was **Dr. Frank Brewster**, Nebraska's first flying doctor. The doctor bought a Curtiss-Wright JN4D biplane in 1919 for $8,000. The airplane was brought to Beaver City by rail in two large boxes. It was assembled and made its first flight May 19, 1919, where some 8,000 people gathered to see **Wade Stevens**, a young World War I veteran, take to the air. Later Stevens became a successful lawyer in McCook, Nebraska.

"Doc" Brewster flew many missions of mercy throughout southwestern Nebraska and northwestern Kansas. For many years his airplane was a familiar and comforting sight to farmers and ranchers of this area.

ATLANTA

ATLANTA (pop. 100), 25 miles east of Arapahoe was the site of a large Prisoner-of-War camp, one of several in Nebraska during World War II. Planning for the camp began in June 1943 and by November, 70 buildings and seven miles of roads were constructed. The first prisoners, captured in the North African and Italian campaigns, included 250 German soldiers who arrived in early December. In February 1944 another 830 arrived. The camp was established to accommodate 4,500 prisoners, guarded and administered by some 600 military and 130 civilian personnel

These prisoners were a valuable source of farm labor in the area during the war years when young men from every walk of life were being drafted. The camp was phased out in 1945. A marker, just east of town, points out the site of POW camp.

HOLDREGE

HOLDREGE (pop. 5,585), seven miles east, is the county seat of Phelps County and was named for **George W. Holdrege**, an official of the Chicago, Burlington & Quincy Railroad. US 6 and 34 intersects with US 183 and Holdrege is only 17 miles south of 1-80.

Holdrege, settled by Scandinavians in 1883, was incorporated in 1884. Today it is a trading center for a large agricultural area.

A museum, on North US 183, is operated by the Phelps County Historical Society and serves as the national headquarters for The Sod House Society. The museum, with an interesting and unique collection of Nebraska history, is open daily from 2 to 5 p.m. The Sod House Society is a nationwide organization formed in 1956 to preserve our heritage through what **Poet John G. Niehardt** described as "those sod house settlers."

FUNK (pop. 188), a small farm town with several grain elevators, is seven miles east of Holdrege.

AXTELL (pop. 602), seven miles east, was settled by Swedes and is home of **Bethpage Mission**, a church operated facility for retarded persons. Bethpage was founded February 19, 1913, by the **Rev. K. G. William Dahl**. The facility, just north of town, is easily identifiable with its several yellow brick buildings.

MINDEN (pop. 2,896) is nine miles east. (See listing in Section 2.)

PHELPS COUNTY MUSEUM—This outstanding county museum is located just north of Holdrege on US 183 and is operated by the Phelps County Historical Society. It also serves as the national headquarters for The Sod House Society.

HARTWELL (pop. 87), 10 miles east, is a small farm community.

KENESAW (pop. 851), seven miles east on US 6 and 34 and three miles north on N1-A Spur, is near the burial site of **Susan Hale**, who died on the Oregon Trail in 1852. Mrs. Hale, traveling west with her husband, drank water from a well poisoned by hostile Indians. She became ill and died on the trail. Her husband made a coffin from the lumber of his wagon, buried her and then went to Omaha where he bought a marble headstone for her grave. He returned to her grave and set up the headstone himself.

JUNIATA (pop. 703), eight miles from the Kenesaw turnoff and a mile north of US 6 and 34, was once the county seat of Adams County. It was named for the Juanita River in Pennsylvania.

32-MILE CREEK STATION, a mile east and five miles south of Juniata, was erected in 1859 and used as a stage and Pony Express station on the Oregon Trail.

HASTINGS is six miles east of the Juniata turnoff on US 6 and 34. (The Hastings listing is in Section 2.) At Hastings US 6 continues directly east 92 miles before turning north and then east again into Lincoln. From Lincoln US 6 follows along the west side of I-80 to Omaha. US 34 runs north through Hastings to a point just south of Grand Island before running east, parallel

153

to I-80 to Lincoln. From Lincoln, US 34 runs 42 miles east to the junction of US 73 and 75 where it joins these two highways running north.

State Seal and Flag

Nebraska's first legislature prescribed the design to be used as the Great Seal of the state in 1867. The blacksmith in the foreground symbolizes the mechanical arts while agriculture is represented by shocks of grain, growing grain and a settler's cabin. The appreciation the state has for transportation which hastened settlement is depicted in the steamboat and train. The State Seal under the signature of the Governor and Secretary of State must be affixed to all official state documents. The Great Seal on a field of national blue comprises the official State Flag of Nebraska. Although this banner first flew over a University of Nebraska football game in 1925, it was not officially adopted by the Legislature until 1963.

Section 5

Six miles east of Arapahoe is the junction of US 136 leading to Catherland, centered at Red Cloud in Webster County; Fairbury, near the site of Rock Creek Station where the legend of "Wild Bill" Hickok was born; Beatrice, near the site of Daniel Freeman's homestead claim, the first claim to be filed in 1863, and to the Missouri River and the unique old town of Brownville.

Red Cloud was the home town of Willa Cather, who won a Pulitzer Prize for her novel, "One of Ours," published in 1922. Catherland is one of the favorite tourist attractions on US 136 and there are several historic spots in this area.

Emigrant wagon trains passed through the Fairbury area on the Oregon Trail for more than two decades. The colorful, short-lived Pony Express and Overland Stage Company routes followed the Oregon Trail.

Northwest, along the Little Blue River, are those areas hardest hit by Indian raiders during the summer of 1864.

In this same area, Charles Fuller and a handful of investors opened a manufacturing plant in 1907 to produce the Fuller car. The plant closed in 1909.

A Union soldier, home on leave, made his name in history when he appeared at the land office in Brownville in the wee hours of January 1, 1863 to file a homestead claim on a quarter section of land near present day Beatrice. Daniel Freeman is believed to be the first American to take advantage of "free" land under the Homestead Act of 1862. The National Homestead Monument, operated by the U.S. Parks Commission near Beatrice, tells the story of Daniel Freeman and other homesteaders.

US 136 finally ends in Nebraska at the Missouri River in the historic town of Brownville.

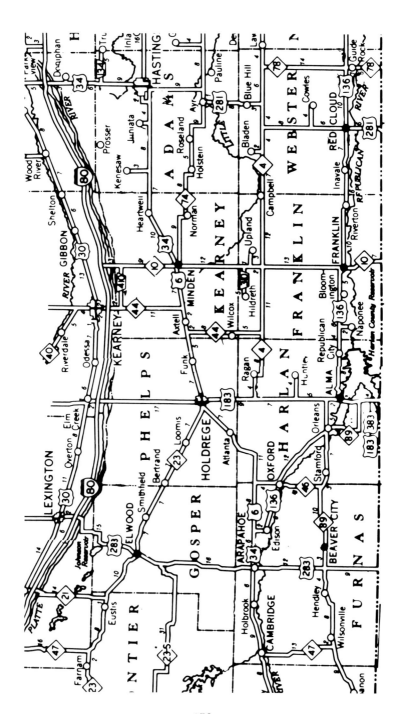

156

US 136 TO CATHERLAND

Just six miles east of Arapahoe is the junction of US 136 which turns southeast to within a half dozen miles of the Kansas state line before turning east. US 136 runs 236 miles east to Brownville on the Missouri River. There are several historic spots and places along this route, including Red Cloud, the heart of Catherland (for Willa Cather, the author), 71 miles from the junction of US 6 and 34. Along this route is the tiny village of Oak, hard hit in 1864 when Indians swooped down on several places along the Oregon Trail in a hopeless effort to stop the white "invasion" of their hunting lands. About 80 miles east of Red Cloud, just southeast of Fairbury is the site of Rock Creek Station, where James Butler Hickok was involved in a shoot out in 1861 to become famous as "Wild Bill" Hickok. Just a little further east, 25 miles to Beatrice, is the site of the Daniel Freeman homestead, the first to be filed in the nation under the Homestead Act of 1862. This route concludes at Brownville, one of the most historic communities in Nebraska, nestled along the Missouri River.

EDISON (pop. 209) is just two miles from the junction of US 6 and 34.

OXFORD (pop. 1,102), eight miles southeast of Edison, was incorporated in 1879. This farming community was hard hit by the Republican River flood of 1935. A historical marker three miles west of town, on US 136, commemorates the disaster.

ORLEANS AND MAJOR CULBERTSON

ORLEANS (pop. 526), 12 miles southeast of Oxford, was named by **Gen. Victor Vifquain**, a Belgian who settled in Saline County and was interested in settling this part of of Nebraska. It was believed the name came from Orleans, Massachusetts, or Orleans, France. Originally, Vifquain planned to call the town **Napoleon**, located on a 320-acre site near present-day Orleans. The area around Orleans was settled in the early 1870s. The village was incorporated in 1880.

Orleans was the burial place of **Maj. Alexander Culbertson**, an early day fur trapper and trader. He was a partner and agent of the powerful Upper Missouri Outfit and established a number of their trading posts on the frontier. He was also helpful in the government's dealings with several Indian tribes.

When he was 30 years old he married 15-year old **Natawista Iksina**—or **Medicine Snake Woman**, daughter of a Blackfoot Indian chief. She was helpful to her husband in dealings with the Indians.

157

After nearly 30 years on the frontier, Culbertson retired with a sizeable fortune, estimated at $300,000. He went to Peoria, Illinois, in the late 1850s, and, as so often happens, soon lost his fortune and went bankrupt.

Culbertson came to Orleans to live with a daughter, Julia (Mrs. George H. Roberts). His wife Natawista went to live with her people in Canada. He died in Orleans August 27, 1879 at the age of 70. A monument recapping his story is placed on his grave.

ALMA—NAMED FOR ALMA COOK

ALMA (pop.1,358) is the county seat of Harlan County, named for Thomas Harlan from Cheyenne, Wyoming. The town was founded in 1871 and incorporated in 1881. The town was named for **Alma Cook**, daughter of N. P. Cook, one of the founders. Alma was involved in an early day dispute over the location of the county seat. Melrose (now defunct) citizens obtained the county records briefly but these were "rescued" one night by the citizens of Alma to settle the dispute.

Construction of the Harlan County Reservoir got underway in the 1940s to avert flooding in the Republican Valley. This construction forced relocation of the southern part of Alma, all of Republican City to the east and 21 miles of Chicago, Burlington & Quincy railroad trackage. The dam was dedicated in 1952 and serves as a flood control and provides irrigation for 50,000 acres of farm land in the region. Harlan County Lake attracts thousands of people annually and is noted for its boating, fishing and camping facilities.

Eight miles west is REPUBLICAN CITY (pop. 231), relocated in the early 1950s with construction of the Harlan Reservoir. It serves boaters and fishermen using Harlan County Lake.

NAPONEE (pop. 16) is four miles east and two miles south, located in Franklin County. Screen and TV actor **David Jansen** (1930-1980), who played the lead role in the TV series, "The Fugitive," was born here.

BLOOMINGTON (pop. 138) is 10 miles east of Republican City, site of a U.S. Land Office in the 1870s. Bloomington became the county seat of Franklin County in 1870 where it remained until 1920.

FRANKLIN (pop. 1,162), five miles east of Bloomington, is the county seat of Franklin County. The town was founded in 1870 by the Republican Land and Claims Association, also called the Knight Colony. A small Negro colony arrived the following spring to try to establish a settlement but failed.

HISTORIC COURTHOUSE—A historical marker on the Franklin County courthouse grounds in Franklin briefly tells the history of this area and serves as a tribute to the early settlers here. The county was organized in 1871.

This entire region was part of the Pawnee Indian buffalo hunting range before 1869. Settlers began arriving the next year. Franklin County was organized in 1871 with Franklin as the county seat. The county seat was moved to Bloomington until 1920 when it was returned to Franklin.

RIVERTON (pop. 212), 10 miles east of Franklin, was founded in 1870 by the Thompson Colony.

INAVALE—BIRTHPLACE OF WILLIAM C. NORRIS

INAVALE is a tiny farm community 16 miles east of Franklin

and seven miles west of Red Cloud. This unincorporated village was founded in 1884 by **William James Vance**, who homesteaded "in a valley," thus the name for his town. The Irish emigrant provided 40 acres for the village site.

William C. Norris, founder and board chairman of Minneapolis-based Control Data Corporation, a giant in the computer industry, was born and raised on a homestead near Inavale. He graduated from Red Cloud High School and earned a degree in electrical engineering at the University of Nebraska. Control Data is listed on *Fortune* magazine's 500 list of top companies in America.

RED CLOUD—HOME OF WILLA CATHER

RED CLOUD (pop. 1,303), seven miles east of Inavale, is the county seat of Webster County and home of famed author, **Willa Cather**, from 1884 to 1890. By action of the Nebraska legislature in 1965, the western half of Webster County has been designated **Catherland**.

Willa Sibert Cather was born in Winchester, Virginia, December 7, 1873. The family moved to Nebraska in 1884. After graduating from the University of Nebraska in 1895, she worked as a journalist and teacher in Pittsburgh. In 1904 she went to New York and the following year had *"The Troll Garden,"* a collection of short stories published. This led her to the editorial staff of the muckraking *McClure's Magazine* in 1906 when she moved to New York. Her first novel, *"Alexander's Bridge,"* was published in 1912, followed the next year with *"O Pioneers!"* dealing with life on the rugged frontier. *"My Antonia,"* a favorite with many Nebraskans, was published in 1918. Her story of the growth of an American farm boy to manhood, *"One of Ours,"* published in 1922, earned her a Pulitzer Prize.

Her other books were *"The Song of the Lark,"* (1915); *"A Lost Lady,"* (1923); *"The Professor's House,"* (1925); *"My Mortal Enemy,"* (1926); *"Death Comes for the Archbishop,"* (1927); *"Shadows on the Rock,"* (1931); *"Lucy Gayheart,"* (1935); and *"Sapphira and the Slave Girl,"* (1940).

Her work won her a worldwide audience and a host of honors. In addition to her Pulitzer, she received the Prix Femina Americaine in France, the Mark Twain Award, the Gold Letter of the National Institute of Arts and Letters and a dozen honorary degrees, including the honorary degree of Doctor of Letters from Columbia University in 1928. Miss Cather was inducted into the Nebraska Hall of Fame in 1963. She never married.

PULITZER PRIZE WINNER—
Willa Cather, who spent several
of her childhood years in Red
Cloud, won a Pulitzer Prize for
her novel, "One of Ours," published in 1922. She was an internationally recognized author.

Willa Cather died in New York City April 24, 1947 of a cerebral hemorrhage. She was buried in the old Jaffrey Cemetery, Jaffrey, New Hampshire.

Webster County's first settlement was in 1869 at **Guide Rock**, on the Republican River. A settlement was started 10 miles west the next year and was named for the famed Sioux Indian chief, **Red Cloud**. The county was formed in 1871, named for **Daniel Webster**, the American statesman, with Red Cloud as the county seat. **Silas Garber**, a leading citizen of the county, was elected Nebraska's third governor.

Two towns in the northern part of the county are worth mentioning here—BLUE HILL (pop. 882), 21 miles north on US 281, and BLADEN (pop. 298), 14 miles north on US 281, four miles west on N-4 and two miles north on N-2. Blue Hill was founded in 1878 as **Belmont** by A. B. Smith, an agent of the Burlington Railroad. The name was changed to Blue Hill when it was learned another town in the state had claimed the name of Belmont. Bladen was platted in 1886 by the Lincoln Land Company and named for **Ellen Bladen Gere**, daughter of the founder of the *Lincoln State Journal* newspaper.

There are a number of historic spots in the county.

WILLA CATHER HISTORICAL CENTER, downtown, is located in a former bank building built in 1889 by Silas Garber. Developed by the Willa Cather Pioneer Memorial and Educational

CATHER PIONEER MEMORIAL—Willa Cather, Nebraska's Pulitzer Prize winning novelist, called Red Cloud home during several of her young days. The Cather home (above) is included in the Memorial to the author.

Foundation, the Center, including six buildings, was turned over to the Nebraska State Historical Society in 1978. The restoration of the buildings, which include the old bank facility, the Cather home, Burlington & Missouri Railroad depot, Episcopal Church and St. Juliana Church buildings, continues.

The Cather home (1894-1904) is located at the corner of 3rd and Cedar Sts. It is a National Historic Landmark.

The bank building houses a number of original Willa Cather letters, manuscripts, first issue books and papers among its collections.

The restored B&M depot was the third depot serving the community and was built in 1897. The other two buildings were destroyed by fire. This building is located at the south edge of town, two blocks west of US 281.

Willa Cather and her parents joined the Episcopal Church, corner of 6th and Cedar Sts. in Red Cloud in 1922. She was a member of the congregation at the time of her death.

St. Juliana's was the first Roman Catholic church in Red Cloud, built in 1883. It was here Willa Cather heard the Mass sung and this church was the setting for the marriage of the prin-

162

WEBSTER COUNTY MUSEUM—Housed in a lovely old home, the Webster County Museum is located in Red Cloud and contains many exhibits and artifacts depicting the lives of the early settlers to this region.

ciple character in her book, *"My Antonia."*

Willa Cather Historical Center is open 8 a.m. to 5 p.m., Monday through Friday year-round, and 1 to 5 p.m., Saturday and Sunday during the summer months.

Five miles south of Red Cloud, off US 281, is the **Willa Cather Memorial Prairie**, a 610-acre tract of native grassland set aside as a memorial to the author.

WEBSTER COUNTY MUSEUM, 721 West 4th Ave. (US 136), is operated by the Webster County Historical Society. The museum occupies a beige brick mansion built in 1905 for **Dr. Robert Dammerall**, an area physician. It contains 21 rooms on four floors, three woodburning fireplaces and a ballroom. Thousands of items are displayed to take the visitor back into the pioneer days on the prairies.

It is open 1 to 5 p.m. daily during the summer months; by appointment year-round. Admission is charged.

THE LITTLE RED SCHOOL HOUSE, at the western outskirts of Red Cloud, was built in 1885. Here pioneer youngsters learned their three "R's." The one-room school, once designated District No. 37, has been restored and is open for public viewing.

THE STARKE BARN, 4½ miles east of Red Cloud on US 136, off to the right, was built in 1902 and is one of the largest of its

163

kind in the nation. This circular structure, 130 feet in diameter and three stories tall, has no nails, spikes or pegs to hold it together. The Starke Barn is listed on the National Register of Historic Places.

PIKE'S RIFLE PITS, a little further east on US 136, are the trenches dug by soldiers commanded by **Lt. Zebulon Pike** on an expedition through this area in 1806. Pike believed he and his men would be attacked by the Pawnee Indians living in the region. At the intersection of US 136 and N-76 is a marker noting the Pike-Pawnee Site.

PIKE-PAWNEE VILLAGE HISTORIC LANDMARK SITE OF 1806 is located on a county road south and west of Guide Rock. About 2,000 Indians, in some 44 lodges, occupied this area in 1806. It is a registered National Historic Landmark and is owned by the Nebraska Historical Society Foundation. It can be reached by taking N-76 about 1½ miles south, then turning west on the county road for nearly four miles. After viewing the area, the visitor may return to Guide Rock over the route used to reach this site or by driving nine and three-tenths miles west to US 281 and then north on US 281 for a little over a mile to Red Cloud.

THE INDIAN RAIDS ON THE LITTLE BLUE

Eleven miles east of Red Cloud, just off US 136, is GUIDE ROCK (pop. 344). Continuing east on US 136 23 miles is NORA (pop. 24) and another five miles east is RUSKIN (pop. 224).

North of Ruskin, a little more than five miles on a county road, is the tiny town of OAK (pop. 79) on the Little Blue River. (Oak can also be reached from N-4, south on N-65A). Nearby was the **Oak Grove Station**, about two miles from present-day Oak, serving Oregon Trail emigrants, the Overland Stage Company and the short-lived Pony Express during the 1860s. This was one of the hardest hit areas during the August 1864 uprisings—when the Sioux and Cheyenne raided 400 miles along the overland trail and closed the frontier between this point and Denver for several weeks.

To set the scene we need to establish the location of the various stations along the trail at that time. Six miles southeast of Oak Grove was **Kiowa Station**, operated by James Douglas; eight miles northwest was **Little Blue Station**, operated by J. M. Comstock; a mile further up the river was **Buffalo Ranch**, which replaced the Little Blue Station when it was burned, and eight miles further up river was **Liberty Farm Station**, operated by

CAPTURED BY THE INDIANS—Sixteen-year old Laura Roper, Danny Marble and Belle Eubanks were captured along the Little Blue River in Nebraska during the 1864 Indian uprising. The children were released a short time later in an exchange in Colorado.

Charles Emery and his wife.

The Indians began their attack along the Little Blue Sunday morning, August 7, 1864. Patrick Burke, of Beatrice, hauling a load of corn to Fort Kearny was attacked near Buffalo Ranch. He was shot several times with arrows and scalped. He died that night of his wounds.

The William Eubanks family of ten had settled in the area four miles north of Oak Grove at a point near the river known as "The Narrows." They had arrived just a few months before the August attack. "The Narrows" was so named because there was just enough room for a wagon to pass between the bluffs and the river below.

In the early afternoon the Eubank brothers, Joe and Fred, were killed near Oak Grove Station while they were cutting hay. About the same time **William Eubanks, Sr.**, their father, and his 13 year old son, James, were killed while returning home from the Joe Eubank's farm.

Later in the afternoon, around 4 o'clock, **William Eubanks, Jr.**, his wife, **Lucinda**, their two children, **Isabelle (Belle)**, 3 years old, and **William J. (Willie)**, 6 months old, left the ranch house they shared with William Jr.'s parents to walk 16 year old **Laura Roper** back to her home about 1½ miles from the Eubank's ranch. Laura's father was **Joe Roper**, one of the ranchers along the Blue. Laura had gone to visit the 24-year old **Lucinda Eubanks**.

Sixteen year old **Dora Eubanks** and **Henry Eubanks**, 11, stayed behind. As the Eubanks and Laura Roper walked down the road they heard Dora scream and William raced back towards the ranch house. The Indians had attacked and Dora had run screaming from her attackers. In the ensuing attack William, Dora and Henry were killed.

Two other members of the Eubanks family, William, Sr.'s wife and their 20 year old daughter, Hannah, escaped the slaughter as they had gone to visit relatives in Quincy, Illinois. Joe Eubanks's wife, **Hattie (Palmer)**, escaped to safety. Her brother, **John Palmer**, was with Joe and Fred during their haying operations on Sunday but had gone back to their cabin when the Indians attacked. We are not told if he escaped or was killed by the Indians.

When **Lucinda Eubanks** realized Indians had attacked their home she gathered up her two children and with **Laura Roper** attempted to hide in a buffalo wallow off the road. The Indian raiders spotted them and took them captive. Laura and little Isabelle were taken with one group; Lucinda and Willie with another. Laura and Isabelle were among four white captives (one of the others was **Danny Marble**, captured in a raid at Plum Creek) released to **Maj. Edward Wynkoop**, 1st Colorado Cavalry, near Fort Lyons, Colorado Territory, September 11, 1864. Lucinda and Willie were not released until May 18, 1865, at Fort Laramie. Isabelle Eubanks was taken to Denver and died November 1, 1864.

Mrs. Eubanks was severely mistreated by her captors. The two Indians who held her at the time of her release were Ogalala Sioux Chief **Black Foot** and **Two Face**. Mrs. Eubanks, almost naked and in poor physical condition upon her release, accused Black Foot and Two Face of abusing her. The commanding officer at Fort Laramie, **Col. Thomas Moonlight**, 11th Kansas Cavalry, was so infuriated he hanged the two Indians immediately.

166

Site of August 1864 Indian Raids

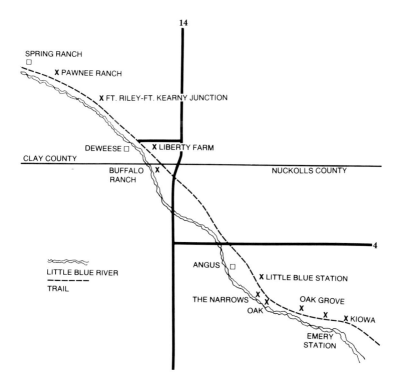

RAIDERS SWOOPED DOWN on the unsuspecting settlers along this route of the Oregon Trail on the Little Blue River in August 1864. A number of settlers along the trail were killed during the initial attack. Several members of the William Eubanks family, who lived near Oak, were killed and a young mother and two of her children were taken captive by hostiles. Also captured in this raid was 16-year old Laura Roper who was released with other captives a few weeks later in Colorado. For several weeks after these attacks more than 400 miles of the Oregon Trail were closed as the Indians continued their rampage.

After her release, Laura Roper returned to the East and in 1866 married Elijah Soper in Pennsylvania. In 1885 she married James K. Vance of Fairbury, Nebraska. Lucinda Eubanks went to Missouri and later to Crawford County, Kansas. She married Dr. D. F. Atkinson in 1893. She died in McCune, Kansas, April 4, 1913.

One of the heroic actions in the early stages of the raids on the Little Blue occurred the early morning of Tuesday, August 9th. **Bob Emery**, a brother of **Charles Emery** in charge of Liberty Farm Station, was driving an overland stage heading east when he passed Buffalo Ranch, a mile from Little Blue Station. Along the trail, at "The Narrows," Emery's stagecoach was attacked by Indians. The driver, recognizing his dilemma, was able to turn his coach around and in a mad dash made it back to the safety of Buffalo Ranch with the raiders hard on his heels. Some of the nine passengers, including seven men and two women, had taken up the fight as well. At the time Bob Emery was making his run for safety, Indian raiders attacked the **Bowie Ranch**, between Oak Grove Station and Kiowa Station, and killed **Mr. and Mrs. William Bowie** and then destroyed their ranch buildings.

More than 50 lives were lost August 7th. When Indians approached Oak Grove Station two men, **J. H. Butler** and **Marshall Kelley**, were working in the yard. They became suspicious but before they could make it to safety they were both killed. Several persons were wounded. The following day several of the stations and equipment were burned, including the Little Blue and Oak Grove Stations. The raids continued for weeks. Several freighters were attacked and a few were killed. Others escaped with their lives and their scalps but lost their freight, wagons and stock. The largest loss of equipment was at Little Blue Station. More than 200 freight wagons were destroyed and horses and oxen were killed or stolen by the Indians. Most of the settlers packed up their belongings and went to Beatrice or Fort Kearny for safety. The Indians held the area for several weeks and terror reigned until order was finally restored by troops.

By late fall the Indians, under the general leadership of **Black Kettle**, were making efforts to sue for peace. This effort went up in smoke and fire at the infamous **Sand Creek Massacre** in late November when troops led by **Col. John M. Chivington** launched a dawn attack on the unsuspecting Sioux and Cheyenne Indians camped at Sand Creek. The Indians, with their squaws and children, believed they were under a flag of truce. Chiving-

THE ANGUS AUTO WORKS—The Fuller automobile (1907-09) was manufactured in this rustic plant in Angus, Nebraska. At one time this plant employed 40 men and several models of the Fuller car were built here.

ton's force, made up of troops from the 1st and 3rd Colorado Cavalry regiments, struck the Indian camp and killed women and children in their fury. This infamous act reunited the Indians and they went on a rampage that lasted for nearly two more years.

The entire area was abandoned in 1867 when the Indians raided along this same route. In 1870 the Indian scare continued to impact the area as reflected in the census taken that year. Only eight persons were listed as residents in the county in that official head count.

Russ Snyder, a Baltimore Oriole outfielder, was born and raised in Oak. He signed with the New York Yankees in 1952 and played on their various farm clubs until 1959 when he was traded to the Kansas City Athletics. In January 1961 he was sold to the Baltimore Orioles and played for several years with them.

ANGUS—HOME OF THE FULLER CAR

ANGUS was a small community about nine miles north of Nora along the west side of the Little Blue River in Sherman Precinct, Nuckolls County. The little town was founded in 1886 by the Lincoln Land Company and named for **J. B. Angus**, a railroad official. Angus is important to Nebraska's history as an early day auto manufacturing center. The **Angus Automobile Company** was organized by a group of Nuckolls County inves-

tors and opened February 16, 1907 and began producing the
Fuller car, named for **Charlie Fuller**, the plant manager. The
company manufactured several models of the Fuller car for three
years. At one point the plant employed 40 men before it closed
down in 1909. The top model, a five-passenger touring car, sold
for $2,500 during the first year of production. There is no record
of the number of Fuller cars manufactured in this country plant.

BACK ON US 136

Back to US 136 at Ruskin from this side trip, the route east
continues through or near several small farm communities. Seven
miles east is DESHLER (pop. 994), named for **John G. Deshler**
in 1887, a land speculator from Columbus, Ohio. Eight miles further is HEBRON (pop. 1,907), founded in 1869, county seat of
Thayer County. Another 10 miles east is GILEAD (pop. 69).

FAIRBURY—ENTER WILD BILL

FAIRBURY (pop. 4,887), 13 miles east, was founded in 1869
and is the county seat of Jefferson County. The Oregon Trail bi-
sects the county from the southeast to the northwest and its
wagon ruts can still be seen from a dozen or so spots through this
area. The area is rich in pioneer history.

The CITY MUSEUM is located on the west side of the courthouse square, on D St. between 4th and 5th Sts., in downtown.

The museum's collections and exhibits focus on the historical
events of the area. It is open from 1 to 5 p.m. Monday, Wednesday and Friday, all year.

About six miles southeast of Fairbury is the famous **Rock
Creek Station** on the Oregon and Pony Express Trails. There
actually were two Rock Creek Stations—West and East—sepa-
rated by Rock Creek. Between 1865-67 **D. C. Jenkins** operated a
toll bridge across the creek between the two stations. It was at
Rock Creek Station (East) that a 24-year old stock tender from
Troy, Illinois, gained the reputation as one of the West's fastest
guns in an incident that occurred July 12, 1861. **James Butler
"Wild Bill" Hickok** became a gunfighter that day when he shot
and killed **David C. McCanles**, who had come to the east station
to settle a dispute with **Horace Wellman**, the operator.
McCanles and two companions, **James Wood** and **James Gordon**, were killed. Hickok went into the combination home and office when he saw McCanles and his friends approaching the station. He opened fire on the trio from behind a door in this building. Hickok killed McCanles from ambush and wounded his
friends. The two wounded men were actually killed by Wellman

170

A LEGEND IS BORN—James Butler Hickok was a 24-year old, nondescript laborer until July 12, 1861 when he shot and killed David McCanles from ambush in a quarrel at Rock Creek Station, southeast of Fairbury. This incident launched the legend of "Wild Bill" Hickok, the gunfighter. Two other men, companions of McCanles, were also killed that day by others at the station.

and a stable hand, **J. W. "Dock" Brink**. Hickok, Wellman and Brink were arrested and tried for murder in Beatrice, but they were acquitted after pleading self-defense.

The station was used by both the Pony Express and Ben Holladay's Stage Line. A State Park Entry Permit ($2 daily, $10 annual) is required to enter Rock Creek Station. It is open the year-round during daylight hours.

Rock Creek Station can be reached by driving south on N-15 across the viaduct, turn left on the south side of the viaduct, follow the blacktop 5½ miles, turn south one mile and east again for a half mile. Near the entrance to the Rock Creek Station State Park, on the right (south), is an Oregon Trail and Pony Express marker. Wagon ruts on the Oregon Trail are visible at the Rock Creek Station area. See the visitor's center for replicas of the toll bridge and buildings as well as some of the more detailed history of this historic site.

Historic STEELE CITY (pop. 137) may be reached through a scenic country drive south to N-8, then a mile east (or 10 miles on N-8 from Fairbury). This small town was founded in 1872 as Freeport, then Steelburg. There are four old buildings worth exploring. The old bank, built in the early 1880s from bricks kilned locally, has been restored and houses a museum. A stone blacksmith shop, built in 1890, has been restored. A stone livery stable, built in 1902, is a rarity and the old stone 1881 Baptist Church is unique.

The return trip to Fairbury, via N-8, takes about 15 to 20

HISTORIC LIME KILN AND LIMESTONE HOUSE—Worel C. Smith built this lime kiln on this site north of Fairbury in 1874. In 1878 he built his limestone house nearby. Both are historical attractions.

minutes on a blacktop road. North of Fairbury are several historic spots to see and visit.

At the west edge of Fairbury, on US 136, is a well maintained county road, following the Union Pacific railroad tracks four miles, leading to the **Smith Lime Kiln** built in the early 1870s. Nearby is the home of **Worel Smith** who operated the kiln. A historical marker at the site tells the story of lime burning and the Smith Lime Kiln. Displays in the house highlight the lime-burning industry. It is open 2 to 4 p.m. Sundays during the summer. Visitors browsing in the area are cautioned about poison ivy.

Continue two miles north to the stop sign (after crossing the railroad tracks twice), turn west and drive two miles to POWELL and at the stop sign west of town, turn north and drive one mile to the Oregon trail and Pony Express monument. **Big Sandy Station** site is about a mile west.

Turn west at this corner and drive two miles to **Alexandria State Recreational Area** with its three man-made lakes, fed by springs. These lakes offer fishing, boating and swimming.

From the recreational area, drive west to the dead end, turn south and drive one mile to the DISTRICT 10 SCHOOL MUSEUM. An Oregon Trail and Pony Express monument grace the museum grounds.

Driving east about five miles (back through Powell) to the **Little Sandy Station** site, a plaque marks the emigrant station of Joel Helvey on the Oregon Trail.

The next stop is at the **George Winslow Monument**, reached by going 3½ miles further east, one mile south and west a half mile. This takes one to the gate of the pasture where the Winslow monument is located. George Winslow of Newton, Massachusetts, died of cholera and was buried here. The brown rock imbedded in the marker is the original stone his friends put on his grave at the time of his death and burial.

Virginia City Station, four miles north of Fairbury along N-15, served as a freight, stage and Pony Express station. This station was also referred to as **Lone Tree** for a solitary oak tree nearby. This station has also been referred to as **"Whiskey Run" Station**. There is a monument marking this site.

About 2½ miles east of Fairbury, on US 136, is an Oregon Trail and Pony Express marker. This is located near the 1904 District 39 school. The trail passed at this point.

Six miles east of Fairbury is JANSEN (pop. 203), settled in 1874-75 by Mennonites led by **Cornelius** and **Peter Jansen**. The town, platted in 1886, was named for Peter Jansen, a noted sheep rancher who gave the land for the town site. He served in the Nebraska legislature in 1898 and 1910 and was active in politics until his death in 1923.

The Mennonites purchased 25,000 acres of land in this area. Originally their community was made up of several so-called "line villages," each made up of several dwellings clustered together along both sides of a section line or road.

BEATRICE

BEATRICE (pop. 12,891),the county seat of Gage County, is located 25 miles east of Fairbury on US 136. It was founded in 1857 by a group called the Nebraska Association. The Association under the leadership of **Judge J. F. Kinney** was responsible for the site selection for the new village. Beatrice is situated along the Blue River in a hilly region.

The GAGE COUNTY HISTORICAL MUSEUM is located in Beatrice on the corner of 2nd and Court Sts. It is housed in the Burlington depot which was built in 1905. The depot was presented to the Gage County Historical Society by the Burlington

The Gage County Historical Society Museum is located in the old train depot in Beatrice.

Northern Railroad. The Museum's displays show the development of industry, the railroad, agricultural progress and the history of the communities and people of Gage County. Listed on the National Register of Historic Places, the museum is open year-round. Hours are 9 a.m. to 12 noon, 1 to 5 p.m. Tuesday through Saturday, 1:30 to 5 p.m. Sunday. Closed Saturday from October 1 through April 30. Closed Thanksgiving, Christmas, New Year's Day and Easter. Admission is free and tourist information is available at the Museum.

The **Gage County Courthouse**, 6th and Grant, was built in 1890-91. It is a historic limestone structure with a clock tower. It has recently been nominated for listing on the National Register of Historic Places.

There are many lovely old homes located in Beatrice. The **Paddock House**, which is a stone structure, is located at 1401 N. 10th St. It was originally built as a farmhouse in 1870 by **Algernon S. Paddock**. He served as Secretary of Nebraska Territory (1861-67) and U.S. Senator (1875-81, 1887-93). Paddock built the original **Paddock Hotel** in Beatrice. An example of brick and concrete Renaissance Revival architecture is located at 701 N. 7th St. It was built in 1904-05 by **S. D. Kilpatrick**, a successful railroad contractor and coal mine owner. Both of these houses are listed on the National Register of Historic Places. The homes are privately owned and are not open for public tours. For more information on other historical homes in the area contact the museum at (402) 228-1679.

Beatrice's downtown business district features some fine examples of cornice detailed storefronts. Many dates of original construction are still visible. The district was restored in 1974 along Court St. Located at the corner of 6th and Court is Paddock Townhouse. It was formerly the Paddock Hotel which was rebuilt in 1923 after the original Paddock Hotel burned. It is an example of early 20th century Renaissance Revival architecture. It has been nominated for listing on the National Register of Historic Places.

The **Beatrice Public Library** is located at 218 N. 5th St. It is a Carnegie Library built in 1904. It is an example of Beaux Arts architecture and is listed on the National Register of Historic Places.

Chautauqua Park is located on the south side of the Blue River. Go south on US 77 and turn east after the bridge. The original Chautauqua Tabernacle, first used in 1889 is still

EXHIBIT AT HOMESTEAD MONUMENT—The Epard-Palmer cabin, originally built in 1867, is one of several exhibits at the Homestead National Monument near Beatrice.

standing. It is listed on the National Register of Historic Places.

There are several historic places in Gage County.

The HOMESTEAD NATIONAL MONUMENT, located 4½ miles northwest of Beatrice on N-4, the monument and museum are tributes to **Daniel** and **Agnes (Suiter) Freeman**, among the first applicants to file under the **Homestead Act of 1862**. The Act, signed into law by President Lincoln May 20, 1862, made it possible for settlers to claim 160 acres of government land by paying a small filing fee of $18. To become full owner, a man or woman 21 years of age or older, was required to build a house, live on the land and till it for five years.

Daniel Freeman, a Union soldier home on furlough, filed the first claim at the land office in Brownville January 1, 1863. Earlier he had established squatter's rights to land on Cub Creek where he had built a log cabin and had broken ground. Freeman's furlough was to be over before he could get to Brownville but he met a young assistant in the land office at a New Year's party and the assistant took him to the office just after midnight and recorded his entry. Daniel was not discharged from the Army until 1865, when he returned with his bride.

The Freemans built themselves a new log cabin and eventually built their farmstead up to 840 acres. In time they replaced the

OLD FILLEY BARN—This unusual barn, constructed in 1874, is located near Filley and is owned by the Gage County Historical Society. Built by Elijah Filley, the barn has been placed on the National Register of Historic Places.

cabin with a brick house, later destroyed by fire.

Senator George W. Norris introduced the bill, passed by Congress in 1936, creating the Freeman Homestead National Monument.

The visitor's center is located near the entrance to the Monument. There are several points of interest in the park which may be seen on a 1½ mile walking tour. Near the visitor's center is the **Palmer-Epard Cabin**, originally built in 1867 and moved to its present site in 1950. Along the trail the visitor will see the approximate site of the squatter's cabin, site of the brick house (1876-1916) and the site of the original homestead cabin (1865-1890). The **Freeman School** is a furnished one-room schoolhouse that served the local community from 1872 to 1968. It was moved to the Homestead National Monument in 1970. The Freeman graves are also located in the park.

The Homestead National Monument, operated by the U.S. National Park Service, is open 8 a.m. to 5 p.m. daily. Admission is free.

The **Filley Stone Barn** is located two miles southwest of FIL-

LEY (which is 12 miles east of Beatrice on US 136). The barn was built in 1874 by **Elijah Filley**. It is a four-story limestone structure measuring 46' x 56'. The barn is listed on the National Register of Historic Places. It is owned by the Gage County Historical Society which sponsors a threshing demonstration each year on the 2nd Sunday of July from 11:30 a.m. to 5 p.m. The quarter section on which Filley is located was purchased in 1882 by Mr. and Mrs. Filley from a person who had homesteaded the land in 1865.

HOLMESVILLE, nine miles southeast of Beatrice, was founded in 1880 by **Morgan L. Holmes**. The rock from the stone quarry in the area was hauled to Lincoln in wagons to be used in the original capitol building in 1868.

BARNESTON, located in southern Gage County, was first the site of the Otoe and Missouri Indian reservation. It was probably settled in 1854-55 with approximately 600 residents. The reservation measured 10 miles by 25 miles encompassing 250 sections. The permanent village (the present site of Barneston) was located along the banks of the Blue River and was occupied for 27 years by the tribe. The Indian village site became Barneston in 1884 named for **F. M. Barnes** who had located at the Otoe Agency about 1870 and established a cattle ranch. His wife was recognized as a member of the tribe. The old boarding schoolhouse called the **Old Mission House** from reservation days is located on the east edge of Barneston. On N-8 near the west entrance of Barneston is a marker designating the site of the **Otoe-Missouri Earth Lodge Village and Agency** which is listed on the National Register of Historic Places.

The town of ADAMS is located about 26 miles northeast of Beatrice on N-41, just west of the intersection of N-43. It is situated on part of the claim of **John O. Adams**, who is believed to be the first permanent white settler in Gage County. Homestead laws had not been enacted at this time so he obtained squatter sovereignty over 160 acres of land in March 1857.

WYMORE (pop. 1,790) is located south of Beatrice 12 miles on US 77. The town was named for **Samuel Wymore**, a young pioneer farmer who provided the land for the town. District 81 School was organized in 1878 in the rural Wymore area. It was moved to McCandles Park in Wymore in 1967 by the Wymore Historical Society. In 1983 the school was donated to the Gage County Historical Society. The building houses many of the items and furnishings used during its days as a country school.

HISTORICAL TECUMSEH—Tecumseh, county seat of Johnson County, was incorporated in 1856. This courthouse was built in the 1880s and is one of several buildings in the community listed on the National Register of Historic Places.

TECUMSEH

TECUMSEH (pop. 1,906), 14 miles east, is the county seat of Johnson County, in the heart of Nebraska's cornbelt. The town was named for **Tecumseh**, famed chief of the Shawnees, by **Col. John Boulware**. The town was incorporated in 1856.

There is a quaint city hall and courthouse, built in the 1880s, and a historic jail, circa 1872, located in the town square. Tecumseh is listed on the Register of Historic Places, not only for these buildings but for many houses in the community of unique architectural structure.

JOHNSON COUNTY HISTORICAL MUSEUM is housed in the former Christian Church, Lincoln St., just off 3rd St. The museum is open daily, May through September, and by appointment at other times.

AUBURN

AUBURN (pop. 3,483), 19 miles east of Tecumseh, was formerly two towns known as **Sheridan** and **Calvert**. Sheridan was surveyed October 19, 1868, and was named in honor of **Gen. Phil S. Sheridan**, a Civil War hero. The Missouri Pacific Railroad arrived in Sheridan on February 4, 1882.

The townsite of Calvert was purchased in early 1881 by the **Lincoln Land Company**, a subsidiary of the Burlington & Missouri railroad. It was platted July 1, 1881, and was named for **Thomas E. Calvert**, an official of the railroad.

The two rival towns agreed to unite and form one town in 1882. **Charles Nixon**, who had an interest in the land through which the Missouri Pacific ran, suggested the town be named Auburn in honor of Auburn, New York.

The County Courthouse was located between the towns. The present courthouse building, built in 1900, is located on the same square.

Half-Breed Tract was set aside by the government in the 1830 Prairie Du Chien Treaty for the half-breeds of the Oto, Iowa, Omaha and Santee Sioux Indian tribes. Early day fur traders often married into Indian tribes and children of these marriages —the half-breeds— had difficulty in establishing claim to Indian lands. The Half-Breed Lands were located between the Little Nemaha and Missouri Rivers and the first patent was issued to **Louis Neal** September 10, 1860.

The owners were not required to live on the land and much of it was sold off to white settlers. Descendants of some pioneer fur traders still live in this area. A historical marker is located three-quarters of a mile east of Auburn on US 136.

BROWNVILLE

BROWNVILLE (pop. 203), US 136 and N-67, presented a busy scene with the rumble of wagons and the shouting of busy men when it was incorporated as a city of second class in 1855. Almost everyone who owned a wagon went into the freighting business. When the great needs of the settlers were met and with the coming of the railroads, Brownville began to decline.

THE CARSON HOUSE—Located in the central part of Brownville is the historic Carson House, built by Richard Brown in 1860. Furnished in period furniture, the home is open for tours by the Brownville Historical Society.

The town was named for **Richard Brown** who arrived on the townsite in 1854. He was quickly followed by other settlers and Brownville grew rapidly. It was here **Daniel Freeman** filed his homestead claim, recognized as the first in the nation. The first telegraph office in Nebraska was established in Brownville.

Robert W. Furnas, who arrived in Brownville to establish a newspaper, *The Advertiser,* in 1856, served as Nebraska's governor in 1873-74. Furnas served with the 2nd Nebraska Cavalry Regiment on the frontier during the Civil War. He joined the cavalry as a captain, commanding Company E, but was soon promoted to the rank of colonel and commanded the regiment. He was founder of the Board of Agriculture October 4, 1858 and was elected its first president. He also was founder and first president of the Nebraska State Historical Society, September 28, 1878.

The **Muir House**, home of **Robert Valentine Muir** (1827-1917), an early resident of Brownville, is located a block north of US 136 in the northeastern part of town. Muir was a prosperous Brownville businessman and was a publisher of *The Advertiser.* The Muir house was built during 1868-1870 and was one of Nebraska's most elegant early homes. It was built of native Nebraska brick in the Italianate style.

Another historic home is the **Carson House**, which dates back to 1860. The original home, a small brick structure, was built by **Richard Brown**, the town founder. **John Carson**, serving with the Union Army, purchased the house in 1863 and began adding to the original structure the following year when he moved his family to Brownville. Carson was a successful pioneer banker and was only one of three Nebraska bankers to survive the 1857 financial crash. The house, as it now stands, was completed in 1872 and has been owned continuously by the Carson family. John Carson was serving as president of the 1st National Bank of Lincoln and the Carson Bank of Auburn at the time of his death in 1898. His wife died in 1902. The Carson House, located on the main street, is open for tours conducted by the Historical Society Sunday afternoons during the months of May, September and October. The house is open every afternoon during the months of June, July and August. The house is furnished in period furniture.

Brownville has been revived in recent years by the formation of the **Brownville Historical Society**. The Society has been restoring the old historic landmarks and buildings and a number of stores have been built and remodeled along the main street in the late 19th century frontier motif.

The *Spirit of Brownville*, an authentic sidewheeler, makes her home in Brownville and takes visitors on scenic Missouri River cruises. The **Nebraska Wesleyan University Theatre in Residence** presents performances at the **Brownville Village Theatre** and the schedule can be obtained from the historical society. Travelers are also encouraged to visit the **Captain Meriwether Lewis**, a restored riverboat museum, which houses Missouri River memorabilia from the early 1900s.

PERU

PERU (pop. 1,002), on N-67 north of US 136 and east of US 75, was incorporated in 1857 on the banks of the Missouri River. The **Nemaha Valley Seminary and Normal Institute**, which was the forerunner of today's **Peru State College** and the oldest college in Nebraska, was established in 1860. The school became Nebraska's first state-supported college in 1867. As a state college, the first classes were held October 24 of that year with an enrollment of 32. Initially the campus contained 60 acres and a single building, Mount Vernon Hall.

During Peru State's existence, thousands of Nebraskans and other young people from throughout the nation have received a college eduction on the "Campus of a Thousand Oaks."

BROCK

BROCK (pop. 187), on N-67 six miles west of US 75, originally named **Dayton**, was located near a belt of timber about 22 miles northwest of Brownville. Brock has had its name changed seven times since it was laid out in 1855. Most of the changes were made at the whims of the early settlers. **Podunk** was the government postoffice name.

After the railroad came, the Missouri Pacific officials changed the name to Brock to honor an official of that railroad.

NEMAHA CITY

NEMAHA CITY (pop. 209), is near the mouth of the Little Nemaha River which flows nearby on its south side. It was incorporated by the Territorial Legislature in 1855. A postoffice was established July 1, 1856, and the Methodists established the first religious organization in 1857.

Nemaha Precinct was created by the Board of County commissioners in 1857. In 1880 a state law changed Nemaha City to a village.

Indian Cave State Park is located east of Nemaha City, on N-67, south of US 136. Named for its ancient Indian petroglyphs, the park is probably the most pristine area of the state, preserved in its natural wilderness beauty.

JOHNSON

JOHNSON (pop. 359), east of N-59, north of US 136, is beautifully situated on the rolling prairie in the center of one of the most fertile farming sections in Nemaha County. **Julius A. Johnson**, the owner of a large body of land in the west central part of the county, laid out the town in 1869.

JULIAN

JULIAN (pop. 87) is located west of US 75 north of N-67. About 1880 a postoffice was established at a farmhouse little more than a mile south of Julian. This postoffice was named Julian in honor of **Julian Bahaud**, a rich French bachelor who lived in the community. Bahaud was known to all his friends and neighbors as "Old Man Julian."

Nebraska's Government

Nebraska's Unicameral is the only one-house legislature in the nation, and senators are elected on a non-partisan basis. Adopted in 1935, the Unicameral is efficient and economical.

The late U.S. Senator George W. Norris was one of the most ambitious advocates of the system and wore out two sets of tires campaigning for the constitutional amendment to form the new system. Campaigners promised that one house would save time, talk and money.

The first year it was in effect, the Unicameral cost one-half as much as the previous two-house session. Only two major changes have been made in the Unicameral since its adoption. The number of senators has been raised from 43 to 49, and they are elected for four years instead of two.

Because of the effectiveness of the Unicameral, other states have been studying it.

In 1964 the people approved a constitutional amendment extending the governor's term from two to four years. Governor Norbert T. Tiemann was the first governor to serve a four-year term. The Constitution of 1875 also provided for a lieutenant governor, and his term was also changed to four years in 1964. All executive officers, including the governor and lieutenant governor, are elected on a partisan basis.

The State Supreme Court consists of a chief justice and six judges. The chief justice is appointed by the Governor from a statewide list of applicants whereas the other six judges are chosen from districts. All judges serve six-year terms, and they too are appointed on a non-partisan basis.

Section 6

This is a very picturesque as well as historic drive (approximately 100 miles one way) along the general route of Lewis and Clark's expedition up the Missouri River in 1804. There are several unique communities along the way.

One of the first is Plattsmouth, just south of Bellevue. Founded in 1854, Plattsmouth served as a busy river port during the early days of the steam boat.

Nebraska City, some 25 miles south, is the home of J. Morton Sterling, founder of Arbor Day. The town was founded as a freighting center in the early days of the state and has many historic homes and buildings still in use. Arbor Lodge is one of the most popular tourist attractions in eastern Nebraska.

Brownville, along the Missouri some 35 miles south of Nebraska City, is another historic, small river town. Many of its old buildings are being restored and an old river boat has been converted to a museum, depicting life in the early days on the river.

Indian Cave State Park offers a glimpse of the wilderness and some of nature's beauty in a primitve setting. The drive, especially in the fall, offers spectacular scenery. It is located adjacent to the Missouri River.

Falls City, near the Kansas state line, is still another old Nebraska community with many attractions. A Kentucky couple, the Stringfields, arrived in 1852 to operate a sawmill. The community was founded in 1857. The first oil production in Nebraska started at Falls City just before World War II.

185

AMONG THE SIGHTS—Along this route are many historical attractions. Nebraska City is the home of Arbor Lodge and the museum (below) captures some of the long and colorful history of Brownville, with many of its old buildings being restored.

ALONG THE LEWIS & CLARK TRAIL
US Highways 73 and 75
The trip south of Omaha and Bellevue, along the old Lewis & Clark Trail on US 73 and 75, is both interesting and colorful. The Lewis & Clark Expedition used a trail along the western bank of the Missouri River as they made their way north from St. Louis in 1804. They went north to the northeastern part of the state before turning westward toward their ultimate destination—the Pacific Ocean.

(Background histories and information about Omaha and Bellevue appear in Section 2).

PLATTSMOUTH
Seventeen miles south of Omaha is PLATTSMOUTH (pop. 6,294), incorporated in 1855 and designated as the county seat of Cass County.

Between 1850 and 1860, the "Golden Age" of steamboating on the Missouri River saw many sidewheelers and sternwheelers put in at Plattsmouth, a busy river port. The **John C. Fremont Expedition of 1842** located their camp two miles south of present day Plattsmouth. As early as 1848, settlers were crossing the Missouri at Plattsmouth enroute to California and the Oregon Country.

In 1860 Plattsmouth served as a stagecoach stop on the route between Ottumwa, Iowa, and Fort Kearny. It was also the terminus for lumber and other supplies shipped from the East and as a shipping point for cattle and grain from the West. The Burlington & Missouri Railroad arrived in Plattsmouth in 1869.

Ferry boats were used to cross the Missouri at this point until 1880 when a bridge was constructed. In 1891 the Missouri Pacific Railroad brought north-south rail transportation to Plattsmouth.

Plattsmouth takes its name from its geographical location at the mouth of the Platte River. This particular spot has been a camping spot and home for hundred of years—first for Indians and then for white settlers. From artifacts found in and around the Plattsmouth area it is believed the earliest inhabitants were Indians of the Omaha and Otoe tribes.

The Main Street Historic District is listed on the National Register of Historic Places. Plattsmouth is home of the CASS COUNTY HISTORICAL MUSEUM.

NEBRASKA CITY
Fifty miles east of Lincoln, via N-2, is the city of NEBRASKA

ARBOR DAY FOUNDER—J. Sterling Morton, a frontier journalist and state leader, urged that trees be planted throughout the state. He was the founder of Arbor Day in 1885.

CITY (pop. 7,075), site of **J. Sterling Morton's** home, **Arbor Lodge**. Morton was founder of **Arbor Day**, the day dedicated to tree planting and a legal holiday in Nebraska.

The first settlement in this area occurred in 1846 with the establishment of old **Fort Kearny** on Table Creek. Only a blockhouse and a few temporary buildings were erected at the fort when it was determined a military post was needed further west on the frontier. Out of that decision came the plan to build a fort out along the Platte River on the emerging Oregon or Overland Trail. (This came to be **Fort Kearny** on the Platte or the "new" Fort Kearny).

Nebraska City is the county seat of Otoe County.

There are several historic places to see and visit in Nebraska City.

ARBOR LODGE STATE HISTORICAL PARK, West 2nd Ave., was the home of the founder of Arbor Day, **J. (for Julius) Sterling Morton** and is one of the most popular tourist attractions in eastern Nebraska.

Morton and his bride, Caroline (French), arrived in Nebraska Territory in 1854 and moved into a log cabin in Bellevue until they moved to Nebraska City the next spring. Morton came to Nebraska City to become editor of the *Nebraska City News.*

In Nebraska City the Mortons settled on a 160-acre parcel of land they gained title to through preemption. They built a four-room, L-shaped frame house with a front porch, a veritable mansion at the time. They immediately set out plants and trees to brighten their surroundings and by 1858 they had not only planted ornamental greenery around their home but had also developed an apple orchard.

OLD FORT KEARNY—A replica of the old fort established in 1846 by Col. Stephen W. Kearny is located at 423 Central Ave., Nebraska City. The fort was abandoned in 1847.

Morton promoted advancements in agriculture and his convictions about the need for tree planting throughout the territory in his writings as a frontier journalist. His active interest in tree planting gained recognition as early as 1872 when as president of the State Board of Agriculture he introduced a resolution calling for a tree planting day to be known as Arbor Day. The state legislature acted in 1885 and **Arbor Day** became an official state holiday April 22nd (Morton's birthday). The idea spread across the U.S. and into several foreign countries.

Caroline Morton died June 29, 1881 at the age of 47.

Morton was involved in Nebraska Territorial politics and served as U.S. Secretary of Agriculture in President Grover Cleveland's second administration (1893-96). He served two terms as Territorial Representative, Secretary and Acting Governor of the Territory (1858-61).

J. Sterling Morton died April 27, 1902 at the home of his son, Mark, in Forest Park, Illinois. He was buried beside Caroline and his son, Carl, in Nebraska City's Wyuka Cemetery, 1½ miles southeast of Arbor Lodge, at 19th St. and 6th Corso.

The 52-room mansion at Arbor Lodge was completed in 1902 by **Joy Morton**, oldest of Morton's four sons and founder of the

189

WILDWOOD PERIOD HOUSE—Located in Steinhardt Park, Nebraska City, this house was built in 1869 and is furnished in the 1860-80 period. It is listed on the National Register of Historic Places.

Morton Salt Company, who inherited the mansion. Joy Morton donated the Lodge to the state in 1923 to be preserved for future generations as a memorial to his father. It is listed on the National Register of Historic Places.

ARBOR LODGE is open 9 a.m. to 5 p.m. daily from mid-April to to October 31. Admission is charged.

OLD FORT KEARNY, 423 Central Ave., is a replica of the old fort established in 1846 by **Col. Stephen W. Kearny**. The post was abandoned the next year in favor of a site further west.

Over several decades the blockhouse was used for many purposes including a printing shop, justice court, jail, drugstore and butcher shop. The fort replica was dedicated in 1938.

OTOE COUNTY COURTHOUSE, 11th St. and Central Ave., erected in 1864, is still in use although the original has had annexes built on. It's the oldest public building still in use in the state. There has been little change made in the original structure. The courthouse is open for walking tours.

WILDWOOD PERIOD HOUSE AND PARK, Steinhart Rd., was built in 1869 by **Jasper A. Ware**, a banker. The ten room brick home is furnished in the 1860-80 period. An 85-key Steinway grand piano, a rose-wood sofa, petit-point picture, pier mirror and marble topped table are among the items of interest in the house. It is listed on the National Register of Historic Places.

Hours: 1 to 5 p.m. daily, except Monday, April 15 through October 15. Admission is charged. Group tours are available.

The original barn has been converted into an art gallery. Admission to the gallery is free.

Other Sites of Historical Interest

JOHN BROWN'S CABIN, N-2 and 19th St., constructed in 1852, is a typical one room, log house and an authentic station on the **"Underground Railroad"** used to help escaped slaves to freedom before the Civil War. It's the oldest Nebraska structure at an original scene. It is open 10 a.m. to 5:30 p.m. daily, March 1 through November 1. Admission is charged.

There are more than 30 residences and other buildings in use in the community that were constructed in the mid and late 19th century. Among these are:

TAYLOR-WESSELL HOUSE, 711 3rd Corso, was built in 1857 and is listed on the National Register of Historic Places.

BISCHOF HARDWARE BUILDING, 701 Central Ave., was built in 1867 and until 1978 was one of the oldest hardware stores in Nebraska.

SLOAN DRUG STORE, 622 Central Ave., was built in 1870 and features high Victorian Italianate brickwork on the second floor with metal window hoods.

WRIGHT-STRAUB HOUSE, 608 1st Ave., was built in 1861.

DENNIS-STEPHENSON HOUSE, 1002 1st Ave., was built in 1865 for Indian Agent **William W. Dennison**.

DILLON-PETERSON HOUSE, 1014 1st Ave., was built in 1864.

METHODIST EPISCOPAL CHURCH, 11th St. and 1st Ave., was originally built in 1855-56 and rebuilt in 1874-75. The earlier church was the first Methodist Church built in Nebraska.

The firm of **Russell, Majors & Waddell**, the wagon train freighters, built three houses in Nebraska City in 1858, one at 517 N. 13th St. and another at 516 N. 14th St. The third, at 407 N. 14th St., was paid for by the U.S. government and was originally occupied by **Maj. J. G. Martin**, Army Quartermaster.

For a complete listing of these older buildings, contact the Nebraska City Chamber of Commerce.

PERU

Driving south on US 73 and 75, 10 miles, one reaches the small farm community of JULIAN (pop. 87) and five miles south is the

OTOE COUNTY COURTHOUSE—The Otoe County Courthouse, located at 11th St. and Central Ave., Nebraska City, was constructed in 1864. The original building has had several annexes added over the years but is still in use. It's the oldest public building in use in Nebraska. Visitors to Nebraska City should not pass up a walking tour of the courthouse.

intersection of US 73 and N-67. Seven miles east on N-67 is PERU (pop. 1,002), incorporated in 1857. (For more information, see Section 5.)

BROWNVILLE

From Peru it is 10 miles to BROWNVILLE, via N-67 and US 136. (See Section 5.)

NEMAHA

Four miles south of Brownville is NEMAHA (pop. 209), en-route on N-67 and Spur-64E to **Indian Cave State Park**.

The 14 mile drive from Brownville to Indian Cave State Park, via N-67, offers spectacular scenery, especially during the fall months. The park includes 3,000 acres of timbered land adjacent to the Missouri River. The state's newest park offers primitive camping and three miles of Missouri River bluffs. There are more than 35 miles of hiking trails. The Indian Cave, the park's name-sake, is located in the southeast corner of the park and can be reached by car.

AUBURN

Returning north to Nebraska City, US 73 and 75 takes one to AUBURN, 20 miles south.

Auburn is the county seat of Nemaha County. The county, created in 1854, was originally called Forney County. The name was changed to Nemaha County in 1855.

Auburn is considered home of the **Cooper Nuclear Station**, less than a dozen miles away on the banks of the Missouri River. The giant utility plant began operation in 1974 and serves electricity to a wide region. (For more on Auburn, see Section 5.)

PODUNK

The mythical town of PODUNK has long been used to describe the ultimate in provincialism. A Podunk did exist in Nebraska for a time in the early days.

BROCK (pop. 187), 12 miles northwest of Auburn on N-67,was called Podunk, officially recognized as such by U.S. postoffice officials. Podunk, or Brock, started out as **Dayton** when it was laid out in 1855. The town's name was changed seven times, almost at the whims of the early day settlers.

After the railroad arrived, Missouri Pacific officials changed the name to Brock to honor an official of that railroad. Missouri Pacific trains began running through Brock in 1882.

FALLS CITY

After leaving Auburn, US 73 and 75 split midway in Richardson County, 17 miles south. It is 10 miles south on US 75 to the Kansas state line. It is 18 miles, via US 73, to FALLS CITY (pop. 5,128), county seat of Richardson County. Founded in 1857, Falls City was named for a nearby waterfall on the Nemaha River. The falls are gone now, victims of progress when the river channel was straightened. The beginnings of Falls City dates back to 1852, when a Kentucky couple moved to Nemaha Falls, just two miles southwest of the present town site. Here, the Stringfields built and operated a rig to saw lumber and grind corn. They sold the business to **James L. Stumbe**, who had a house guest, **John A. Burbank**. Mr. Burbank, an easterner, had traveled west looking for a place to start a new town.

In 1857 **Jim Lane**, a noted free-soil leader, along with Burbank and two others formed the Town Company. Purchased for $50, the land was platted and recorded as Falls City by the men. This occurred three years after the opening of the Kansas-Nebraska territories for settlement, which involved a bloody struggle between pro-slave and anti-slave settlers. Falls City was located on the Lane Trail nearest the northern boundary of Kansas, through which free-state emigrants could be funneled into the territory.

Falls City became the county seat of Richardson County in 1860 after being approved by the legislature.

Scenic and Historical Points Near Falls City

BUCHOLZ NO. 1, opened in 1939, was the first oil well in Nebraska. Located three miles west of Falls City on N-8 is a historical marker on the site of the rich find. From this location visitors can see existing oil wells pumping and and also have a good view of the Nemaha River Valley.

RICHARDSON COUNTY HISTORICAL SOCIETY MUSEUM, 312 West 17th, three blocks west on N-73, is located in Prichard Auditorium. The museum has displays of artifacts that are related to the development of Richardson County and southeastern Nebraska. Tours can be arranged by contacting city employees in the building.

RICHARDSON COUNTY COURTHOUSE, 18th and N-73, built in 1924-25, is a three story brick structure and is a pretentious example of Classic Revival Architecture of the early 20th century. The district courtroom on the third floor shouldn't be missed.

IRON MONUMENT is located several miles south of Rulo on the Kansas-Nebraska border. This seven foot obelisk-shaped monument marking the starting point of all Nebraska surveys was erected high in the bluffs just west of the Missouri River in 1855.

LEARY-KELLY SITE is also located south of Rulo. An undeveloped Registered National Historic Landmark, it is a multi-component site yielding Nebraska culture, Oneota and historic Indian material. This area was visited by Lewis and Clark in July, 1804.

Section 7

The particular area covered in this tour is usually
referred to as Lewis and Clark Country or Lewis and
Clark Land. It was here the two American explorers
spent some time with the Indians before heading to the
Pacific. Many other early day American explorers followed
Lewis and Clark to this region.

There is a lot of country to see in this recommended
tour of northeastern Nebraska. Fort Atkinson
was the first fort built in the territory and it was
here the first school was built. It is Indian country
and it is farm country.

Part of the route follows the old Mormon Trail for
several miles west. There are many historic spots along
this old trail, opened in the 1840s and used for more
than a quarter of a century.

Bancroft, one of the small towns on the route, is
site for the Neihardt Center, built in honor of John
G. Neihardt, Nebraska's Poet Laureate. He was an expert
on Nebraska Indian culture and traditions and authored
more than 25 volumes of poetry, fiction and philosophy.

Famed TV Host Johnny Carson was raised in Norfolk
and Columbus. He began his broadcast career in Nebraska
after graduating from the University of Nebraska.

There are several historic spots along the way throughout
this tour. There is the old Neligh Mill, for example, which
has been fully restored and there is the town of Niobrara,
settled in 1856, which had to be moved in its entirety in 1977.
There is much to see and learn about this region.

195

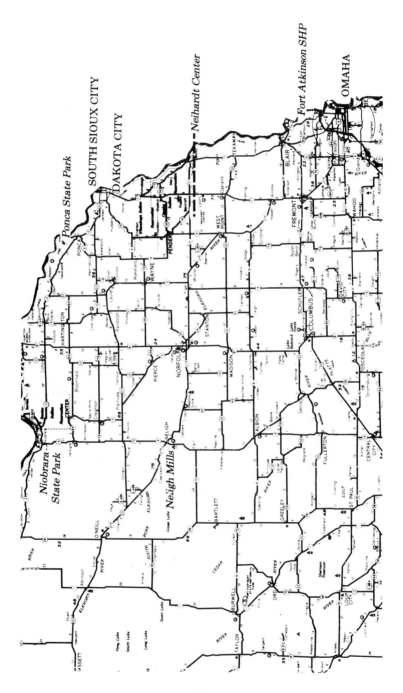

LEWIS AND CLARK TOUR
Through Northeast Nebraska

Lewis and Clark Land was among the last areas of the wilderness to be settled by pioneers on their way west to the new frontier.

Some of the early explorers to the region included **Etienne Venyard de Bourgmont**, a French adventurer who ascended the Missouri River to the mouth of the Platte River. In 1720 a Spanish expedition under **Col. Pedro de Vallasur** was massacred along the Platte by Pawnee Indians. **Peter** and **Paul Mallet** of France were among the first explorers, crossing the region from east to west in 1739-40, and are credited with naming the Platte River. In 1804 **President Thomas Jefferson** commissioned **Meriwether Lewis** and **William Clark** to explore the West. The Lewis & Clark Expedition mapped the eastern boundary of Nebraska along the Missouri River.

In the half century following the Louisiana Purchase in 1803, exploration by Lewis and Clark (1804-06), **Lt. Zebulon M. Pike** (1806), the **Hunt Party** (1811), **Maj. Stephen H. Long** (1819-20), **Col. Henry Dodge** (1835), **Lt. John C. Fremont** (1842-44), and **Lt. G. K. Warren** (1855-57) made known important facts about the region. Among the early trading groups was the **St. Louis Missouri Fur Company**. **Manuel Lisa** established a post for this company in 1812 in present-day Washington County. In 1820 a nearby camp became a permanent Army post, **Fort Atkinson**. It was established to discourage British encroachment and to protect the frontier.

FORT CALHOUN

This tour begins 15 miles north of Omaha at the site of **Fort Atkinson** in the community of FORT CALHOUN (pop. 638) on US 73 (take Exit 454 in Omaha).

Lewis and Clark set up camp in the area July 30, 1804. They held council with the Otoe and Missouri Indian tribes on August 3rd. The pow wow gave the locale its name of "Council Bluffs," and Clark later recommended the site for use as a fort.

In 1819 **Col. Henry Atkinson** was given command of the **Yellowstone Expedition** to establish a chain of military outposts from the mouth of the Missouri River to the Yellowstone River to protect U.S. fur traders and establish American influence over the area acquired in the Louisiana Purchase.

Atkinson's command reached this point late in the fall and established a winter camp 1½ miles north and called it **Canton-**

197

THIS MARKER TELLS THE STORY—DeSoto, incorporated in 1855, once provided a landing for steamboats plying the Missouri River. The town grew rapidly and it became the county seat of Washington County. Its future looked bright. A depression hit and the railroad bypassed the frontier settlement in favor of Blair and eventually the town died.

ment Missouri. More than 100 members of the expedition died during the winter. The camp was moved to higher ground in the spring and a fort established and named for Colonel Atkinson. In the meantime Congress scuttled plans to build the chain of forts.

Fort Atkinson was the largest military post in the West with over 1,000 troops during its active period. Among the units assigned here were the Rifle Regiment and the 6th U.S. Infantry.

FORT ATKINSON (1820-27)—Reconstruction of some of the barracks at Fort Atkinson, established to protect American interests in the region, continue under the auspices of the Nebraska Game and Parks Commission. Visitors are welcome to explore the site and visit the musuem.

The only major military campaign launched from Fort Atkinson was an expedition, commanded by **Col. Henry Leavenworth**, against the Arikara Indian in 1823 for their raid on a party of fur traders.

The fort was abandoned in 1827 and the troops were transferred to Jefferson Barracks at St. Louis.

During the seven years Fort Atkinson was in existence, the first school and a library were built. A large-scale agricultural project was developed and a sawmill, brickyard and gristmill were constructed.

Visitors are welcome to explore the site and tour the museum. The historical park is undergoing continuing development. The park is open the year-round, however, the visitor's center is open daily, 9 a.m. to 5 p.m. during the summer. A State Park Entry Permit ($2 daily, $10 annual) is required.

Fort Calhoun is also the home of the WASHINGTON COUNTY HISTORICAL SOCIETY MUSEUM. The museum is open 1 to 4:30 p.m. Wednesday, Friday and weekends, April 1 through mid-November.

DANA'S "OLD MAIN"—Lutheran Pastor A.M. Andersen was the founder of Dana College in Blair. The school began in 1884 as Trinity Seminary and the name was not changed to "Dana" until 1903. "Dana," which rhymes with "Anna," is the poetic word for Denmark. Both names derive from the legendary King Dan, progenitor of the Danes and founder of the kingdom of Denmark. Pictured here is "Old Main" on the Dana College campus.

BLAIR

BLAIR (pop. 6,277), county seat of Washington County, is nine miles north of Fort Calhoun on US 73. Blair is home of **DeSoto National Wildlife Refuge.** The Visitors Center here features exhibits and artifacts salvaged from the sunken steamboat *Bertrand* that sank in the Missouri River in 1865. The Center is open 9 a.m. to 4:30 p.m. daily. The Refuge is open from 6 a.m. to 10 p.m. daily, April 15 through September 30. It has two self-guiding nature trails.

Blair is also home of **Dana College**, established in 1886.

Blair was established in 1869 following the demise of the town of **DeSoto**, platted in 1854 and incorporated in 1855. DeSoto, promoted as a "gateway to the West" by its ambitious and enthusiastic citizens, was the county seat of Washington County from 1858 to 1866. DeSoto's three banks were forced to close in the Panic of 1857 and many of its residents fled to the newly discovered gold fields in Colorado in 1859. The railroad decided to bypass DeSoto in favor of Blair and soon the town went out of existence.

Several Missouri River boats sank in the river nearby, notably the *Cora* and the *Bertrand.*

The *Steamboat Bertrand,* which was discovered in 1968, a victim of the Missouri River, has been raised from its watery grave and salvage is displayed in the museum.

FREMONT—ARLINGTON—AMES

FREMONT (pop. 26,800), on US 30 22 miles west of Blair, is named for **Gen. John C. Fremont**, the "Pathfinder," and was settled in 1856. It is the county seat of Dodge County.

A Pawnee Indian village, home of about 1,500 Indians, was located about four miles southeast of the new town in 1856. The Indian chief sent a messenger to the townsite demanding its abandonment within three days or they would exterminate the small band of whites. **James G. Smith** was dispatched to Omaha to seek help from territorial governor **Mark W. Izard**. He was given a box of muskets, ammunition and eight soldiers. By marching and counter-marching, setting fires here and there, they were able to give the impression that a large army had moved in. On the third day a messenger came with a white flag and word that the Indians would not bother them. His word was kept and the Indians never bothered Fremont.

THE MAJOR LONG MONUMENT is located four miles north of Fremont on the south slope of a bluff. Here the expedition of Major Long passed during the year 1820, enroute to explore the Rocky Mountain area of Colorado. He and his men crossed the Elkhorn River at a point south of present ARLINGTON (pop. 1,117), after traveling over the highlands from Fort Atkinson. This was the first trail and the first traveled road up the Platte Valley and for 24 years was the only one.

LOUIS E. MAY MUSEUM, 1643 N. Nye Ave., houses the collections of the Dodge County Historical Society. Named for the Trust which made the purchase of the house possible, it was built by Fremont's first mayor, **Theron Nye**, in 1874.

The museum is open 1:30 to 4:30 p.m. Wednesday through Sunday. Admission is free.

JAMESTOWN MARKER was erected on the site of the original Jamestown postoffice, and also on the trail of the Major Long expedition of 1820.

THE FREMONT MARKER stands on the site of where **Abram McNeal** established the first home in the area, two miles west of present Fremont, on the north side of the Mormon Trail and Military Road in 1856.

AMES is seven miles west of Fremont on US 30. THE MORMON TRAIL AND MILITARY ROAD MARKER stands on the townsite of the original postoffice, **Lincoln**, which existed from 1856 to 1868. The town was first called Albion, for the Albion Ranch or Albion Hotel established here. Later it was renamed **Timberville** until Ames was established. The Mormons established the trail passing this point in 1847. In 1856 it was surveyed and staked as the Military Road serving Fort Kearny.

NORTH BEND

NORTH BEND (pop. 1,374) is 15 miles west of Fremont on US 30. The NORTH BEND MARKER was dedicated in 1956 to mark the site of the first home of this area, established in 1856.

The PURPLE CANE MARKER stands eight miles northwest of North Bend on a farm on the east line of the NE ¼ Section 30-18-5. The Purple Cane postoffice was established on this homestead in 1872 by **S. Rufus Mason**. This marker is also on the Major Long Trail and the trail used by the Pawnee and Omaha Indians until after homestead days.

SCHUYLER

SCHUYLER (pop. 4,557), 15 miles west of North Bend, was platted in 1869 and became the county seat of Colfax County. The community and county were named in honor of **Schuyler Colfax**, Vice President of the United States at the time.

Schuyler was the first point on the Union Pacific railroad from which Texas cattle were shipped.

COLUMBUS

COLUMBUS (pop. 17,317), 47 miles west of Fremont on US 30 and 81, was founded in 1856. Nine years later, Columbus was incorporated as the "Town of Columbus." The Loup and Platte

PAWNEE SCOUTS LEADER —Major Frank North, of Columbus, recruited and organized the famous Pawnee Scouts, who operated out of Fort Kearny on numerous occasions during the Indian uprisings and during the construction of the railroad after the Civil War.

Luther North was the other half of "The Fighting Norths."

203

GREW UP IN NEBRASKA—
Johnny Carson, host of the
long-running "Tonight Show"
on NBC-TV, was raised in Norfolk and Columbus, Nebraska.
He received his degree from
the University of Nebraska in
1949 and began his broadcast-
ing career at KFAB, Lincoln.
Carson was born October 23,
1925 in Corning, Iowa.

Rivers join near the city, and in the 1870s a ferry transported wagons across the Loup River on their way to the northwest. In the 1860s and 70s Columbus was a major outfitting post for pioneers. It is the county seat of Platte County.

Maj. Frank North and his brother, **Luther**, organized the friendly Pawnee Indians to serve as scouts for the Army and fight marauding Indian bands that threatened both the settlers in the early 1860s and workers on the Union Pacific railroad after the Civil War. The "Fighting Norths," as the brothers became known, settled in Columbus in 1858 and operated a road ranche (general store-hotel) 20 miles south of the Pawnee Indian reservation. Frank learned their language and won their confidence by the time of the Civil War. The **Pawnee Scouts** operated as a military unit, under his command, on the Plains for 13 years. His Pawnee Scouts revered their leader and called him **Pani Leshar** ("Pawnee Chief").

Luther North also understood and could speak the Indian language and served as an officer with the Scouts.

While serving with the Army, Major North met the now legendary **William F. "Buffalo Bill" Cody**. Cody and North first joined forces while attached to the military and participated together in the **Battle of Summit Springs** in 1869, led by **Maj. Eugene A. Carr**. This campaign cleared the Republican Valley, to the west, of hostile Indians. The Pawnee Scouts participated in several campaigns in the Powder River Country and were used to guard work crews during the construction of the transcontinental railroad. In 1883 Cody joined with the North brothers and other noted Indian fighters to organize and stage the first **"Buffalo Bill's Wild West Show"** at Columbus. An official state historical monument commemorating these pioneers was dedicated in 1970 at the Columbus Area Chamber of Commerce site.

CENTRAL CITY

CENTRAL CITY (pop. 3,080), county seat of Merrick County, is located 41 miles southwest of Columbus on US 30. The **Hord Lake State Recreation Area** is near here.

Central City was platted in 1864 and, in a sense, replaced **Lone Tree**, a stopping place on the Old California Trail. Lone Tree, a giant, solitary cottonwood, was a noted Platte River landmark. The town that emerged as Lone Tree was renamed Central City. The original tree finally died as hundreds of passing travelers stopped to carve their initials or names on its massive trunk. It stood on the north side of the river about three miles southwest of present-day Central City and the site is marked by a stone in the form of a tree trunk. The tree was finally destroyed in a storm in 1865.

From Central City, turn north on N-14 to FULLERTON (pop. 1,500), county seat of Nance County; ALBION (pop. 1,996), county seat of Boone County; and NELIGH, county seat of Antelope County.

FULLERTON—GENOA

FULLERTON, platted in 1878, is 18 miles north of Central City. Nearby, along the Loup River, was a Mormon pioneer campsite used by several hundred "Saints" on their historic trip to the Great Salt Lake Valley in 1847.

Nineteen miles northeast of Fullerton, on N-22 and N-39, is GENOA (pop. 1,096), one of the temporary settlements established by the Mormons in 1857. This was one of the way-stations for the **Brigham Young Express and Carrying Company**, which held a government mail contract to Salt Lake City. These stations also served as rest stops and supply depots for the Mormon emigrants.

In 1859 the Genoa settlement became part of the newly created Pawnee Indian Reservation and Genoa served as the Pawnee Indian Agency until 1876 when the Pawnees were resettled in the Indian Territory (Oklahoma) and the reservation lands sold. **Petalesharo** was the chief of the Pawnees during the period 1859-1876. The Pawnees suffered major losses in their battle with the Sioux in 1873 in Massacre Canyon (near Trenton).

The Mormon Trail started from Winter Quarters (Omaha) and went west to the Platte River, followed the north side of the Platte to Columbus. From Columbus it followed the north bank of the Loup to the western-most edge of Merrick County before dropping south to the Platte about 14 miles northeast of Grand Island. From this point the Mormon Trail moved west along the Platte to a point just east of North Platte where the Platte splits into the North and South Platte Rivers. The Mormon Trail continued along the North Platte River into present-day Wyoming.

ALBION

ALBION, platted in 1872, is 22 miles north of Fullerton on N-14. The town was originally called **Hammond**, for **John Hammond**. A dispute arose over the renaming of the town a short time later. **Loran Clark** favored the name Albion for his hometown in New York, while **S. D. Avery** wanted the name of Manchester for his hometown in Massachusetts. The argument was settled in a game of euchre with the players favoring Albion the winners.

Boone County, named in honor of the legendary frontiersman, **Daniel Boone**, was surveyed in 1870 and came into existence in 1871. The first group of settlers, 14 in number, arrived April 13, 1871. They built a 14 x18 sod house and all occupied it for two weeks. Many of the settlers that followed were Civil War veterans.

The Boone County Historical Society operates a museum in Albion.

NELIGH

NELIGH (pop. 1,891), 33 miles north of Albion on N-14 and US 275, is the site of **Neligh Mills**, built from locally fired brick in 1873 by **John D. Neligh** in the newly platted town of Neligh. Milling operations began in 1874. Some of the best known brands of flour milled were *Neligh Patent Flour* and *So-Lite Flour*. Crescent brand feeds were also popular brands produced here.

The Nebraska State Historical Society acquired the mill in

NELIGH MILLS—The old mill in Neligh served customers in the Elkhorn Valley from 1874 to 1952. The flour milling equipment is still in place and is fully restored. It is listed on the National Register of Historic Places.

1969. It is listed on the National Register of Historic Places.

Half-mile north and two blocks east of the Neligh cemetery is a marker recalling the death of **White Buffalo Girl** of the Ponca tribe. The death of the child, daughter of **Black Elk** and **Moon Hawk,** symbolized the tragic 1877 removal of the Ponca from their homeland on the Niobrara River to the Indian Territory (Oklahoma). White Buffalo Girl was one of several Indian children to perish along this route southward which became known as the Ponca **"Trail of Tears."** White Buffalo Girl was given a Christian burial by the people of Neligh and it was her father's last wish that her grave would be honored and cared for by the people of Neligh. In 1913 a marble monument was erected in her honor.

Neligh was incorporated in 1873.

At this point, the tour can follow three directions—north (via N-14), east or west on US 275. First, a tour to the east.

BATTLE CREEK

BATTLE CREEK (pop. 940), 27 miles southeast of Neligh on N-121 off US 275, was the scene of the Pawnee War of July 12, 1859. On June 21, while the state militia and Army troops prepared to punish the Indians for raids on white settlers in the Platte River and Elkhorn Valleys, a large party of Pawnee raiders, some 700 in number, stole 100 head of cattle. Messengers were sent to the territorial capital in Omaha requesting aid from the governor.

The governor was not available so the order to call out the militia was given by Territorial Secretary **J. Sterling Morton**. **Gen. John M. Thayer** led six companies of militia in the expedition. He was joined by **1st Lt. Beverly H. Robertson**, leading Company K, 2nd Dragoons, from Fort Kearny on the Platte.

The Indians surrendered without a shot being fired. Although no battle actually took place, the stream where the Indians were camped was named Battle Creek and the community took the same name when founded in 1867.

STANTON—PILGER—WISNER

STANTON (pop. 1,597), 41 miles east of Neligh on N-24 south of US 275, was platted in 1870 and incorporated in 1871. It is the county seat of Stanton County, named for Secretary of War **Edwin M. Stanton** in 1863. PILGER (pop. 405), eight miles west of WISNER (pop. 1,338) on US 275, was platted the next year and named for **Peter Pilger**, who owned the original townsite. The town was incorporated in 1887. A historical marker, three miles west of Pilger on US 275, relates the history of Stanton County.

WISNER was platted in 1871 and named for an official of the Sioux City & Pacific Railroad.

EWING—NIOBRARA—SANTEE—CROFTON

From Neligh this tour begins on US 275 west. It is 19 miles to Ewing on US 275.

EWING (pop. 517) was the scene of some of Nebraska's earliest experiments with heavier-than-air flight. This was the home of the **Savidge brothers**, sons of **Martin P. Savidge**, aviation pioneers.

The Savidge brothers became interested in flight before 1907. They built model gliders, full-sized gliders and finally a self-powered airplane. Their first public flying demonstration was held Sunday, May 7, 1911. For the next five years the brothers barnstormed throughout the Great Plains and during this time they built and flew three different biplanes. Their aviation careers ended when **Matt Savidge** was killed during a test flight June 17, 1916.

NIOBRARA (pop. 419) is located 43 miles north of Neligh on N-14 and N-70. (See Section 8 for more details).

The Santee Indian Reservation is just to the east of Niobrara. This is one of three Indian reservations in Nebraska, the other two belonging to the Winnebagos and the Omahas. For a view of Lewis and Clark Lake, take S-54D after entering the reservation to SANTEE (pop. 395). This small community was named for the Santee Sioux moved here from their lands in Minnesota and the Dakota Territory after the Minnesota Massacre in 1862.

CROFTON (pop. 949), named for Crofton Court, England, is 36 miles east of Niobrara on N-12.

PONCA—MACY

PONCA (pop. 1,061), the county seat of Dixon County, is 44 miles east of Crofton on N-12. The townsite was surveyed and platted in 1856.

The C.O. BOOK BLACKSMITH SHOP, built in 1884, has been restored as museum by the City of Ponca and the Ponca Historical Society. It is on the National Register of Historic Places.

Driving south on N-9, the traveler will pass through the **Winnebago** and **Omaha Indian Reservations**. Indian pow wows are staged here during the summer months. In 1983 there were approximately 14,500 Indians in Nebraska. In Knox county there were approximately 420 Santee-Sioux. On separate tracts in Thurston County live 800 Winnebago and 1,100 Omaha Indians. The Santee-Sioux live on 3,500 acres of land in Knox County where they are governed by a tribal council. Ceremonial dances are held annually at Winnebago where for two days in August the Indians celebrate old times, hold councils, revive ancient songs and legends.

MACY, site of the original Omaha tribe, is situated on US 73, three miles south of N-94, in the Omaha Reservation. It is the center of community life. Perhaps the most interesting cultural ceremony surviving among the Omaha is the annual Pow Wow Council held in August just outside of Macy. Symbolic dances, traditions, myths and songs are part of these ceremonies.

BANCROFT

BANCROFT (pop. 549), on N-16 north of N-51, is the site of NEIHARDT CENTER. Built in honor of poet **John G. Neihardt**, the center features architectual themes from his book, *"Black Elk Speaks."*

Bancroft was named in honor of historian **George Bancroft**.

John Gneisenau Neihardt, born January 8, 1881, moved from Sharpsburg, Illinois, to a sod house in northwestern Kansas in 1886; then to Kansas City in 1888 and finally to Wayne, Nebraska, in 1891. Neihardt graduated from Wayne Normal College with a B.S. degree at the age of 16 and then taught school. He began writing poetry at the age of 13. He was a bookkeeper with an Indian trader and later became editor of the *Bancroft Blade*. His acquaintance with the Omaha and Winnebago Indians led him to an interest in the Sioux, their customs and traditions. He published *"The Divine Enchantment"* when he was 19 years old. Neihardt married Mona Martinsen, the daughter of Rudolph Vincent Martinsen and Adah Ernst, in 1908. They had three daughters, Enid, Hilda and Alice, and a son, Sigurd. When he was 31 years old, Neihardt began his major work, *"A Cycle of the West,"* which he completed in 1941. *"A Cycle of the West"* was selected by men and women of letters as one of 3,000 important books in 3,000 years from **Homer** to **Ernest Hemingway**. The Nebraska legislature selected Neihardt as Nebraska Poet Laureate in 1921. Neihardt died November 3, 1973, at the age of 92. Author of some 25 other volumes of poetry, fiction and philosophy, Neihardt's credits include: *"The River and I," "The Stranger at the Gate," "The Splendid Wayfaring," "The Song of the Indian Wars," "Black Elk Speaks,"* and his autobiographies, *"All Is But a Beginning"* and *"Patterns and Coincidences."*

The fascinating **Sioux Prayer Garden** was planted here under Neihardt's supervision.

NEIHARDT CENTER is at Elm and Washington Sts. in Bancroft. It is open 8 a.m. to 5 p.m. Monday through Saturday; 1 to 5 p.m. Sunday, April 1 through November 15. The hours are 8 a.m. to 5 p.m. weekdays November 16 through March 31. Special tours by appointment can be arranged by telephoning (402) 648-3388. Admission is charged.

TEKAMAH—OAKLAND

An 18 mile side trip south to Oakland and Tekamah may be interesting to many tourists.

TEKAMAH (pop. 1,886) is located at US 73 and N-32, 14 miles

THE POET LAUREATE—
John Gneisenau Neihardt was
named Nebraska's Poet Laureate in 1921. He wrote more
than 25 volumes of poetry, fiction and philosophy. The Neihardt Center is located in Bancroft.

east of OAKLAND (pop. 1,393). Oakland can be reached via
N-51 and US 77 from Bancroft.

Tekamah was incorporated as a city on March 14, 1855, and became the county seat at the same time. The first settlers arrived
in 1854.

On July 18, 1855 a small colony that had settled just north of
Silver Creek moved to Tekamah for safety after hearing of the
killing and scalping of two white men near Fontanelle. Fear of Indians was great and slowed the development of the country.

Edward "Hoot" Gibson, born August 6, 1892, a popular actor
appearing in many early Western films, and **Frances Burt**, the
first governor of Nebraska, are two notables from Tekamah.

WAYNE—WEST POINT

WAYNE (pop. 5,094), county seat of Wayne County, is located
35 miles northwest of Bancroft via N-16 and N-35. The city and
county were named for Revolutionary War **Gen. "Mad" Anthony Wayne**. The county was organized in 1870 and LaPorte,
about six miles southeast of Wayne was named the county seat.
The town of Wayne was laid out in 1881 and a short time later
became the county seat and LaPorte became a ghost town.

Lutheran Academy opened as a private college in 1887 and
classes were held until 1890. Nebraska Normal College was established in 1891. Since 1963 it has been called **Wayne State College**.

The WAYNE COUNTY MUSEUM is housed in the 12-room
Ley House, built in 1900, and located at 702 Lincoln St. in

Wayne. It is open 2 to 4 p.m. Sunday. Special tours may be arranged through the Wayne Historical Society.

WEST POINT (pop. 3,597), county seat of Cuming County, is 19 miles south of the Neihardt Center and is reached via N-51 and N-9. It was incorporated in 1858. The town was founded in 1857 by **John D. Neligh**, who set up a brickyard and sawmill here.

SCRIBNER—DODGE—HOOPER—WINSLOW

SCRIBNER (pop. 1,010) is located on US 275, south of N-91. The PEBBLE CREEK MARKER describes the site of the town of **Pebble** and where **H. J. Robinson** built the first gristmill in the area during 1868-69. The location is one mile west and ½ mile south of Scribner on the south bank of the Elkhorn River where the **Fremont, Elkhorn & Missouri Valley Railroad** was built, which missed the site a mile distant and the town of Scribner sprang up to leave the Pebble site with but an inland town.

John J. Blair, an early-day railroad official, named the town for his son-in-law, **Charles Scribner**, founder of the Scribner publishing firm in New York.

DODGE (pop. 813) was the site of the first white settler of the area and is marked by the GLENCO MARKER, which stands five miles south and one and a half miles east of Dodge. Dodge is on N-91, east of US 275.

HOOPER (pop. 927) is seven miles south of Scribner on US 275. The JALAPA MARKER was established at the point three miles south of Hooper, on the bluff slope, on the south side of Maple Creek. It marks the site of the Jalapa Postoffice of 1858 and commemorates the date of July 1859, when volunteers of the area met here and organized a little army to punish the Pawnee Indians for killing cattle while enroute to their reservation near Genoa.

WINSLOW (pop. 143), US 75 north of US 275, features the location of the LOGAN MONUMENT. The monument marks the site of the **Briggs Flour Mill** on the east bank of Logan Creek about three miles north of Winslow and about 60 rods west of the highway, but at the time of erection was at the site of the main north and south highway. It was also at the site of the old **Black Hills Trail** leading from Omaha via Fontanelle to the northwest.

This ends the tour of Lewis and Clark Land.

Section 8

This particular tour follows US Highway 20 west from South Sioux City to Gordon in the Sandhills Country. It is about a 430 mile trip that begins in a fairly well populated area and ends up in the wide open spaces of the Nebraska Sandhills.

There are many historic spots along this route and several unique places to visit. For instance, there is O'Neill, the "Irish Capital of Nebraska," out in Holt County. Further west is Bassett where two of Nebraska's badmen, "Doc" Middleton and "Kid" Wade, often hung out with a band of outlaws and renegades who called themselves the Pony Gang. Vigilantes finally decided the town had enough of the antics of the Pony Gang and took "Kid" Wade into custody and then strung him up on a pole nor far from town.

Valentine is considered the crossroads of the Sandhills. The cattle town has two museums and nearby was the site of Fort Niobrara. A young soldier stationed at this lonely frontier outpost—John J. "Black Jack" Pershing—became a famous general. Several unusual fossil finds have been discovered in Cherry County.

It is rugged country, too, where the visitors will see large cattle ranches and hay operations. Cowboys still ride the range but in pickup trucks and jeeps, equipped with two-way radios, instead of cow ponies. People out here are friendly and helpful.

Further west, out in Gordon, is Old Jules Country, made famous by author Mari Sandoz. Old Jules was her father and was a wild and rugged individual who believed in this country and its future. Miss Sandoz was a prolific writer and based many of her stories on her experiences in the Sandhills Country.

213

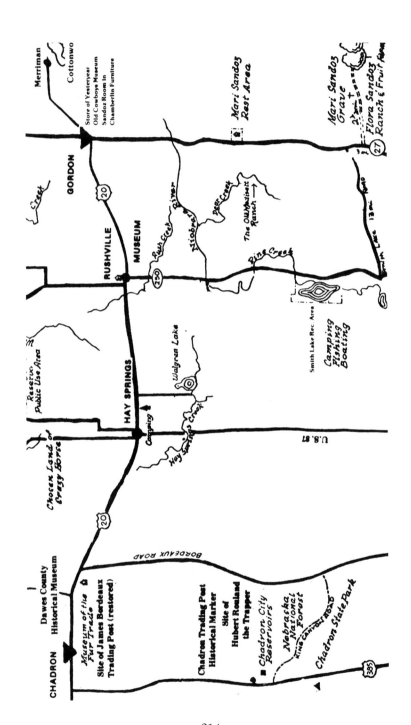

214

ROUTE US—20 TO THE SANDHILLS

This route starts in eastern Nebraska at SOUTH SIOUX CITY (pop. 9,093), founded in 1887. It serves a rich agricultural area.

Gustave Pecaut, a Frenchman, is believed to have been the first white settler in what is now South Sioux City. He built his tiny cabin near the river in 1854. In 1856 a small town was established and called **Pacific City**. It was soon abandoned because of flooding. **Harney City** was laid out on paper in 1856, but never became a reality. The original South Sioux City was platted in 1857 but the town, as known today, was not incorporated until 1887 and included the old town of **Pacific City** and **Stanton**. **Covington**, another small town, was joined to **South Sioux City** in 1893.

STANTON and COVINGTON were incorporated in 1870 and became noted as two of the frontier's wild, rip-roaring towns. Both communities boasted several saloons and gambling establishments. The **Pea Green**, a sporting house overhanging the Missouri River, is said to have had a trap door for the convenient disposal of bodies of those reluctant to part with their money.

South Sioux City has often been the victim of floods. The most devastating in recent years was the flood which occurred on Easter in 1952. This flood reached depths of seven feet in the city.

Driving west five or six miles from South Sioux City on US 20 is JACKSON (pop. 288), which came into existence in 1893 with the establishment of St. Catherine's Academy, staffed by Dominican Sisters. This was a boarding and day school, closed in 1940. About a mile and a half north of Jackson is the site of old **St. John's**, founded in 1856 by **Father Jeremiah Trecy** who settled there June 2, 1856 with a colony of 60 persons he brought from the Garryowen Parish near Dubuque, Iowa. He named his town, platted June 24, 1856, in honor of St. John the Baptist. Father Trecy became an Army chaplain during the Civil War and never returned to his Nebraska colony. St John's was finally abandoned because of flood threats and most of the residents moved to the new town of Jackson.

Thirty-one miles west of Jackson is LAUREL (pop. 505) and five miles west is BELDEN (pop. 151). Sixteen miles north of Belden via N-15 is HARTINGTON (pop. 1,735), county seat of Cedar County. Named in honor of **Lord Hartington**, the town was founded in 1883. It is a farm center. Hartington is the home-

State Colleges and Universities

Nebraska has 14 colleges and universities accredited by the North Central Association of Colleges and Schools. This list is as follows:

Chadron State College, Chadron, founded in 1911.

Concordia Teachers College, Seward, founded in 1894.

Creighton University, Omaha, founded in 1878.

Dana College, Blair, founded in 1884.

Doane College, Crete, founded in 1858.

Hastings College, Hastings, founded in 1882.

Kearney State College, Kearney, founded in 1905.

Midland Lutheran College, Fremont, founded in 1887.

Nebraska Wesleyan University, Lincoln, founded in 1887.

Peru State College, Peru, founded in 1867.

Saint Mary College, Omaha, founded in 1923.

Union College, Lincoln, founded in 1891.

University of Nebraska, Lincoln, founded in 1871.

Wayne State College, Wayne, founded in 1891.

town of **Governor Charles Thone** and **Lt. Governor Dwight Burney**, who became governor upon the death of **Governor Ralph G. Brooks** in September 1960.

Continuing west on US 20 from Belden 20 miles is OSMOND (pop. 880), 10 miles west is PLAINVIEW (pop. 1,483), then ROYAL (pop. 85) is 17 miles further west. ORCHARD (pop. 474) is six miles west and 11 miles further is the junction of US 20 and US 275. The two highways run northwest 13 miles to O'Neill where US 275 terminates.

NIOBRARA—THE NEW OLD TOWN

A side trip to NIOBRARA (pop. 419), 12 miles west of Plainview and 20 miles north on N-14, may be of interest to many travelers through the area. Niobrara is situated near the Nebraska-South Dakota state line and the Missouri River. The old Lewis and Clark Trail ran just north of the Niobrara townsite. One mile west on N-12 is Niobrara State Park. A Park Entry Permit is required and user fees apply.

Niobrara was settled by fur traders in 1856 and is believed to be Nebraska's third oldest community. Construction of the **Gavin Point Dam** in 1957, creating **Lewis and Clark Lake**, caused the ground water table to rise and created a siltation problem. These conditions often meant the residents of Niobrara had problems with flooding basements and other water conditions. In 1973 it was determined the town had to be relocated on higher ground and over the next four years 90 percent of the business establishments and 25 percent of the homes were moved to the new location. The $14 million project was completed in the spring of 1977. The new town was dedicated in a three-day ceremony held July 1-3, 1977 and the old town was demolished in 1978.

Niobrara was the hometown of **Gary** (22), **Gregory** (21) and **Kelly** (19) **Sage**, sons of **Mr. and Mrs. Ernest Sage**. The Sage brothers were among 74 American sailors lost at sea when their ship, the *USS Frank E. Evans,* and the Australian aircraft carrier, *Melbourne,* collided in the South China Sea June 2, 1969. A historical marker in their memory has been erected at the southern edge of town.

This area was the homeland of the Ponca Indians until they were forcibly moved to a reservation in the Indian Territory (Oklahoma) in 1877. The Poncas had been guaranteed their lands in a treaty with the U.S. government in 1858. Ten years later the government, in the Treaty of Fort Laramie, gave the Ponca lands

217

to the Sioux and sent the Poncas to the Indian Territory.

In January 1879, **Chief Standing Bear** and a small band of Poncas left the Indian Territory to return to their Nebraska homelands to bury Standing Bear's son, who had died on the reservation. Standing Bear and his band were arrested in Nebraska and a white journalist came to Standing Bear's defense in a trial where it was determined that "an Indian is a person within the meaning of the law." This decision did much to provide legal rights to Indians. A historical marker has been erected to honor the Ponca Indians about two miles south of Niobrara on a scenic turnout on N-14.

O'NEILL—THE SHAMROCK CITY

O'NEILL (pop. 4,052), county seat of Holt County, is called the "Irish Capital of Nebraska." **Governor Norbert Tiemann** officially bestowed this title upon the city on St. Patrick's Day in 1969.

Gen. John O'Neill, a native of Ireland and a veteran of the Civil War, was the founder of the town bringing his first colonists to the county May 12, 1874. He brought three other groups of colonists to the community by 1877, the year before he died. O'Neill became the county seat in 1874 and was incorporated in 1882. The town was originally called **Holt City** but the name was changed to O'Neill by **Col. James H. Noteware**, a state official.

Holt County was named in honor of **Joseph Holt** of Kentucky, who served as Postmaster General and Secretary of War under President James Buchanan. Later he served as Judge Advocate of the Army under President Abraham Lincoln. The county boundaries were set January 9, 1862. At one time there were 59 communities in the county. Today there are nine.

The Holt County Historical Society has acquired the **Kinkaid Bank Building**, a National Historic Site. The building, located in O'Neill, is being developed into a historical site, under the direction of the Nebraska State Historical Society, and is expected to open sometime in the mid-1980s. The building was owned by **Moses Kinkaid**, who served in Congress from 1903 to 1922. On April 28, 1904, the Kinkaid Act was approved and two months later to the day, land in Holt County was thrown open to settlers. This act made it possible for settlers to homestead a section (640 acres) of land instead of just a quarter section.

The small farm community of EMMET (pop. 73) is located eight miles west of O'Neill along the Elkhorn River. The **William Maloy** family settled in O'Neill in 1876 from Sheboygan,

Wisconsin. Maloy was the first judge elected in Holt County in 1879. Judge Maloy was instrumental in platting the town of Emmet in 1882. He and his co-workers named the new village Emmet, as it was the birthday of **Robert Emmet**.

ATKINSON (pop. 1,477) is 10 miles west of Emmet. **Atkinson Lake State Recreation Area** has facilities for camping.

In March 1876, **John Crimmins** made the first entry on the land where Atkinson now stands. **Col. John Atkins**, a friend of General O'Neill's, came to the community in 1877 from Detroit, Michigan. He began the town, named in his honor, on land owned by **Frank Bitney**.

Ten miles further west is STUART (pop. 640), site of the WHITE HORSE MUSEUM. This museum houses antiques from **Calvin Thompson's White Horse Ranch**. This museum is open from 12 noon to 5 p.m. daily from May 30 through Labor Day. Admission is charged.

John Carberry is given the distinction of having founded the town of Stuart in 1878. He named the town **Stuart** after his father-in-law, **Peter Stuart**, its first postmaster.

NEWPORT (pop. 141), established in 1884, is nine miles west in Rock County. The town was founded by **J. H. Davenport** and named for a bridge across the Niobrara River called the Newport Bridge. Just west of Newport is Spring Valley Park established by **Vic** and **Maude Thompson** in 1938 and is believed to be Nebraska's first roadside rest area. In 1966 the Thompsons dedicated the **Centennial Memorial Forest** and proclaimed their ranch a wildlife refuge, free to all.

Newport, in the early days, was a major hay shipping center with thousands of tons of hay being exported annually. There have been many prairie fires in this region with the most devastating occurring in 1904 when 40 miles of hay fields in the northern part of the county were destroyed. There were large losses of farm property in this fire and for a time the village of Newport was threatened.

BASSETT

BASSETT (pop. 987) is the county seat of Rock County, which has only three communities. The third little town in the county is ROSE, serving the ranchers in the southern part of the county. Rose is 28 miles south of Bassett on US 183.

Bassett was named for **A. N. Bassett**, a rancher who brought 600 head of cattle into the county in 1878. Rock County was part of Brown County until 1888 when it was divided. Rock County was named after Rock Creek which is located northeast of Bassett. The town was located along the old Black Hills Trail which was used in the 1870s.

The folks of Bassett awoke the morning of February 8, 1884 to learn that **Albert "Kid" Wade**, a member of **David C. "Doc" Middleton's** gang of horse thieves, had been strung up by the vigilantes on a pole about a mile east of town. The "Kid" had been captured and was held in the Bassett jail awaiting transfer to Ainsworth for trial. About midnight the jailers were overpowered by well-armed, masked men who spirited Wade from his jail cell. The vigilantes believed their swift type of justice would end the horse stealing in this part of the country.

"Doc" Middleton, alias Henry Shepherd, alias James Riley, was an early-day horse thief and well-known Nebraska outlaw. He gained his reputation early when he organized the **Hoodoo Gang** to get rid of vigilantes operating in the Sandhills country. In the mid-1870s he was rustling cattle and stealing horses from the ranges of the Niobrara. He was in the state penitentiary from 1879 to 1883 for horse stealing. He worked from time to time as a saloonkeeper at Gordon, Rushville and Valentine. He spent three weeks with **"Buffalo Bill's" Wild West Show** in the early 1890s. Tales about "Doc" Middleton flourished in the Sandhills and he obviously was his own publicity man in promoting his notoriety. The old outlaw died in the Douglas, Wyoming, jail of erysipelas with pneumonia complications December 13, 1913.

AINSWORTH

Eighteen miles west of Bassett is AINSWORTH (pop. 2,238), county seat of Brown County. Named for **Capt. J. E. Ainsworth**, a railroader, the town was incorporated in 1883. Ainsworth was in charge of the railroad building which arrived in the area in 1882. The town of Ainsworth became the county seat of the new Brown County in 1888.

For several years outlaw gangs and the vigilantes struggled against each other. **"Doc" Middleton** and his gang of horse thieves operated in the area for several years before Middleton was finally captured and imprisoned in 1879. Middleton came to Nebraska in the early 1870s from Arizona Territory and was one of the state's best known and most feared outlaws although he was not known for violent acts.

Today Ainsworth serves as a major trading center for farmers and ranchers.

TWO MUSEUMS IN VALENTINE—There are two museums, four blocks apart, in Valentine. Above is the Cherry County Historical Society Museum. Below is the Sandhills Museum. Information on area tours is available at the Information Center, corner of Main St. and US 20 during the tourist season.

VALENTINE—CROSSROADS OF THE SANDHILLS

Forty-nine miles west of Ainsworth is VALENTINE (pop. 2,824), county seat of Cherry County. Two small Sandhill ranch towns—JOHNSTOWN (pop. 71), 10 miles west of Ainsworth, and WOOD LAKE (pop. 89), 11 miles further west—are situated on the route between Ainsworth and Valentine.

Cherry County was formed in 1883 and named for **2nd Lt. Samuel A. Cherry**, killed by one of his men. Thirty-one year old Cherry, stationed at Fort Niobrara, was killed May 11, 1881 by **Pvt. Thomas W. Locke** while Cherry was leading a detachment of troops ordered to track down three would-be robbers. The record is unclear what caused Locke to turn against his commanding officer and fellow soldiers. Valentine, founded in 1882, was named for **Congressman E. K. Valentine**, who served in Congress in 1883-85. The town was incorporated in 1884.

In order to provide protection for homesteaders and to bring law and order to the frontier, **Fort Niobrara** was established four miles east of Valentine in 1880 The military reservation included 34,000 acres of land. **2nd Lt. John J. Pershing**, Troop A, 6th Cavalry, who led the American Expeditionary Forces in World War I as a general, was stationed at the fort in early 1891. Pershing was an instructor in military tactics at the University of Nebraska (1891-95), where he earned a law degree in 1893. He was promoted to the rank of 1st lieutenant in the fall of 1895 and assigned to Troop L, 10th Cavalry. Fort Niobrara was abandoned in 1906. Today the remaining 16,000 acres of fort lands makeup the Fort Niobrara National Wildlife Refuge.

There are two museums in Valentine, both on US 20—CHERRY COUNTY HISTORICAL MUSEUM and four blocks west, the SANDHILLS MUSEUM. The county museum is open April 15 through October 15, Tuesdays, Thursdays and Saturdays, 9 a.m. to 5 p.m., other days by appointment. The Sandhills Museum is open May 30 to Labor Day, 9 a.m. to 6 p.m. daily; by appointment during off-season. Admission at both museums is free.

The Valentine Chamber of Commerce has developed several area tours. Maps and information may be obtained from the Information Center at the intersection of Main Street and US 20.

GORDON—OLD JULES COUNTRY

It is 91 miles from Valentine to GORDON (pop. 2,167). There are several small farm communities enroute—CROOKSTON (pop. 86), incorporated in 1919; KILGORE (pop. 76), incorporated in 1913; NENZEL (pop. 28), incorporated in 1923; CODY (pop. 178), incorporated in 1901; and MERRIMAN (pop. 159), incorporated October 7, 1902.

BOWRING RANCH STATE HISTORICAL PARK, near Merriman, was developed as a working cattle ranch beginning in 1894 by **Arthur Bowring**, son of **Henry** and **Jane Bowring** who had homesteaded near Gordon in 1886. Arthur and his second wife, Eva, eventually put together a 12,000-acre spread (the **Bar 99 Ranch**) stocked with Hereford cattle. Arthur Bowring died in 1944 and for the next 41 years Eva ran the Bar 99 single-handedly. She was dedicated to the idea of public service and was involved in Republican Party politics as well as serving as a member of the National Institute of Health, member of the U. S. Board of Parole, and U.S. Senator, the first woman from Nebraska to enter Congress. Eva Bowring died on January 8, 1985, one day before her 93rd birthday. She outlived her three sons so she turned the 7,202-acre Bar 99 Ranch over to the Nebraska Game and Parks Foundation to be preserved as a State Historical Park. Her only stipulations were that the Foundation pay the annual taxes to the county, that part of her Hereford bloodline be kept and worked so the ranch would be a living history museum, and that her home and its collections be retained intact so that visitors could see what a 19th century ranch looked like.

The interpretive center illustrates the history of the Sandhills, the Nebraska cattle ranching business and the lives and careers of Arthur and Eva Bowring. The ranch house was opened to the public July 18, 1987. It is open 9 a.m. to 5 p.m. daily during the summer months. It can be reached via N-61 north out of Merriman. A State Park Entry Permit ($2 daily, $10 annual) is required. For more information, contact the park superintendent, (308) 684-3426.

Gordon is a major Sandhills trading center and was incorporated in 1921. Gordon was named for **John Gordon**, a leader of a mining party making an illegal entry into the Black Hills gold fields in 1875. His party was apprehended by soldiers southeast of the present day town. Their wagon train was destroyed.

Points of interest include the STORE OF YESTERYEAR, the OLD COWBOY MUSEUM and the SANDOZ ROOM upstairs in Hobb's Furniture, 122 N. Main St. The Store of Yesteryear, 3rd and Main Sts. is only open on special occasions. Admission is free. The Old Cowboy Museum, located in the city park, 3rd and Oak Sts., is open 1 to 5 p.m. daily from June 15 to September 15.

STORE OF YESTERYEAR—This small museum is located at 3rd and Main Sts. in Gordon. The Old Cowboy Museum is located in the City Park.

Admission is free. The Sandoz Room is open during regular store hours of Hobb's Furniture. Admission is free.

Twenty-eight miles south, on N-27, is the birthplace and grave of **Mari Sandoz**, author and historian of the Nebraska Plains. She was born in 1896 in a two-room, unpainted shack, the second child of the fourth wife of **Jules Sandoz**, a hot-tempered, violent, gun-toting Swiss emigrant who had settled in Sheridan County in the 1880s. His first two wives ran away and he deserted his third. He died in Alliance in 1928. Miss Sandoz's

THE SANDHILLS AUTHOR—
Noted Nebraska author Mari
Sandoz (1896-1966) was born
and raised in the Sandhills
country. Possibly her best work
was "Old Jules," the story of
her father. She is buried south
of Gordon.

mother, also a Swiss emigrant, died here in 1938.

The story of her crusty, indomitable father, published under the title *"Old Jules,"* won Miss Sandoz the Atlantic Monthly prize of $5,000 for "the most interesting and distinctive work of non-fiction" submitted in a 1935 contest. In 1925, Miss Sandoz received honorable mention in the Harper Intercollegiate Short Story Contest and when her father received the news he sent his daughter a one-line message: "You know I consider writers and artists the maggots of society."

Miss Sandoz, who did most of her writing in New York City where she had access to libraries, wrote more than a score of books. Her subjects for the most part were the lore of the American land that stretches from the Mississippi to the Rockies, the Indians and the cavalry, the cattlemen and the homesteaders, the trappers and the oil men, and the others who conquered the land and exploited it and fought and died there.

Other books written by Miss Sandoz are *"Slogum House,"* 1938, banned in McCook and Omaha libraries because of the strong language used; *"Capital City"* (1939); *"Crazy Horse"* (1942); *"The Tom-Walker"* (1947); *"Miss Morissa"* (1955); *The Horsecatcher"* (1957); *"The Cattlemen"* (1958); *"Hostiles and*

SHERIDAN COUNTY MUSEUM—This museum complex is located on US 20 in Rushville. At the right is the postoffice where "Old Jules" Sandoz often visited.

Friendlies" (1959); *"Son of the Gamblin' Man"* (1960); *Love Song to the Plains"* (1961); *"These Were the Sioux"* (1961); *"The Story Catcher"* (1963); and *"The Beaver Men"* (1964). Her book *"Cheyenne Autumn"* served as the basis of a movie by the same name released in 1964. This was an account of the flight of the Northern Cheyennes in 1878 from their enforced encampment on a government reservation in Oklahoma to their destination in Montana, about 1,500 miles away.

Miss Sandoz died of cancer in New York City March 10, 1966. She was 69 years old.

On N-27 is the Mari Sandoz Rest Area, about 21 miles south of Gordon, and a few miles south is her grave and the Flora Sandoz Ranch and Fruit Farm. Just south of the entry to the farm is the Mari Sandoz historical marker.

About eight miles east of Gordon is a historical marker explaining the opening of the Sandhills. Five miles south of this marker, on the Niobrara River, **E. S. Newman** established the first cattle ranch in the area in 1877. In 1879, several of the ranchers that had joined Newman discovered some of their cattle had drifted south of the Niobrara into the rugged Sandhills, believed to be dangerous and too sparse to support cattle. Instead the ranchers

Nebraska Symbols

State Tree...Cottonwood
State Grass...Little Bluestem
State Rock...Prairie Agate
State Gem..Chalcedony
State Fossil...Mammoth
State Nickname ....Cornhuskers
State Bird...Meadowlark
State Insect...Honey Bee
State Flower...Goldenrod
State Song ...."Beautiful Nebraska"
State Mammal.......................................White-tailed Deer

found their strays in good condition as there was adequate food, water and shelter to support grazing cattle.

RUSHVILLE (pop. 1,240), 15 miles west, is the county seat of Sheridan County. It was founded about 1885. Rushville is the hub of the story *"Old Jules."* SHERIDAN COUNTY MUSEUM, on US 20 in Rushville, has many exhibits relating to the book, *"Old Jules."* The old Rushville postoffice, used in 1885, is included in the museum complex. The museum is open from noon to 4 p.m. daily from Memorial Day to Labor Day and by appointment at other times. Admission is free.

Eleven miles west of Rushville is HAY SPRINGS (pop. 793).

MARI SANDOZ COUNTRY—The novelist Mari Sandoz was born in Sheridan County but lived most of her adult life in the East. This marker is not far from her grave in the Sandhills country. She gained fame as a writer in 1935 upon publication of "Old Jules," the story of her father's life in the Sandhills. Her greatest work is the series of six related books as it developed on life with the Indian and white man in the trans-Missouri country. She was internationally known as an expert on Indian history.

Section 9

At Chadron, one enters Nebraska's Pine Ridge Country.
a beautiful area with a rich heritage. Fur traders were
in the region as early as the 1840s.

The area actually opened to white settlers with the
coming of the railroad. It became a cattle raising center
when it was learned that cattle thrived on the rich
sandhill grasses. "The Great 1,000 Mile Horse Race"
was sponsored by Chadron businessmen and ranchers in
1893. It started when someone asked the question, "how
much could a Western horse stand?"

Indians roamed the territory long before the white
man came upon the scene and for a period created problems
for settlers and travelers through the area.

Fort Robinson was established as a military post at
the Red Cloud Agency in 1874 when it appeared there
may be trouble brewing with some of the 13,000 Indians
living at the Agency. After the Indians problems were
settled the fort was used for many purposes and was not
closed down until after World War II. It is a popular
tourist attraction.

One of the Army officers stationed at Fort Robinson
in the early days was Captain Walter Reed (1851—1902)
who went on to conquer Yellow Fever. Outlaws, the likes
of "Doc" Middleton, were often seen in the area and
"Calamity Jane" once spent several days in Crawford
in search of dance hall girls for a hall in Dakota
Territory.

There are many unusual sights to see in this area.
Toadstool Park, north of Fort Robinson, is just one
such attraction. A trip to this area will be most
rewarding to many tourists and visitors.

229

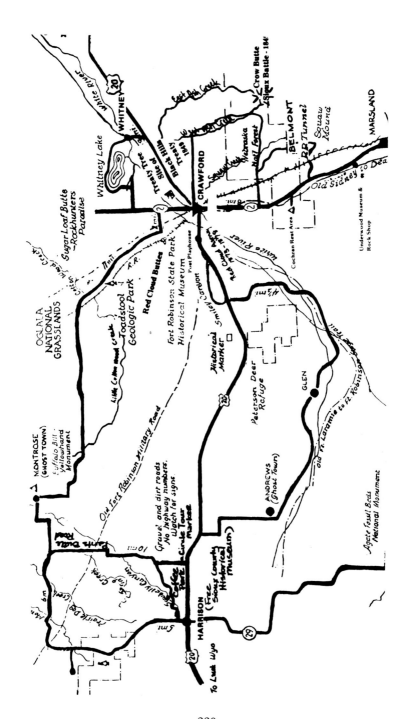

230

CHADRON AND THE PINE RIDGE COUNTRY

Nestled in the corner of Nebraska's Panhandle is the beautiful Pine Ridge area. History tells the story of the formation of the breath-taking, 3,528 square mile Pine Ridge—it was once the bottom of a fresh water lake disrupted either by earthquakes or volcanoes. Now it stands as beautiful buttes and canyons, which were carved into the earth by raging rivers long ago. Fossils of plants and animals embedded in the earth here declare the history of this region thousands of years ago.

CHADRON (pop. 5,972), 20 miles northwest of Hay Springs, was begun in 1884 as a small town on the White River northwest of the present city. At this site it was called **O'Linn** for **Fannie O'Linn**, who owned the land. At the time this area was part of Sioux County and Sidney was the county seat.

The railroad's arrival in the summer of 1885 caused the town to relocate to its present site. It is said Mrs. O'Linn, a tough-minded business woman, and the railroad townsite company could not reach an agreement over the purchase of her land on the White River.

Railroad officials first called the new town **Bordeaux** but local citizens insisted on the name **Chadron**, for **Louis Chartran**, a fur trader from Illinois who operated a trading post eight miles south on Chadron Creek in the early 1840s. Mrs. O'Linn had been named the postmistress for her little town May 14, 1885. The railroad and its first passenger service to Chadron officially arrived August 1, 1885 on the **Fremont, Elkhorn & Missouri Valley Railroad**. The FE&MV became the Wyoming division of the Chicago & NorthWestern in 1903. The first train load of cattle was shipped from Chadron to Chicago August 15th by **Charles F. Coffee**, a Wyoming cattle rancher. On August 20th the Sidney and Deadwood stage line changed their railroad connection from Sidney to Chadron and operated between Chadron and Deadwood. The line had previously connected with the Union Pacific at Sidney.

Dawes County, established in 1885, was divided in 1886 with the southern part becoming Box Butte County. The county was named for **Governor James W. Dawes**, governor of Nebraska at the time. Chadron continued as the county seat for Dawes County and Alliance became the county seat of the newly established Box Butte County.

Long before white settlers arrived, **James Bordeaux**, from a French settlement near St. Louis, established an Indian trading

MUSEUM OF FUR TRADE—This is the site of the James Bordeaux Trading Post, just east of Chadron, which is listed on the National Register of Historic Places. The museum is open from June through Labor Day.

post 3.5 miles east of present-day Chadron about 1840. The post was operated until 1876. Hostile Crow warriors once attacked the post and set the buildings aflame before being driven off by a friendly Sioux force. Bordeaux was a well-known fur trapper and trader in the Upper Missouri Basin for nearly 40 years (1840s-1870s).

In one of the great publicity stunts of the time, Chadron businessmen and ranchers sponsored **"The Great 1,000 Mile Horse Race"** or **"The Cowboy Endurance Race"** in June 1893. Purpose of the race was said to test the endurance of Western cow ponies and cowboys. **James Dahlman**, later to become the popular "Mayor Jim of Omaha," spotted a mud-caked cow pony on a rainy day in 1892 and casually asked: "How much could a Western horse stand? Had there been a test of it?" A local newspaper editor picked up on the question and soon a committee was formed to put the project into motion. One thousand dollars was raised by subscription. In considering the route, the Chicago goal was favored for its World's Fair appeal. A second reason for favoring the Windy City was **"Buffalo Bill's" Wild West Show**, making a summer stand there. **Col. William F. Cody** was Nebraska's most celebrated personality of the time.

The race was to be from Chadron to Chicago with each rider entered allowed two mounts. Cody put up a $500 purse and requested his show grounds be made the finish line in Chicago. The Colt Manufacturing Company donated a gold-plated, ivory-handled six shooter and Montgomery Wards put up a fancy hand-tooled saddle as prizes.

Three hundred riders were expected to enter the race but when registration ended June 1 only nine riders had signed up. The race was on and was to start at 5 a.m. June 13. The riders included **David "Doc" Middleton**, 43-year old renegade and reformed horse thief; **John Berry**, 40-year old railroad right-of-way agent; **Joe Gillespie**, 58-year old Chadron rancher; **Joe Campbell**, a Denver cowboy; **Jim "Rattlesnake Pete" Stephens**, a Kansas cowboy; **Emmett Albright**, a Texas cowboy; **David Douglas**, a Hemingford cowboy, and two cowboys from South Dakota, **Charles W. Smith** and **George Jones**. The route, starting from Chadron, went through Long Pine, O'Neill, Wausa, across the Missouri River into Iowa and Sioux City, Galva, Fort Dodge, Iowa Falls, Waterloo, Manchester, Dubuque, and into Illinois and Freeport, DeKalb and Chicago.

The starting pistol was fired at 5:30 a.m. Sunday, June 13. Thirteen days, 16 hours and 30 minutes later John Berry, ready to pitch out of the saddle atop his pony, "Poison," rode to the finish line at 9:30 a.m. Sunday, June 27, to be greeted by Cody and a large reception committee. Gillespie came in second and Smith third. Ironically the sheriff holding the $1,000 prize money back in Chadron had lost it so Berry wound up with Cody's $500, a gold-plated pistol and a hand-tooled saddle for his 1,040 mile horseback ride.

Nebraska State Normal School, the state's fourth such school, was designated for Chadron by the state legislature in 1910. The first classes were held the following summer. **Chadron State College** evolved to a rapidly growing, multi-purpose educational institution and has received many national awards for its innovative approaches to teaching.

On August 6, 1910, the C&NW railroad roundhouse and shops were destroyed by fire. Also lost in the fire were 16 locomotives, all coaled and ready to go on their runs.

DAWES COUNTY HISTORICAL MUSEUM, three miles south of Chadron on US 385, adjacent to the golf course, features local pioneer artifacts. Open summers, 1 to 5 p.m. Admission is free.

South of the golf course on US 385, before arriving in Chadron State Park, is the site of a cabin occupied by **Hubert Rouleau**, an old French-Canadian trapper, during the period 1873-76. Francis Parkman described him at Fort Laramie in 1846.

Ten miles south of Chadron on US 365, **Chadron State Park** is an excellent center for exploring the Pine Ridge. It was established in 1921 as Nebraska's first state park. A replica of the old **Chartran Trading Post** is located in the park and is open weekdays during the summer months. Here one can see a buckskinner tanning hides as the Indians and fur trappers did in the 1800s. One can also try his or her skill at throwing a tomahawk at this site. The original Chartan post operated on Chadron Creek during 1841-45. A historical marker describes this early day trading station.

Just northwest of Bordeaux's trading post, east of Chadron, is the site of the **Bissonette Trading Post** (1872-1877) and the **J. B. Nelson Saloon** and **Postoffice** (1878). South of Bordeaux's on the Big Bordeaux River, is **Spotted Tail's Camp** (1870-1872).

North, on Slim Buttes, is the site of the **Whetstone Agency**, the first Indian agency in what is now Dawes County, which was operated in 1873-74. It was established to aid and assist the Brule Sioux Indians. The agency was moved in 1875 to Beaver Creek and renamed **Spotted Tail Agency**.

The C&NW Railroad ended passenger service in Nebraska in 1958. The last train, No. 13, arrived from Omaha July 6. When No. 14 left Chadron that afternoon it put an end to 73 years of continuous railroad passenger service.

There are several historical spots to visit in the area.

THE MUSEUM OF THE FUR TRADE, 3.5 miles east of Chadron on US 20, presents materials and exhibits concerned with the commerce of the fur trade and the daily lives of traders, trappers and Indians. The museum grounds includes the site of Bordeaux's trading house and warehouse. When **James Bordeaux** left the station in 1872, **Francis Boucher** occupied it until August 1876 when a U.S. cavalry unit confiscated illegal ammunition being sold to hostile Indians and Boucher abandoned the post. The Bordeaux Trading Post has been entered on the National Register of Historic Places. The museum is highly recommended to persons of all ages interested in our early American history.

HOURS: The museum is open 8 a.m. to 6 p.m. daily from June 1 through Labor Day. It may be open at other times by appointment, (308) 432-3843. Admission is charged.

MARI SANDOZ HERITAGE ROOM in the Chadron State

234

CHADRON STATE COLLEGE—This state college was authorized by the Nebraska legislature in 1910 and was opened the following year. The administration building was constructed in 1911.

College Library is open to visitors by appointment, (308) 432-6271. It contains artifacts from Miss Sandoz' life and the region she wrote about. It includes some of the research materials about **Mari Sandoz**. The room is maintained by the Mari Sandoz Heritage Gallery.

EARTH SCIENCE MUSEUM is located on the Chadron State College campus and is open from September to May 15, Monday through Friday, by appointment. Admission is free.

CHADRON STATE PARK, south of Chadron on US 385, is open from Memorial Day to Labor Day. The park has 22 modern, two-bedroom, housekeeping cabins and each is equipped with bedding, bathrooms and furnished kitchenette. Reservations must be made in advance and are accepted for only two or more nights and an advance deposit is required. A special feature is the trapper's stew cookout and film programs held at sunset on Mondays, Wednesdays and Fridays. Trail rides are available daily 8 a.m. to 5 p.m. For reservations, write: Chadron State Park, Chadron, NE 69337 or call (308) 432-2036. A Park Entry Permit required.

BUTTE COUNTRY

In the 23 miles between Chadron and Crawford, off to the

235

south, is **Butte Country** possibly one of the most historical and geographical landmarks in Nebraska. From the historical marker (on the south side of US 20) one can look southward and see **Crow Butte**, site of a legendary battle in 1849 between the Sioux and Crow Indians. The Crow Indians had attacked the trading post of James Bordeaux and had been driven off by friendly Sioux warriors. The Sioux chased the Crow raiders to the butte where the hostiles took refuge. That night two or three Crow Indians danced and sang all night to divert the attention of the Sioux who held them at bay. The other Crow warriors were able to escape during the diversion and when the Sioux attacked the next morning all they found were the two or three left behind. These Crow warriors were killed and the butte became known as **Crow Butte** or **Dancer's Hill**. Looking west one can see Red Cloud Buttes. From these well-known buttes one can see the town of Crawford to the east, Fort Robinson to the south and the site of the Red Cloud Agency to the southeast.

About a half mile northwest of this historical marker is the site of **Treaty Tree** where, in September 1875, the **Allison Commission** unsuccessfully tried to buy the Black Hills area from the Indians. Thousands of Sioux were present as spectators at this meeting led by **Red Cloud, Spotted Tail, Little Big Man** and other chiefs. It was not until after the bloody campaigns of 1876 that the Sioux Commission, led by **George Manypenny**, succeeded in purchasing the Black Hills land.

CRAWFORD

CRAWFORD (pop. 1,311), named for **Capt. Emmet Crawford**, a Fort Robinson Army officer, is 23 miles west of Chadron. The town sprang up as a tent city on land owned by homesteader-newspaper correspondent **William E. Annin** in 1886 with the arrival of the **Fremont, Elkhorn & Missouri Valley Railroad**. To incorporate the town, editor **William Edgar** supplemented civilian signatures with those of obliging soldiers stationed at Fort Robinson. After the Burlington railroad passed northward in 1887, Crawford became a supply depot and entertainment center for troops assigned to the nearby post. Passing through this area was the **Fort Laramie-Fort Pierre Trail** of the 1840s and the **Sidney-Black Hills Trail** active during the Black Hills gold rush of the 1870s.

Crawford has been the host or home to such personages as **Sioux Chief Red Cloud**, reformed badman **"Doc" Middleton**, poet-scout **John Wallace ("Captain Jack") Crawford**, fron-

KILLED BY INDIANS—Lt. Levi Robinson, for whom Fort Robinson was named, was killed by Indians in 1874.

tierswoman **Martha "Calamity Jane" Canary**, Army scout **Baptiste "Little Bat" Garnier**, Army surgeon **Walter Reed**, and **President Theodore Roosevelt**.

Captain Jack Crawford's best known poem was *"Have You Heard the Death of Our Beloved Young Custer?"* He was well liked on the frontier.

Badman "Doc" Middleton's second wife, Irene, is buried in Crawford. After spending more than a decade as a horse thief and three years in the penitentiary, "Doc" went straight. He died in a Douglas, Wyoming jail and is buried in Douglas.

"Calamity Jane" (1852-1903) came to Crawford from Deadwood in search of 10 dance-hall girls for a saloon in Dakota Territory. She lived in a tent by the railroad tracks during her stay.

Capt. Walter Reed (1851-1902), the medical officer who conquered Yellow Fever, was stationed at Fort Robinson from 1884-1887. **Jules Sandoz**, who crushed an ankle while digging a well with two friends out on Mirage Flats, was a patient of Dr. Reed for several weeks.

"Little Bat" Garnier, a noted chief of Army scouts, was shot by bartender **Jim Haguewood** in **George Dietrich's** Crawford saloon December 15, 1900. In an apparent dispute over a bar bill the bartender shot the scout as he stood at the bar. The wounded Garnier was shot a second time as he left the bar and fell, badly wounded, within a few feet of the southeast corner of the crosswalks in front of the Forbes block. He died at 3:15 a.m. the next day.

Fort Robinson, three miles west of Crawford, was authorized

FAMOUS FRONTIER DOC-
TOR—Capt. Walter Reed
(1851-1902), the Army medical
officer who was instrumental in
conquering Yellow Fever, was
stationed at Fort Robinson
from 1884-87.

as a military camp at the Red Cloud Indian Agency on the White River in March 1874. The agency, housing some 13,000 Indians, most of whom were hostile, was one of the most troublesome spots on the Plains. The camp was named **Camp Robinson** in honor of **2nd Lt. Levi H. Robinson**, who had been killed by Indians that February. In May, the camp was relocated to its permanent site and in December, 1878, officially became **Fort Robinson**.

Levi Robinson was born in Vermont in 1840. He joined the Army when he was 21 years old and served as a sergeant with the 10th Vermont Volunteer Infantry during most of the Civil War. In February 1865 he was commissioned a second lieutenant and assigned to the 119th Colored Regiment. A short time later he was assigned to the 14th Infantry Regiment for frontier service. He was killed February 9, 1874 in an ambush near Fort Laramie by Indians from the Red Cloud Agency. He was buried in New Britain, Connecticut. September 5, 1934 a stone monument was dedicated at the fort in his honor.

The fort played an important role in the Indian wars from 1876 to 1890. **Crazy Horse**, the famed Oglala Sioux war chieftan, surrendered here May 6, 1877. In 1875 the government ordered Crazy Horse and other Sioux warriors to a reservation and they refused. In 1876, troops attacked a Cheyenne village believing it was one of Crazy Horse's camps. Seeking revenge Crazy Horse

238

FORT ROBINSON MUSEUM—This unique museum is located in the old fort's headquarters building. Fort Robinson and the area offer visitors many unusual attractions and is steeped in frontier history.

led the Indians in the Sioux War of 1876. Crazy Horse, with others, led the Sioux and Cheyenne that defeated **Gen. George Crook** in the battle of the Rosebud, Montana, and eight days later were responsible for the **Custer Massacre** at the Little Big Horn. Crazy Horse was stabbed about 6 p.m. and died shortly before midnight September 5, 1877 while resisting imprisonment.

January 9, 1879, the fort was the scene of a major battle resulting from the **Cheyenne Outbreak**, led by **Chief Dull Knife**. Dull Knife had led 300 Northern Cheyenne from an Oklahoma reservation in the fall of 1878 in a flight northward to their old hunting grounds. After creating a reign of terror in western Kansas and Nebraska, killing settlers and destroying property, 150 of them were captured, including Dull Knife, on October 23 and confined at Fort Robinson. A total of 149 escaped from the fort January 9. Of those who escaped, 64 were killed, 58 sent to the Cheyenne Agency, 20 returned to Oklahoma and the rest were left dead or dying in the hills. Dull Knife first was taken to the Pine Ridge Indian Reservation and later to Lame Deer, Montana, where he died.

Fort Robinson remained an active military post through World War II...as the world's largest Quartermaster Remount Depot... Olympic equestrian training grounds...field artillery testing station...the last great gathering place of the Sioux nation...Prisoner-of-War Camp...K-9 Reception/Training Center...and now Nebraska's largest state park with nearly 24,000 acres of land. Fort Robinson State Park was established in 1956. The U.S. Department of Agriculture operated a Beef Cattle Research Center at the fort from 1949 to 1971.

The park offers many attractions.

FORT ROBINSON MUSEUM is open daily and is headquarters for the Nebraska State Historical Society branch. This building served as headquarters for the military when the fort was active. Additional exhibit buildings include: 1874 Guardhouse and Adjutant's Office, 1887 Officers' Adobe Quarters, as well as wheelwright, blacksmith and harness repair shops. There is also a 1908 Veterinary Hospital. Consult the guide schedule at the Fort Robinson Museum. Open April 1 to November 1, Monday through Saturday, 8 a.m. to 5 p.m.; Sunday 1:30 to 5 p.m. Winter hours: 8 am. to 5 p.m. weekdays. Admission is charged.

TRAILSIDE MUSEUM is operated by the University of Nebraska State Museum. This museum interprets the area's geologic and natural history. On display is a 14-foot mammoth found just north of the park, other prehistoric fossils and informative displays about the unique Pine Ridge landscape. Open Memorial Day through Labor Day, 8 a.m. to 5 p.m., Monday through Saturday; 9 a.m. to 5 p.m., Sunday. Admission is free.

Other Information

There are accommodations in the park including lodging facilities in the 1909 enlisted men's barracks (the Lodge) as well as in some of the 1909 officer's quarters (providing modern housekeeping cabins). Campgrounds, with shower house, electrical hookups, a trailer dump, grills, picnic tables and water pumps, are also available. Reservations for lodgings are accepted after January 1 for the following season. Minimum cabin reservations are for two nights and a deposit is required. There is no deposit required for rooms in the Lodge. Campground facilities are open on a non-reservation basis. For information write: Superintendent, Fort Robinson State Park, Box 392, Crawford, NE 69339 or telephone (308) 665-2660. A Park Entry Permit is required.

There are other activities at the park including swimming, horseback riding, train rides, jeep rides, van tours and stage coach rides. The Post Playhouse is open nightly, six days a week, between Memorial Day and Labor Day. Performances by the Post Playhouse Company include melodramas and comedies. For reservations write: Post Playhouse, Box 271, Crawford, NE 69339 or after May 1 telephone (308) 665-1976. A must for all visitors is the Fort Robinson's famed buffalo chuckwagon cookout.

East of Fort Robinson is site of the **Red Cloud Agency** established in 1873 for **Chief Red Cloud** and his Oglala band as well as other northern plains Indians as part of **President Ulysses S. Grant's** Indian Peace Policy. The agency served some 13,000 Indians until 1877 when it was moved to the Pine Ridge Agency, Dakota Territory. **Dr. J. J. Saville** was appointed the first agent for the Red Cloud Agency which served as an issuing point for supplies to the Indians.

Toadstool Geologic Park is located five miles north of Crawford on N-2 and 10 miles west on an all-weather road with its strange and unique rock formations. The park has been described as "moon-like badlands." This is part of the **Oglala National Grasslands**, managed by the U.S. Forest Service Office, Chadron. Other attractions in the Grasslands are the rock hounding areas and the War Bonnet Creek Battlefield site. Persons visiting Toadstool Park are warned to watch carefully for rattlesnakes. The best way to enjoy these "badlands" is to leave the parking-picnic table area and hike into the rock formations. The Park Service has provided shaded picnic tables and there are primitive outhouses as well as water pumping services. Camping is permitted.

From Crawford, **War Bonnet Creek Battlefield** is located five miles north on N-2, two miles west on a gravel road, turn right, proceed one mile past Toadstool Park turnoff, turn left, cross the tracks and follow the main gravel road to **Church of Montrose.** North of the church is a high, conical hill with a stone monument to the 5th Cavalry. Southeast is a monument to **Buffalo Bill** and **Yellow Hand**, a Cheyenne sub-chieftan. It was here, the early morning of Tuesday, July 17, 1876, **Bvt. Maj. Gen. Wesley Merritt**, leading 400 men of the 5th Cavalry, intercepted a large force of Cheyenne warriors who had fled from the Red Cloud Agency, planning to meet **Sitting Bull** who had been one of the leaders who defeated **Gen. George Crook** at the battle on the Rosebud June 17 and **Custer** at the Little Big Horn. **"Buffalo Bill" Cody** was Merritt's chief of scouts; **Baptiste "Little Bat" Garnier**, a scout-interpreter. As the two forces met,

Cody and Yellow Hand (whose name was Hayowei which actually translates to Yellow Hair) charged each other and both lost their horses. As they fell to the ground Cody got off a shot and killed Yellow Hand and quickly scalped him, crying out "the first scalp for Custer." In the fierce battle that followed the Indians were defeated and most retreated to the Agency. There are many colorful tales about the Cody-Yellow Hand "duel."

In 1890, during the **Ghost Dance** troubles, this same hilltop was the site of a civilian fort. It was to be used in case of anticipated Indian attacks, which fortunately never occurred. Parts of this outpost are still visible.

Sugar Loaf Buttes, also north of Crawford, are described as a "rockhunter's paradise."

Pine Canyon Museum and Rock Shop is located 12 miles south of Crawford on N-2 and N-71.

HARRISON

Twenty seven miles west of Crawford on US 20 is HARRISON (pop. 368), county seat of Sioux County. The town began in 1884 as a Chicago and NorthWestern railroad construction camp, called **Summit**. When the railroad arrived they called their station **Bowen** but there was already a Bowen in Nebraska so the name was changed to **Harrison** in honor of **President Benjamin Harrison.**

Sioux county at one time extended west from Brown County and occupied most of the Panhandle. By 1886 this vast territory had been divided into several counties. The first whites to settle in this particular area were ranchers and the first ranch, owned by **Emmons & Brewster**, was built in 1878 about 10 miles northwest of present day Harrison. The first farmer-settlers arrived about 1881 and settled around Fort Robinson for the protection it offered.

John W. Hunter, one of the settlers on Hat Creek, applied for a postoffice to be operated from his store. Hunter's little daughter's name was "Oressa," which was suggested as the name for the postoffice. Meantime, down in Texas, a community had applied for a postoffice, asking that it be named "Bodarc," for a small shrub that grew in the area. In some inexplicable way, postal officials got the names crossed and the Texas postoffice was called "Oressa" and the Nebraska postoffice, "Bodarc." Hunter and C. F. Slingerland established a newspaper, the *Bordarc Record* and the partners worked hard to have their small

The Grasshopper Plagues

Many difficulties faced settlers in Nebraska. The prairie was hard, there was little water and almost no wood. Weather conditions were extreme; hot winds in the summer and bitter cold in the winter.

During 1874-77 they were besieged by swarms of grasshoppers. The insects would suddenly appear in great clouds that at times blocked out the sun and in a few days destroyed growing crops. There are many stories about them eating handles off axes and other wooden handled tools.

No one knew where they came from or where they went. No one seems to know why suddenly they did not reappear.

community named the county seat of Sioux County. Harrison won this battle.

Harrison is the home of the SIOUX COUNTY MUSEUM, located on Main St. The museum houses items common to area homesteaders and ranchers in the early days. The old postoffice has been restored and is part of this complex. Fifteen miles north of town is the **Oglala National Grasslands**, including 95,000 acres of prairie grasses.

Twenty five miles south of Harrison, via N-29, is a historical marker pointing out the **Fort Laramie-Fort Robinson Trail**. It tells the story of this military road between two of the major forts of the Indian Wars. This was originally a fur trade route.

South of Harrison is the ghost town of **Andrews**.

Nine miles west of Harrison is the Wyoming state line.

Nebraska's 1919 Race Riot

On Sunday, September 28, 1919, thousands of Omahans charged the Douglas County courthouse to remove Will Brown, a black suspected of assaulting Agnes Loebeck, a young white girl, the night of September 25th. Miss Loebeck, in the company of Milton Hoffman, was returning home about midnight that evening when she was assaulted.

Will Brown was identified as their assailant and was jailed.

The suspect was finally given over to the mob, dragged out into the street and hanged. His body was riddled with bullets, then brought down and dragged behind a car for four blocks before it was cremated. Still later the charred body was dragged behind a car through downtown Omaha streets.

Two others were killed during the riot. They were 16-year old Louis Young, one of the mob's leaders, and 34-year old businessman, James Hiykel, both white. They were accidentally shot by the mob. Thirty-one persons were injured and thousands of dollars in damage to the courthouse were recorded.

The mob, according to newspaper reports, searched the streets, attacking blacks everywhere. By 3 a.m. troops had been called in to restore the peace.

No one was ever brought to trial for the murder of Will Brown.

The riot was believed to have been fueled by articles about the attacks on white women by black men and racial strife around the country, published in an Omaha newspaper. Critics claimed the newspaper concentrated on the racial issues of the time, often on its front pages.

Section 10

There are many ways to tour the 20,000 square mile Nebraska Sandhills Country. One of the routes is US 20 across the northern part of the state. The other, as we recommend here, covers some of the out-of-the-way places and small farm and ranch towns that serve the cattle ranchers in this vast land.

For instance, one of the most unique towns in the Sandhills is Arthur (population 124 in the last census). Arthur is the home of the Baled Hay Church and one of the line shacks from "Buffalo Bill's" Ranch up on the Dismal River has been brought into town for display. Old cowboy boots adorn many of the fence posts coming into the town from the south. (After several visits we are still unable to explain what this symbolizes.)

The ranches here usually include very large parcels of land, many several thousand acres in size. Small one-room country schools still serve many of the children in this rugged land.

Most of the towns in the western section are small, service communities. Some have small museums. In the eastern section, in the Loup Valley area, are the towns of Burwell and Broken Bow, both cowboy towns. Fort Hartsuff State Historical Park, just north of Burwell, continues to be restored and expanded. Fort Hartsuff was established in 1874 and abandoned in 1881. Ord, also in this area, was the hometown of famous aviatrix, Evelyn Sharp. She flew the mail into Ord when she was only 19 years old and was killed while ferrying a P-38 fighter plane in Pennsylvania in 1944. Nearby is the Scotia Chalk Mine, opened in 1877. A person really hasn't seen Nebraska until they've visited the Sandhills Country.

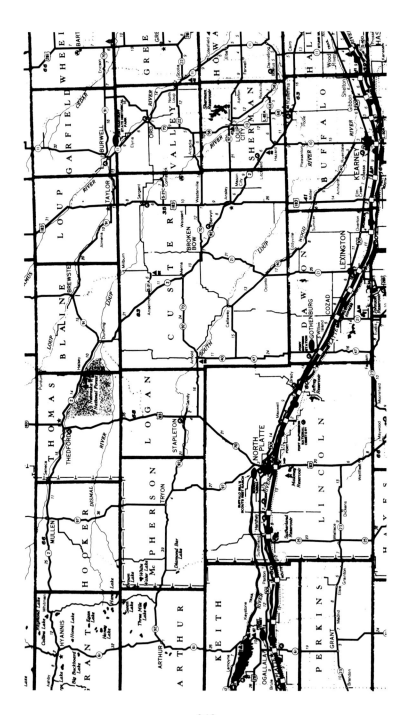

SANDHILLS CATTLE COUNTRY TOUR

The Sandhills region of Nebraska, covering some 20,000 square miles, is noted for its large, sprawling cattle ranches and for its rugged physical appearance. The soil here consists of fine sand piled up by the wind to form low hills and ridges. Grasses, ideal for grazing, cover most of the Sandhills country to hold the sand in place. There is an adequate water supply with running streams, all spring-fed, and well water.

Visitors to the Sandhills should make certain they have an adequate gasoline supply because towns are few and far between and services at times are minimal. Cowboys still roam the ranges here and cattle are branded to prove ownership. One will see many of these brands on signposts at entries into ranches. The people are friendly and helpful and it's well worth a stop in any of the small communities serving the area. Nature's beauty abounds in this open, quiet land.

For the purpose of this trip we will start from North Platte and drive north on US 83 25 miles to Stapleton, turn west on N-92 and drive 65 miles west to Arthur, go north 34 miles on N-61 to Hyannis, then drive east on N-2 for 132 miles to Broken Bow. (Back at Hyannis, one may wish to drive the 58 miles west, via N-2, to Alliance at the westernmost edge of the Sandhills country.)

Between Broken Bow and Anselmo, driving west, is a highway sign advising motorists they are entering the Sandhills and gives the mileage (about 175 miles) to Alliance. From Broken Bow one can return to North Platte via N-70 and N-92 to US 83 or to Grand Island and other points southeast via N-2.

THE SANDHILLS TOUR

Leave North Platte (for attractions, see Section 2) and drive north 25 miles to STAPLETON (pop. 340), county seat of Logan County. There is only one other small community in this sparsely settled county, GANDY (pop. 53), just two miles east of Stapleton.

TRYON

Twenty-five miles west on N-92 is TRYON, county seat of McPherson County. This is the only town in the county. The ranches in this area are extensive.

Tryon, originally called **McPherson**, is an unincorporated village, founded in 1896. McPherson County was organized in 1891 and included present Arthur County just to the west. The county was split in 1913 to form Arthur County. The story goes that the

247

BELIEVE IT OR NOT—This church in Arthur was built with baled hay and plastered inside and out in 1928. The old church was used up until recently and was featured in a "Ripley's Believe It or Not" column.

town got its current name from a comment made when wagons got into the Sandhills and travel became difficult. Those travelers were encouraged to "try on." The county, with a population of 593, was named in honor of **Maj. Gen. James B. McPherson**, a Civil War hero killed in action July 22, 1864 in the Battle of Atlanta.

ARTHUR

It is 40 miles on N-92 to ARTHUR (pop. 124), the county seat and only community in Arthur County. The Sandhills country was divided into counties by the state legislature in 1886-87 and Arthur County was named for **President Chester Arthur** (1881-1885). The county was not officially organized until 1913. (The county had been administered by McPherson County just to the east up to this time.)

Arthur's first county seat was housed in a covered wagon. Later a tent was put up and a fence built around it to keep the cattle out. Still later a homesteader's shack was moved into town

OLD CODY LINE SHACK—This building, restored and set up in Arthur, is believed to be an old line shack once used on William F. "Buffalo Bill" Cody's ranch up on the Dismal River. The historic structure has been restored by members of the local Lions Club.

to serve as the first courthouse and postoffice. The one-room used from 1914 to 1962, now housing a county museum, was famous for being the smallest courthouse in the country.

In 1928 a church was built in the community constructed of baled hay. This structure was featured in "Ripley's Believe It or Not" and is the only church of its kind in the U.S. Used regularly by the Pilgrim Holiness Church, the structure was built of baled hay and plastered inside and out.

HYANNIS

It is 34 miles north, on N-61, to HYANNIS (pop. 334), county seat of Grant County. There are only two other small communities in the county; ASHBY, eight miles west, and WHITMAN, 12 miles east, both on N-2.

ALLIANCE

It is 58 miles west via N-2 to ALLIANCE (pop. 9,865), county seat of Box Butte County. Alliance was settled in 1888 when the Burlington & Missouri Railroad arrived. The railroad owned the property and promoted land sales through a heavy advertising campaign and ran special excursion trains to the area. Alliance replaced the small settlement of **Grand Lake** nearby.

Jules Sandoz and one of his wives are buried in the Alliance Cemetery.

KNIGHT MUSEUM IN ALLIANCE—The Knight Museum, 908 Yellowstone, in Alliance, houses many exhibits depicting the pioneer way-of-life in this area.

The KNIGHT MUSEUM is located at 908 Yellowstone (in the city park). There are many exhibits depicting the early pioneer life styles as well as tools and equipment used in the development of the frontier here.

Fifteen miles east of Alliance is the abandoned town of **Antioch**, once a thriving town of 6,000 because of the potash boom during World War I. The mining operations began in 1916. At one time five factories operated 24-hours a day mining potash for the war effort. The boom ended abruptly after the war and the people moved on.

MULLEN

MULLEN (pop. 712), county seat and the only community in Hooker County, is 37 miles east of Hyannis on N-2. About four miles west of Mullen was the turnoff to the site of the **The North and Cody Ranch**, established by **Maj. Frank North**, **Capt. Luther North** and **"Buffalo Bill" Cody** in 1877. Many notables were guests at this Sandhills ranch covering several thousand acres.

Just across the Thomas County line, 11 mile east, is SENECA (pop. 91).

THEDFORD—HALSEY

Twenty-six miles east of Mullen on N-2 is THEDFORD (pop. 313), county seat of Thomas County. A historical marker, located

NEBRASKA HISTORICAL MARKERS—Markers like this dot the Nebraska countryside, noting historical events and happenings as well as unusual people in the state's long history. These markers are provided and maintained by the Nebraska State Historical Society in cooperation with county historical societies.

at the intersection of US 83 and N-2, 1½ miles east of Thedford, briefly relates the history of the Sandhills Country. In the eastern part of the county is the **Nebraska National Forest**, one mile west on N-2 and then south from HALSEY (pop. 143). Halsey, named in honor of **Halsey Yates** of Lincoln, one of the railroad surveyors who worked in this district, is 14 miles east of Thedford.

Nebraska National Forest is the largest man-planted forest in the country. Visit the ranger's lookout tower for a panoramic view. Open Memorial Day to Labor Day for swimming. Open year-round for camping. Fees apply for swimming and camping.

OLD SODDY EXHIBIT—This replica of an old sod house is on display in Anselmo's park. The old jailhouse built in Victoria has been moved to Anselmo and is another historic attraction.

ANSELMO—MERNA

ANSELMO (pop. 187), south on N-2, has three interesting historical attractions. These include an early-day sod house, an 1890s jail house and firebell and hand-drawn hose cart

MERNA (pop. 385) is 11 miles south of Anselmo on N-2.

BROKEN BOW

BROKEN BOW (pop. 3,974), founded in 1879 as site of a post-office by **Wilson Hewitt**, is the county seat of Custer County. It is 10 miles south of Merna.

Custer County, twice the size of the state of Rhode Island, was organized in 1877 and named in memory of **Gen. George Armstrong Custer**, killed at the Little Big Horn June 25, 1876. The log house of **Rancher Milo F. Young**, located near present-day Callaway, was designated as the temporary county seat. It was in this building hearings were held December 17, 1880 which led to the **Print Olive-Fred Fisher** trial for the lynching of **Ami Ketchum** and **Luther Mitchell**, the state's most noted feud between ranchers and homesteaders.

Broken Bow got its name from Postmaster Wilson Hewitt. Three other names submitted to the Post Office Department had been rejected when Hewitt recalled a broken bow found nearby.

He submitted the name "Broken Bow," which was accepted. Broken Bow became the county seat in 1882.

June 28, 1904 was the date of the mammoth land drawing for more than two million acres in Custer and eight other counties in northwest Nebraska, thrown open for settlement under the **Kinkaid Homestead Act**. The drawing lasted for 10 days. Over 2,000 people gathered on opening day, forcing a call-out of the militia to maintain order.

There are several historical attractions in Broken Bow and the area.

The BROKEN BOW HISTORICAL MUSEUM is located downtown in the old library building. This museum of pioneer and Indian history is open week-day afternoons.

The Custer County Historical Society has acquired the Security State Bank of Broken Bow for use as a research center for Solomon D. Butcher's historical photographs, family research and a museum featuring early banking artifacts. The bank ceased operation in December 1985 and was purchased by P. G. Richardson who then turned it over to the historical society. The facility is open week-day afternoons.

The Historical Society has also acquired the contents of the Westcott, Gibbons and Bragg Store at Comstock and has established the GENERAL STORE MUSEUM in the old Central Nebraska Drug Store building on the south side of the square in Broken Bow.

The first Grange was organized near Broken Bow. A marker, on N-2 between Broken Bow and Merna, 10 miles north, commemorates the site where this historic event took place.

The National Grange of the Patrons of Husbandry was organized in Washington, D.C. in 1867. The Nebraska State Grange was first organized in 1872 but did not succeed until 1911. **James D. Ream**, one of the early pioneers who settled in the region in 1880, was the first Master of both the Custer Center and Nebraska State Granges. He developed his homestead into beautiful **Cedar Lawn Farm**.

The Custer County Race Course was host to the first pari-mutuel Quarter Horse racing in the state. The annual race meeting, which takes place in late summer over several weekends, attracts the finest quarter horses in the nation to Broken Bow.

The **Lewis Dowse Sod House** near Comstock is listed on the National Register of Historic Places. COMSTOCK (pop. 168) is located 29 miles northeast of Broken Bow, off N-183.

Another trip from Broken Bow takes the traveler to CALL-AWAY, 35 miles southwest. To reach Callaway from Broken Bow, drive south 21 miles via N-21 to OCONTO (pop. 176). At Oconto, turn northwest on N-40, for a 14-mile drive to Callaway.

CALLAWAY

CALLAWAY (pop. 550) is near the site of the famous (or infamous) **Print Olive Ranch**. Print Olive was the leader of the cattlemen responsible for the lynching of two homesteaders, **Ami Ketchum** and **Luther Mitchell**, in a feud between cattlemen and homesteaders.

The feud between Olive and Ketchum and Mitchell stemmed from charges and counter charges made by both parties. The Olives accused Ketchum and Mitchell of stealing cattle. The homesteaders, in turn, claimed the cattlemen drove their cattle into their cornfields to destroy their crops.

Finally, the Olives obtained a warrant for Ami Ketchum's arrest for stealing cattle. When Bob Olive rode out to the Ketchum-Mitchell farm with a small posse a gunfight ensued and Bob Olive was mortally wounded. Later the pair was "captured" by Print Olive's men at Plum Creek (today's Lexington) and brought into Custer County where Olive ordered them to be hanged. The two men were lynched and their bodies burned. The burned bodies were photographed and the photos received wide press coverage.

Print Olive and his men were arrested and a trial was held in Hastings. Print Olive and Fred Fisher, an accomplice, were convicted and sentenced to the state penitentiary. They were finally released from prison on a legal technicality to be retried. This retrial was never held.

The **Olive Ranch** is located on private land. For information about the ranch and the nearby Ketchum-Mitchell lynching site, inquire at the Seven Valleys Museum.

The SEVEN VALLEYS MUSEUM is located in Callaway and contains a collection of Indian artifacts and area memorabilia. The museum is open from 2 to 5 p.m. daily except Mondays. Admission is free.

The first **Custer County Courthouse** is located in Callaway's Morgan Park. This log building, originally located on or near the Olive Ranch, is furnished in 1870s and 1880s styles. For more information inquire at the Seven Valleys Museum.

From Callaway one can end the tour by driving west 15 miles and south 24 miles on N-47 to Gothenburg or by driving north 11

FIRST CUSTER COUNTY COURTHOUSE—This small, primitive building, built in 1876, housed Custer County's first courthouse. It is now displayed in Callaway's Morgan Park.

CONTROVERSIAL COWBOY —I. P. "Print" Olive was a Texas cattleman who settled in Nebraska. He was involved in the lynching of two farmers, Ami Ketchum and Luther Mitchell, near Callaway. The trial of Print Olive and the other cattlemen involved was held in Hastings.

miles on N-40 to ARNOLD (pop. 810), then west 16 miles on N-92 to the intersection of US 83, then south 21 miles on N-70 and US 83 to North Platte.

This trip can be added to with a drive further east from Thedford after reaching Dunning. At Dunning, turn east on N-91 and drive for 60 miles to Burwell, then south on N-11, following the general route of the North Loup River, to Scotia. This is one of the routes to Fort Hartsuff State Historical Park as well as to historic Ord.

BREWSTER

BREWSTER (pop. 46), county seat of Blaine County, is 39 miles east of Thedford (24 miles on N-2 to Dunning, 15 miles northeast on N-91 from Dunning).

TAYLOR

It is 31 miles east on N-91 to TAYLOR (pop. 274) on US 183. Taylor, founded in 1881, is the county seat of Loup County. It was named for Ed Taylor, a local pioneer.

BURWELL

BURWELL (pop. 1,382), county seat of Garfield County, is 15 miles east of Taylor on N-91. Burwell is noted for its rodeo, largest of Nebraska's such events, which is held in early August.

Burwell was to have been named Webstertown for **Frank A. Webster**, county surveyor and son of Dr. Sam Webster, who, along with I. B. Nelson, donated the land for a settlement.

FORT HARTSUFF STATE HISTORICAL PARK—Fort Hartsuff, named in honor of a Civil War hero, was established in 1874 to protect settlers against Indian raiders and was closed in 1881. The old fort has been developed into a state historical park and is open to the public for tours. Above is one of the exhibits.

Frank's brother was engaged to **Ada Burwell** and he was killed when a tree fell on him. Frank and I. B. Nelson called the settlement Burwell in honor of Ada and platted it in 1884.

GARFIELD COUNTY HISTORICAL MUSEUM is located in a former Burwell residence. It contains various artifacts and memorabilia of settlement as well as pre-settlement days.

ELYRIA—FORT HARTSUFF

Nine miles south of Burwell on N-11 is ELYRIA (pop. 62) and about three miles north is **Fort Hartsuff**, established September 5, 1874 to protect settlers moving into the North Loup Valley. The fort, initially called the **"Post on the North Loup,"** was named for **Maj. Gen. George L. Hartsuff** (1830-1874), a Civil War hero, December 9, 1874. General Hartsuff was wounded several times during the war.

The years between 1873-75 were hard years in this area particularly because of drought, grasshopper plagues and general economic depression. Construction of the fort provided employment opportunities for many in the region.

257

Troop strength at Fort Hartsuff usually was less than 100 men —a company of infantry. During the seven years of operations, units of the 9th, 14th and 23rd Infantry Regiments served here. Their principal duty was to scout the area and assist civil authorities in pursuit of horse thieves, murderers and train robbers.

The major engagement with the Sioux occurred April 28, 1876 in the **"Battle of the Blowout,"** northwest of Burwell. A detachment of Company A, 23rd Infantry, was sent out to protect white settlers from being harrassed by a party of Sioux braves. A fight ensued and at least one soldier, **Sgt. William Doughtery**, was killed. Three others received the **Congressional Medal of Honor** for their heroism in this engagement. They were **2nd Lt. Charles H. Heyl** and Cpls. **Patrick Leonard** and **Jeptha L. Lytton**. Doughtery had received the medal for bravery in action against the Indians in Arizona in 1868 while serving with Company B, 8th Cavalry.

Shortly before Fort Hartsuff was built a fight occurred not far from Elyria. This was the **Battle of Pebble Creek**, a skirmish between settlers and a band of Sioux warriors during the early morning hours of January 19, 1874. The day before the Indians had raided several of the homes of the settlers, including **Richard Climans** and **Harry Colby**, small farms and a trapper's cabin. The settlers gave chase and caught up with the Indians the following morning camped along Pebble Creek, feasting on one of Colby's cows they had stolen and butchered. The Indians withdrew after an exchange of shots with the settlers but not before 21-year old **Marion Littlefield**, a settler, was killed.

Fort Hartsuff was abandoned April 13, 1881. The property was sold to the Union Pacific Railroad for $5,000 on July 20, 1881 and later was sold to private parties and farmed. In 1961 **Dr. Glen Auble** of Ord presented the site to the State of Nebraska for preservation and interpretation as a historical park. It is operated by the Game and Parks Commission.

Several buildings have been restored and guides are uniformed in period style. The park is open year-round (weather permitting) from sunup to sundown. Buildings open 10 a.m. to 8 p.m. May 12 to September 4. A Park Entry Permit ($2 daily, $10 annual) is required.

ORD—HOME OF EVELYN SHARP

Six miles south of Elyria on N-11 is ORD (pop. 2,661), county seat of Valley County. This was the hometown of the noted aviatrix, **Evelyn Genevieve Sharp**.

ORD HEROINE—Ord was hometown of Evelyn Sharp, noted aviatrix. She became interested in flying when she was 14 years old and by the time she was 19 she had gained her commercial pilot's license. She flew the first airmail into Ord in 1938 at the age of 19. Miss Sharp was killed in a crash in Pennsylvania in 1944 while ferrying a fighter plane for the U.S. Army Air Corps.

Evelyn Sharp

At the age of 19 she delivered Ord's first airmail in a flight May 19, 1938, to become the nation's first woman airmail pilot. Born October 1, 1919, to **Mr. and Mrs. John E. Sharp** in Melrose, Montana, Evelyn grew up in Ord. She became interested in flying at age 14 and soloed when she was 16. Two years later she received her commercial pilot's license, one of the youngest persons to receive this rating. Evelyn purchased an airplane, helped by Ord businessmen, and repaid her creditors through profits she earned on barnstorming tours.

At the age of 20, Evelyn became an instructor and when World War II erupted, she joined the WASPs (Women's Auxiliary Pilot Squadron), organized by **Gen. H. H. "Hap" Arnold.** This elite group was made up of expert pilots to fly aircraft from factory sites to shipping points. Evelyn was qualified to fly everything from training aircraft to big bombers. Evelyn Sharp was killed April 3, 1944 near Middleton, Pennsylvania, when the P-38 fighter plane she was piloting crashed. She was only 24 years old. She is buried in Ord and a historical marker has been erected at the Ord airport in her memory.

The Blizzard of 1888, or **"the school children's storm,"** is considered one of the worst blizzards in the state's history. It struck January 12, 1888 with temperatures plummeting to 30 to 40 degrees below zero and howling winds sweeping over the plains for 12 to 18 hours. The blizzard caught many children at school and many acts of heroism were recorded in this natural disaster which is estimated to have taken some 40 to 100 lives (an actual count was never completed). One of these heroic acts was performed by **Minnie Freeman**, a teenage teacher, teaching in a sod schoolhouse about nine miles south of Ord. Minnie was able to lead her students to a farmhouse a half mile away when the fierce winds ripped the roof off the primitive school building. A historical marker has been erected on N-70 in honor of Minnie Freeman, a symbol to the many acts of heroism performed January 12-13, 1888.

Valley County was formed in 1873 and Ord became the county seat. The town was laid out in 1874 and named in honor of **Maj. Gen. Edward Ortho Cresap Ord** (1818-1883), a Civil War hero. For a time the townsite was known among settlers as **Chin City**.

In 1881, the entire town was threatened by a fire but only the **H. W. Nelson** livery barn was destroyed by flames. Another fire, in 1882, broke out in a building on the south side of the village square and several buildings were destroyed. Ord was incorporated as a village June 23, 1881.

SCOTIA

Seventeen miles south of Ord via N-11 is SCOTIA (pop. 350), near the site of an old chalk mine, now a state recreation area. The mine, opened in 1877 by **Ed Wright**, is located two miles south of town. A chalk building, constructed in 1877 for a general store, still stands in Scotia.

The highest hill in the state recreation area is known as "**Happy Jack's Peak**" that served as an Indian lookout point for **Jack Swearengen**, a trapper, guide and government scout who settled here in 1872.

The other communities with historical museums are Anselmo on N-2; Broken Bow, 21 miles south; and Callaway, 33 miles southwest of Broken Bow, all listed in the previous Section.

Section 11

Often the most interesting trips are those off the beaten path. This is true in Nebraska where most travelers get on I-80 and travel along at breakneck speed complaining there is nothing to see in the state. For that reason we have included a tour through part of the state using Nebraska State Highway 92.

This is a narrow, two-lane highway and traffic can be slowed by a creeping tractor moving from one field to another. The road is winding in spots as well.

But where will you see a torpedo, surrounded in a field of tiny American flags, on a courthouse lawn? How about Wahoo where the community still honors the memory of the crew that went down when the submarine USS Wahoo was sunk by the Japanese during World War II? Wahoo has some famous sons — Movie Producer Darryl Zanuck, Pulitzer Prize Winning Music Composer Howard Hanson, Nobel Prize Winning Geneticist Dr. George Beadle and Baseball's Hall of Famer Sam "Wahoo" Crawford. It's a town worth visiting.

Just a little west is the town of Rising City where Dr. Walter H. Judd, medical missionary to China and a U.S. Congressman, grew up as a boy.

On this route is the town of Stromsburg, "Swede Capital of Nebraska." And, of course, there is the town of Surprise and we will leave that as a surprise for you.

Put a little adventure in your soul, schedule a little more time for your trip or weekend drive and you will find Nebraska has much to offer.

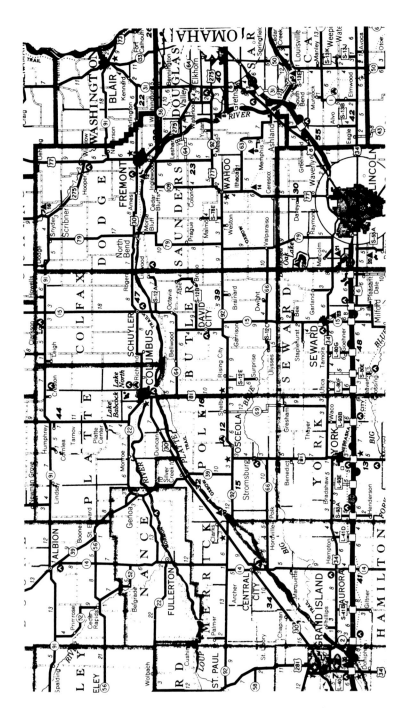

HANSON HISTORICAL HOUSE—This house, located at the corner of 12th and Linden, Wahoo, is the birthplace of Pulitzer Prize-winning music composer Dr. Howard Hanson. It also honors five of Wahoo's most famous men.

TRAVEL ALONG NEBRASKA HIGHWAY 92

An alternate route west, from Omaha, is N-92 which actually runs from the Missouri River some 330 miles west to Arthur in the Sandhills. Travel may be a little slower but the trip through this part of Nebraskaland has its own special beauty. Out of Omaha N-92 is merged with US 275 to the intersection of US 6.

WAHOO

From this intersection it is nine miles west along N-92 to YUTAN (pop. 636) and Saunders County. Saunders County was formed in 1867 with **Ashland** as the first county seat.

Five miles west is MEAD (pop. 507) and it is another nine miles to WAHOO (pop. 3,579), the county seat. The town was founded in 1865. Wahoo is the Indian name for the flaming red bushes which grew along the creek banks. The community is the childhood home of five men who have achieved national recognition—**Clarence W. Anderson**, artist; **Dr. George Beadle**, world famous geneticist and winner of the Nobel Prize in 1958; **Sam "Wahoo" Crawford**, elected to Baseball's Hall of Fame in 1957; **Dr. Howard Hanson**, Pulitzer Prize winning music composer; and **Darryl F. Zanuck**, movie producer and founder of 20th Century-Fox Studios. Anderson (1891-1971) was renowned for his sketches of horses. He published more than 40 books. Dr. Beadle served as president of Chicago University, 1961 to 1968. Dr. Hanson served as director of Eastman School of Music, Rochester, New York, from 1924 to 1964. The internationally known composer-conductor received the Pulitzer Prize in 1944 for his "Symphony No. 4."

A torpedo displayed on the courthouse front lawn is in memory of the crew of the submarine *USS Wahoo (SS 238)*, sunk by the Japanese, October 11, 1943, in the Pacific after sinking 20 enemy ships. The crew members, listed on the plaque on this site, are noted as "still on patrol." Small American flags surround this unique monument.

The Saunders County Historical Society owns and operates the SAUNDERS COUNTY HISTORICAL COMPLEX. The museum, in Joe Bowers Historical Park, is open April through October, 9 a.m. to 12 and 1 to 5 p.m., Saturdays, and 2 to 5 p.m. Sundays. The museum will open weekdays by appointment by calling 443-4315 or 443-4576. The HANSON HISTORICAL HOUSE, at the corner of 12th and Linden, is the birthplace of **Dr. Howard Hanson** and honors Wahoo's five famous men. Other facilities in the historical complex include a Burlington Railroad Depot, constructed in 1886; a one-room school house, built in 1878; a pioneer church built in 1889 by Methodist Episcopals and used until 1977; and the Joe Bowers Home. Bowers, who donated land for the museum, served as the Burlington Railroad agent for 34 years.

WESTON—BRAINARD—DAVID CITY—RISING CITY

Five miles west and a mile south of Wahoo is WESTON (pop. 286) and 13 miles west and a mile south is BRAINARD (pop. 275), in Butler County. Seven miles west and three miles north is DAVID CITY (pop. 2,492), county seat of Butler County. A trade and processing center, David City was incorporated in 1878.

Back on N-92, nine miles west of the David City turnoff is RISING CITY (pop. 395), platted in 1878. Originally called Rising, the town was named for **S. W. Rising** and his son, **A. W.**, who each donated 40 acres of land to the Omaha & Republican Valley Railroad and for the townsite. Agriculture is the basis of the area economy and corn, milo and soybeans are the major crops.

Dr. Walter H. Judd, medical missionary to China and a U.S. Congressman from the 5th District in Minnesota for 20 years,

264

TORPEDO DISPLAY HONORS USS WAHOO CREW—This tor-
pedo, displayed on the Saunders County courthouse front lawn in
Wahoo, is a memorial to the crew lost aboard the submarine USS
Wahoo sunk in 1943.

BUILT ON INDIAN BURIAL SITE—The Saunders County courthouse was built in 1905 on the site of an old Indian burial ground
from which many relics have been unearthed. The courthouse building is in Wahoo.

was raised in Rising City and graduated from the local high school. Dr. Judd, who gave the keynote address at the 1960 National Republican Convention, was a recognized expert on Far East affairs and sought-after speaker.

SURPRISE

A mile west and six miles south of Rising City on N-Spur 12E, is SURPRISE (pop. 60). **George Miller** arrived in the area in 1881 to establish a gristmill on the Blue River. The story goes Miller was so surprised to find enough water there to run a mill he named it the Surprise Mill. The town that developed in 1884, became the town of Surprise.

Surprise became a unique attraction in the decade of 1910-20 when the Chautauqua came to town. The Chautauquas were a traveling troupe of entertainers, educational and recreational, who would perform each afternoon and evening in a huge circus tent. It is estimated as many as 4,000 persons attended some of those events.

The town's population high was 323 reached in the 1940s. Fires and a 1945 tornado destroyed many of the buildings in Surprise.

OSCEOLA

Back on N-92 the next town west, six miles, is SHELBY (pop. 729), three miles into Polk County. Six miles west is OSCEOLA (pop. 977), county seat of Polk County. Osceola, named for the

A Mile Wide and a Foot Deep

Nebraska's principal river, the Platte, has been described as being "a mile wide and a foot deep." It is actually a mile wide in some places and is too shallow for navigation.

The North Platte and South Platte rivers join to make up the Platte River at the City of North Platte. The North Platte flows into the state from Wyoming; the South Platte from Colorado. The Platte River flows into the Missouri River at Plattsmouth.

famous Seminole chief, was platted in June 1872.

STROMSBURG—THE SWEDE CAPITAL

Three miles west and four miles south on US 81 is STROMS-BURG (pop. 1,292), the "Swede Capital of Nebraska." The town is a farm center whose many elevators handle more than five million bushels of grain per year. Stromsburg was settled by Swedes in 1872 and incorporated as a town in 1883.

Leaving Osceola the highway cuts across the old **Oxbow Trail** and then across the Platte River. The Oxbow Trail was the early day trail used to supply Fort Kearny from the river city of Nebraska City. It wound along the south side of the Platte River from Fort Kearny to a point near Columbus and then dropped down southeast, via a circuitous route, to Nebraska City. Some 15 years later the **Nebraska City-Fort Kearny Cutoff** was established for a more direct and shorter route. This cutoff trail follows the general direction of I-80 to Lincoln and in the general area of N-2 east to the Missouri River port. It is 15 miles from Osceola to the intersection of N-92 and US 30.

CLARKS—ST. PAUL

At this point, three miles south of CLARKS (pop. 447), the traveler may wish to take US 30 to Grand Island, 40 miles southwest. This route takes one through Central City, known to those who traveled the Mormon Trail in the early days as **Lone Tree**.

Clarks was named for **Silas Clark**, a Union Pacific Railroad official. The first white settler arrived in 1867. Just west and south of the US 30 and N-92 intersection is the site of the GRAND PAWNEE HUNTING AND BURIAL GROUNDS and site of a Pawnee village.

Thirty one miles west on N-92 is ST. PAUL (pop. 2,081), county seat of Howard County. This farm community was founded in 1871.

St. Paul was founded by **James N. Paul**, a surveyor who visited the area with **Maj. Frank North** of the Pawnee Scouts in 1870. Paul returned the following year with 31 other settlers and they named their new town **Athens** because of the physical surroundings. Nebraska already had an "Athens" so the name as changed to St. Paul, suggested by Senator P. W. Hitchcock. It was settled by Danes.

Another Danish community in Howard County is DANNEN-BROG, 12 miles southeast of St. Paul. It began as a postoffice in 1872 on the homestead of **Lars Hannibal** and was named for Denmark's national emblem.

LOUP CITY

Twenty eight miles west of St. Paul is LOUP CITY (pop. 1,368), county seat of Sherman County. There are two tiny farm communities along this route—FARWELL (pop. 165), nine miles west of St. Paul and ASHTON (pop. 272), 10 miles east of Loup City. Located on the Middle Loup River, Loup City was settled in 1873.

Loup City was the scene of a farm strike, led by the Communist organizer, **"Mother" Ella Bloor**, during the Depression years of the 1930s. "Mother" Bloor embraced Communism as a young woman and even with a large family she traveled throughout the country espousing the cause.

From Loup City N-92 takes the traveler through the Sandhills Cattle Country—43 miles to Broken Bow to Stapleton, 25 miles from Stapleton to Tryon and 39 miles from Tryon to Arthur. (See listing for the Sandhills Cattle Country Tour.)

The Cornhusker State

Nebraska's official nickname is the *Cornhusker State.* The name comes from corn, the state's leading crop, and from the cornhusking bees (contests) that once were held each fall in many of the farm communities.

The name *Nebraska* comes from an Oto Indian word *nebrathka,* meaning *flat water* and was the Indian's name for the Platte River.

Section 12

A group of Chambers of Commerce offer The Blue Valley Trail Tour through the communities of Crete, Wilber, Fairbury and Beatrice, south of Lincoln, the state capital, These are smaller Nebraska communities in a rich farm section of the state.

Many of the first settlers arrived in this area in the 1860s and there are many buildings here that have been listed on the National Register of Historic Places. There are several small museums open to the public. Wilber, founded in 1873, claims the title of "Czech Capital of Nebraska," and has done much to maintain the Czech culture and heritage. Thousands of people flock to the annual Czech festival held the first Saturday and Sunday in August.

In our tour we have added a couple of stops — Dorchester, home of the Dorchester County Museum, and Tobias, which became the final resting place for Sergeant Leodegar Schnyder, who served in the U.S. Army longer than any other non-commissioned officer — a total of 53 years with 37 of these at Fort Laramie.

Fairbury has a number of historic spots to see and visit. Not far away is the site of Rock Creek Station where "Wild Bill" Hickok earned his reputation as a gunfighter in a bizarre shoot-out. The Oregon Trail ran just east of the town and there are a number of attractions on the old trail.

This tour ends in Beatrice, home of the National Homestead Monument and several other historic attractions. This is a trip worth taking and can be done easily in a day.

Take the Blue Valley Trail!

TO OMAHA

LINCOLN

W E
S

11 MILES

Nebraska's First Chautauqua
CRETE
33
14 MILES
103
Doane College

TO Blue Stem

77

Czech Capital of Nebraska
WILBER
11 MILES

23 MILES

15

29 MILES

Rockford Lake

TO Alexandria Lakes

OREGON TRAIL

BIG

BEATRICE

Homestead National Monumen

Winslow Grave

& PONY

136

27 MILES

RIVER

FAIRBURY
Crystal Springs Park

EXPRESS

Rock Creek State Park

Tri-County Oregon Trail Marker

LITTLE BLUE

This map furnished through the courtesy of the Wilber Chamber of Commerce. Also participating in the Blue Valley Trail tour are the Crete and Fairbury Chambers of Commerce.

HOTEL WILBER—Constructed in 1895, Hotel Wilber has been restored and is listed on the National Register of Historic Buildings.

BLUE VALLEY TRAIL TOUR

This tour begins in Lincoln. From Lincoln, take US 77 11 miles south to N-33, turn west on N-33 and a short distance to **Blue Stem Lake**, part of the Salt Valley lakes. This state park is open for fishing, boating and camping. A permit is required.

CRETE

Continuing west (14 miles from the US 77 turnoff) is CRETE (pop. 4,871), founded by **Jesse C. Bickle**, the first white settler. Bickle, a native Ohioan, arrived in the 1860s as a homesteader. The first postoffice was established on his homestead and Jesse called it **Blue River City**. His wife, a native of Crete, Illinois, had other ideas and the postoffice became known as **Crete**. The town was incorporated in 1871.

"THE MAPLES," just off 13th St. downtown, was the home of Jesse Bickle and today is one of the several Crete homes listed on the National Register of Historic Places. The building originated as a two-room log cabin and later expanded into a two-story frame house. This home and the adjoining property which make up "The Maples," is open the third Sunday of every month from 2 to 5 p.m. or by appointment.

Doane College, Crete, Nebraska's first independent, co-educational, liberal arts college, was founded in 1872. It was named for

271

Thomas Doane, the chief civil engineer for the Burlington Railroad.

TUXEDO PARK, located on the banks of the Big Blue River, was the site of Nebraska's first Chautauqua. A marker in the park tells the Chautauqua story. One of the old Chautauqua buildings still stands.

DORCHESTER

The SALINE COUNTY MUSEUM is located seven miles west of Crete at the south edge of DORCHESTER (pop. 613) on N-33.

The five-acre site accommodates nine buildings containing artifacts of all kinds dating from 1880. The museum is open from 1 to 5 p.m every Sunday or by appointment. Admission is free.

WILBER

WILBER (pop. 1,519) is located 11 miles south of Crete at the junction of N-41 and N-103 and claims the title as "Czech Capital of Nebraska." Between Crete and Wilber is the CZECH SETTLER'S MONUMENT, commemorating Czech settlement in the valley dating from 1865. The Czech influence permeates the community where the visitor can find a variety of Czech goods— crafts, foods, imports, costumes, handloomed rugs and fine glassware to name a few. A CZECH MUSEUM is open 2 to 5 p.m. Sunday or by appointment.

Wilber, founded in 1873, is the county seat of Saline County. The town was named for **Charles Dana Wilber** (1830-1891), of Aurora, Illinois, who owned railroad land and donated it to start the town. The town's benefactor, an internationally known geologist, never became a resident of Wilber. In 1881, he published a book, *"The Great Valleys and Prairies of Nebraska and the Northwest,"* that popularized the theory that "rainfall follows the plow." This book was widely circulated by the railroads as part of their land sales promotional efforts.

The first permanent settlers to this region arrived in 1858. The county, organized in 1867, was named for the salt water springs in the area. **Swan City** was located about five miles south of Wilber on N-103 and was the first county seat and served as such from 1867 to 1871. In an 1871 election the county seat was moved to **Pleasant Hill** until the November 1877 election when voters approved Wilber as the new seat of government. The county records were moved to Wilber January 1, 1878. Swan City and Pleasant Hill soon disappeared.

Two early day pioneers in this particular area were **Tobias Castor** and **Jacob** and **Susan Hunt** who arrived in 1862. Castor

SALINE COUNTY MUSEUM—The Saline County Museum is located in Dorchester, seven miles west of Crete on N-33. The museum is open Sunday afternoons and by appointment.

operated the first postoffice in this area.

In the early afternoon of July 26, 1874 grasshoppers by the millions suddenly appeared in the sky through this general area. There were so many of the insects they blotted out the sunlight and it became so dark by mid-afternoon the chickens went to roost. The 'hoppers ate everything growing, including leaves from the trees, and then went on to gnaw on shingles and boards. There are stories told about the 'hoppers eating the handles off axes left in the yards. The grasshopper infestation created unbelievable devastation.

An annual Czech festival is held the first Saturday and Sunday in August and is highlighted with parades, pageants, music and tasty Czech foods. It draws thousands of visitors.

Hotel Wilber, built in 1895, has been restored to its original decor. It is listed on the National Register of Historic Buildings.

From Wilber drive west 11 miles on N-41 to N-15, turn south on N-15 to Fairbury, a 23 mile trip. About four miles north of Fairbury, just off to the west, is the **George Winslow Monument**. It was here George Winslow, an emigrant on the Oregon Trail, died of cholera and was buried in June 1849.

TOBIAS

An interesting side trip is suggested here if the traveler has time. TOBIAS (pop. 140), four miles south of the N-41 and N-15 junction and eight miles west on N-74, is well worth a visit because of its historical background. The village of Tobias was platted in 1884 as the town of **Castor**, for **Tobias Castor**, a Burlington Railroad right-of-way agent. Postal authorities, however, refused to accept the name of Castor so the name was changed to Tobias. The town came into being as a railroad depot and grew rapidly. In 1891 a fire destroyed 22 of the 60 buildings in the town. Many did not rebuild. The **Tobias Community Historical Society** has two museum buildings. The former Citizen State Bank building houses their general museum exhibits and the former Tobias Print Shop serves as a depository for old newspapers and school records. The general museum is open by appointment. Admission is free; donations are accepted.

Ordnance Sgt. Leodegar Schnyder, buried in nearby Altanta Center Cemetery, served in the U.S. Army longer than any other non-commissioned officer—53 years with 37 years spent at Fort Laramie (1849-1886). He retired from the Army in 1890 and settled on a farm near Tobias with his second wife, Julia. He died here December 19, 1896. Born in Switzerland in 1814, Schnyder

ONE OF THE ETHNIC FESTIVALS—One of Nebraska's most popular ethnic festivals is the Czech Festival held in Wilber the first Saturday and Sunday in August. Thousands of visitors flock to "Nebraska's Czech Capital" for this annual event.

came to America in 1829 and joined the Army in 1837. Schnyder was married twice while serving at Fort Laramie and raised his children at this Wyoming post.

FAIRBURY—BEATRICE

To rejoin the Blue Valley Trail tour from Tobias, return to N-15 by backtracking the eight miles east on N-74. Turn south on N-15 for Fairbury.

About a mile south of the George Winslow gravesite, on N-15, is the site of the old **Virginia Station** along the Oregon Trail. A

275

historical marker describes this site.

(For more information about the Fairbury and Beatrice areas, please see Section 5.)

Three miles south is FAIRBURY (pop. 4,887), county seat of Jefferson County. The Oregon Trail and Pony Express route ran from the southeast corner of the county to the northwest and there are six monuments marking the trail through the county. Six miles southeast of Fairbury is the site of **Rock Creek Station** where young **James Butler Hickok** gained his reputation as a gunfighter in 1861. Twelve miles southeast of Fairbury is the tiny village of **Steele City** where visitors may view four unusual buildings dating back to the 1880s. There is an excellent museum in downtown Fairbuy.

From Fairbury the Blue Valley Trail heads east on US 136 to BEATRICE (pop. 12,871), county seat of Gage County. This trip is 27 miles through Nebraska farm country. There are a number of historic places in the Beatrice area including the HOMESTEAD NATIONAL MONUMENT, 3.5 miles northwest of town on N-4; GAGE COUNTY HISTORICAL MUSEUM, CHAUTAUQUA PARK, PADDOCK HOUSE, GAGE COUNTY COURTHOUSE, and FILLEY STONE BARN.

The trip back to Lincoln is 40 miles north on US 77.

The Nebraska Press

The first newspaper in Nebraska, the *Nebraska Palladium and Platte Valley Advocate*, was edited by Thomas Morton in Bellevue in 1854-55. Soon after the *Arrow* appeared in Omaha, the *Nebraska News* in Nebraska City and the *Nebraska Advertiser* in Brownville. Robert W. Furnas started the Brownville newspaper in 1856.

The *Huntsman's Echo* was started in 1858 by Mormon Joseph E. Johnson. He operated the newspaper at a bend in Wood River near today's Shelton and circulated it to immigrants and freighters on the Oregon Trail.

Section 13

*This section contains information about the stations
along the route of the Oregon or Overland Trail.
This was the route of the Overland Stage Lines and the
colorful Pony Express as well as thousands of
emigrants who saw their future on the West Coast.
These emigrants searched for gold and silver and they
looked for new, fertile land.*

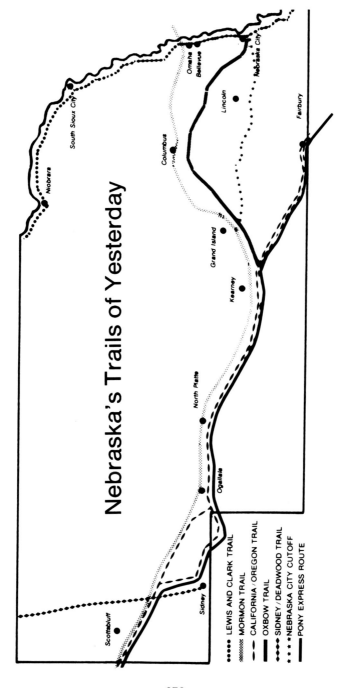

Nebraska's Trails of Yesterday

Scottsbluff

Sidney

Ogallala

North Platte

Kearney

Grand Island

Niobrara

South Sioux City

Columbus

Omaha
Bellevue

Nebraska City

Lincoln

Fairbury

•••• LEWIS AND CLARK TRAIL

▨▨▨ MORMON TRAIL

– – CALIFORNIA / OREGON TRAIL

◆◆◆ OXBOW TRAIL

◆◆◆ SIDNEY / DEADWOOD TRAIL

∗∗∗ NEBRASKA CITY CUTOFF

——— PONY EXPRESS ROUTE

278

Route of the Oregon Trail

The major departure point of the Oregon Trail was Independence, Missouri, and was the "jumping off place" for one of the very first emigrant trains, the Smith-Jackson-Sublette expedition to the Wind River country in the Rocky Mountains in 1830. By the early 1840s, the trail had already seen hundreds of emigrants in their wagon trains headed westward to the Oregon Country or California.

The trail was also called the Fort Leavenworth-Fort Kearny Military Road from the fort just across from Weston, Missouri, to as far west as Fort Kearny. The Pony Express eastern terminus was St. Joseph.

This trail entered Nebraska in the tip of the southwest corner of Gage County. From a point five miles east of Steele City, just across the Jefferson County line, the trail turned northwest along the Little Blue River for three miles then crossed Rock Creek and moved four miles north just east of Fairbury, where it intersects N-15. The trail then moved west across Little Sandy, into Thayer County, south of Alexandria to just north of Hebron and then followed the east bank of the Little Blue River generally northwest, through the northeast corner of Nuckolls County, southwest corner of Clay County and running through Adams County, to a point north of Kenesaw where it turned west and followed south bank of the Platte River for some 180 miles.

The Platte River split just east of North Platte to form the North and South Forks of the Platte River. The Oregon Trail followed the South Fork of the river westward for a number of miles. Up to 1859 users of the trail crossed the South Fork to reach the North Platte River via Ash Hollow (near Lewellen). There were three such crossings.

The Lower Crossing was southwest of Sutherland. At the crossing here it was only about two miles to the south bank of the North Platte River.

The Middle Crossing was just a few miles east of Ogallala and it was about nine miles to the south bank of the North Platte at this crossing. The trail along this part of the North Platte River is partially covered today by Lake McConaughy.

Upper Crossing (also called at various times, Kearny's Ford, Beauvais' Crossing, Laramie Crossing, Ash Hollow Crossing or California Crossing), a few miles west of Brule, was the most popular crossing for emigrants heading for California and Oregon. It was 15 to 18 miles from this point to the south bank of the North Platte.

From this point, at Ash Hollow the Oregon Trail, regardless of the crossing used, followed the south bank of the North Platte all the way to today's Nebraska-Wyoming state line, a distance of about 120 miles.

After 1859, a more popular route followed the Lower California Crossing, south along the South Platte to Julesburg and then turned northwest and then north for about 75 miles to join the trail on the south bank of the North Platte River at Bridgeport. This route was selected because it was easier to travel. It basically followed US 385 from Julesburg to a point just north of Sidney then north to Bridgeport.

The stage routes followed this new crossing at Julesburg. So did the Pony Express and the telegraph.

Early in the development of the Oregon Trail, along all the routes and cutoffs, entrepeneurs established road ranches (usually trading posts) to service emigrants who needed food and supplies. The ranches often served as havens for emigrants against Indian raiders. In the Indian uprisings of 1864-65, many were destroyed or abandoned.

With the establishment of commercial travel and communications—the advent of stage coach service, the Pony Express and telegraph service—stations were established. For the stage companies and Pony Express it was a place for changes of horses, a place to eat and a place to rest.

There continues to be some confusion over the location of every station along the route but the following are those most experts agree upon:

Rock House Station—three miles northeast of Steele City, Jefferson County, just after crossing into Nebraska from Kansas.

Rock Creek Station—six miles southwest of Fairbury. This was the setting of the James B. Hickok-David McCanles shootout where Hickok earned the sobriquet, "Wild Bill," July 12, 1861.

Virginia City Station—four miles north of Fairbury.

Big Sandy Station—three miles east of Alexandria.

Thompson's Station—seven miles northeast of Hebron.

Kiowa Station—10 miles northwest of Hebron.

Oak Grove Station—in the northeast corner of Nuckolls County. It was here the Indians struck hardest during their August 7, 1864 raids along the Little Blue River. Several settlers were killed and two women, Lucinda Eubanks and Laura Roper, and Mrs. Eubanks' small daughter and son were taken captive. The little community of Oak has held a number of programs commemorating this tragedy.

Little Blue Station—four miles northwest of Oak Grove.

Liberty Farm—just north of DeWeese in Clay County.

Spring Ranch—just across in Adams County.

Thirty-Two Mile Creek—six miles southwest of Hastings. Also called Dinner Station or Elm Creek Station.

Sand Hill—one and a half miles south of Kenesaw. Also referred to as Summit Station.

Junction—about eight miles east of Fort Kearny. This was also referred to as Dogtown or Valley Station.

Fort Kearny—southeast of present day Kearney.

Dobytown—two miles west of Fort Kearny. Also referred to as Kearney City.

Keeler's Ranch—eight miles west of Dobytown.

Craig's Stage Station—about five miles southwest of present-day Kearney. Also referred to as Platt's or O'Brien's.

Burton's Seventeen Mile Station—two miles west of Craig's. Also referred to as McClain's and Russell's Ranche.

Garden—six miles southeast of Elm Creek. Also referred to as Platte Stage Station, Biddleman's Ranch and Sydenham's Ranche.

Plum Creek Station—10 miles southeast of present-day Lexington. Near this site was the spot of the Plum Creek Massacre August 7, 1864 when 11 men were killed and Mrs. Nancy Morton and a youngster, Danny Marble, were captured by Indian raiders.

Freeman's Ranch—six miles west of Plum Creek Station.

Willow Island—six miles west of Freeman's. Also referred to as Willow Bend, or Mullally's Ranche, Stage Station and Military Post. The original cabin here has been moved to Cozad as a tourist attraction.

Smithe's Ranche—nine miles west of Willow Island. Also referred to as Miller and Penneston's Ranche and Stage Station or Miller's Ranch.

Midway Station—five miles west of Smithe's. It was described as "one of the best eating places on the Platte."

Dan Smith's Ranche, Stage Station and Military Post—five miles west of Midway. It was near here Mark Twain described a rider streaking by his stagecoach, "swinging away like the belated fragment of a storm."

Gilman's Station—eight miles west of Gothenburg. It was here Pvt. Francis W. Lohnes, Company H, 1st Nebraska Cavalry, earned the Congressional Medal of Honor May 12, 1865 for his gallantry in fighting off attacking Indians.

Dan Trout's Station—south of Brady. Also referred to as Joe Bower's Ranche, Boken Ranche or Machette's. The original building has been moved to Ehmen Park in Gothenburg.

Cottonwood Springs—one mile southeast of Fort McPherson National Cemetery, near Maxwell. Also referred to as Cottonwood Station or McDonald's Station.

Fort McPherson—a mile south of Maxwell.

Box Elder Stage Station and Telegraph Office—three miles west of Fort McPherson.

Jack Morrow's Ranche—just below the confluence of the North and South forks of the Platte River. Also referred to as Junction House. This was one of the best known stations on the route and Morrow was one of the region's characters. He was famed as a scout and fairly popular with the Indians.

Cold Springs Ranche and Stage Station—due south of present-day North Platte.

Fremont Station—halfway between North Platte and Hershey. Also referred to as Bishop's Station or Bishop's Ranche.

Fremont Springs Pony Express and Stage Station—opposite Hershey. Also referred to as Buffalo Ranch.

O'Fallon's Bluff Station—two miles west of Fremont Springs.

Bob Williams Ranche—opposite Sutherland.

Moore's Ranche—three miles west of Bob Williams. Also referred to as the O'Fallon Road Ranche.

Elkhorn Station—two miles west of Moore's. Also referred to as Dansey's, Dorsey, Elk Horn State Station or Half Way House.

Alkali Station, Telegraph Office and Military Post—seven miles west of Paxton. Also referred to as Pike's Peak Station.

Sand Hill Stage Station—opposite Ogallala. Also referred to as Gill's.

Diamond Springs—less than a mile west of Brule.

Beauvais' Ranche—four miles west of Brule. Also referred to the Upper Crossing, Old California Crossing or Star Ranche.

Julesburg—just across in Colorado and two miles east of present-day Julesburg. The original Julesburg was burned by the Indians in early February 1865. The town started in 1859 as a trading post owned by Jules Beni, later killed by the infamous Jack Slade. Nearby was Fort Rankin, later renamed Fort Sedgwick.

Nine Mile Station—back into Nebraska, two miles southeast of Chappell.

Pole Creek Station No. 2—in the vicinity of Lodgepole.

Pole Creek Station No. 3—three and a half miles east of Sidney. Also referred to as Rouliette and Pringle stage ranch and St. George cattle ranch.

Government Well—three miles south and a mile west of Gurley on US 385.

Mud Springs Station—12 miles southeast of Bridgeport. From here the trail split heading north. The Pony Express used the left trail to Pumpkinseed Crossing southwest of Court House Rock. The main trail passed the landmark to the north. The Battle of Mud Springs occurred early in February 1865. A handful of soldiers and crew at the station were able to hold off a large force of Indians long enough to be rescued by the 11th Ohio Cavalry from Fort Mitchell and Fort Laramie.

Court House Rock Station—five miles west and a mile south of Bridgeport.

Ficklin's Springs Station—one mile west of Melbeta, just off N-92.

Scott's Bluff Station—near Scott's Bluff National Monument.

Fort Mitchell—on N-92, two miles west of Scott's Bluff. The fort was established as a one-company post in 1864 because of the Indian crisis and abandoned in 1867.

Horse Creek Station—two miles northeast of Lyman.

From just west of this point the Oregon Trail enters Wyoming.

Two National Forests

Nebraska has two national forests. Nebraska National Forest covers part of Blaine, Dawes, Sioux and Thomas counties in the northwest corner of the state. Samuel Roy McKelvie National Forest is located in Cherry County, also in the northern part of the state.

The McKelvie National Forest is the only national forest planted entirely by foresters.

For Maps and Other Information

Nebraska has a variety of tourist information services. There are information centers at some of the rest areas on I-80 during the summer months and trained Nebraska Vacation Guides, at several of these stops, will be glad to answer your questions and provide travel literature.

When the Guides are not available, consult one of the Visitor Information displays at the rest areas. These displays provide information about Nebraska history and other special topics, and include information about attractions and travel services in the immediate area.

For year-round Nebraska travel information and an excellent state map, write:

Travel and Tourism Division
Nebraska Department of Economic Development
P. O. Box 94666, Lincoln, NE 68509
or telephone
800-742-7595 (in-state) and **800-228-4307** (out-state)

The Nebraska State Historical Society is also extremely cooperative and helpful. The Society's museum in Lincoln is a must for the history buff. For information about the Nebraska State Historical Society and its offerings, write:

Nebraska State Historical Society
1500 P St., Lincoln, NE 68508

The Nebraska Game and Parks Commission provides information on several facets of Nebraska life, including outstanding printed materials for vacationers. It also operates several State Historical Parks. For more information, write:

Nebraska Game and Parks Commissions
P. O. Box 30370, Lincoln, NE 68503

Most of the state's Chambers of Commerce have printed materials about their communities and service areas. Most will respond promptly to any inquiries.

A Nebraska Photo Album

A FUTURE GOVERNOR—Robert W. Furnas served as a colonel and commanded the 2nd Nebraska Volunteers in 1862-63. The regiment, recruited to serve nine months, was sent to guard the frontier. Furnas, who also served as a newspaper editor and publisher, was elected governor of Nebraska in the 1870s.

TWO PAWNEE SCOUTS—Blue Hawk and Coming Around With the Herd served with the Pawnee Scouts, formed during the Civil War by Frank North of Columbus. The Pawnee Scouts were formed to serve as scouts for the Army on the frontier. They served intermittenly for several years.

THE COLORFUL MOSES SYDENHAM—When Moses Sydenham, who had served as postmaster at Fort Kearny for nearly 14 years, learned that the Army post was to be closed he began a drive to have the nation's capital moved to the military reservation which occupied 10 square miles, the size of the District of Columbia. Moses contended that with the nation's capital located in the central part of the country, all sectors would benefit financially. He proposed the new city be called New Washington. He is shown in this photo on the old military site long after it was abandoned.

287

HOME OF THE BIG RED—Nebraska is football country! Memorial Stadium in Lincoln becomes Nebraska's third largest city on football Saturdays every fall. It is here that more than 76,000 red-clad fans cheer on the Cornhuskers, perenially one of the nation's top 10 grid teams.

DINOSAURS ONCE ROAMED THE PLAINS—Gigantic dinosaurs once roamed the plains of the Nebraska. These exhibits in the State Museum on the campus of the University of Nebraska tell the story of the dinosaurs and other strange mammals that once inhabited the land.

MARKS TRAGEDY—This stone monument on the Oregon Trail commemorates the men and women who lost their lives in the Plum Creek Massacre of August 7, 1864. The Oregon Trail is well marked in Nebraska.

THE CAUSE OF FIGHTING—The buffalo was a pri[n] food, clothing and shelter for the Indian. When he sa[w] encroaching upon his hunting lands he went to w fighting between the whites and Indians in Nebra 1864-65. One of those who had some understandin was Nebraska author Mari Sandoz (1896-1966). Mis several books on the plight of the Indians including tumn," which became the basis of a motion picture She is buried south of Gordon, in the Sandhills.

BRONC RIDING INTRODUCED—The rodeo, as we know it today, is said to have been the brainchild of Col. William F. "Buffalo Bill" Cody as a result of his bronc riding contest held July 4, 1882. After this event, Cody included the rodeo in his internationally famous Wild West Show. His show drew large audiences around the country and in Europe for over three decades. The North Platte Rodeo is the only rodeo held annually seven nights a week during the summer. North Platte also served as headquarters for "Buffalo Bill" for a number of years.

THE SOD HOUSE FRONTIER—The area around Broken Bow was the center of what eventually became known as the Sod House Frontier. As homesteaders began to enter this largely treeless region, they made their first homes of prairie sod, which they cut into strips. Early churches, schools and some business places were also made of sod. While most of the sod structures were single story or a story and a half at least one homesteader constructed a full two story sod house.

LOCAL MUSEUMS FLOURISH—County museums like these in Fort Calhoun (top) and Bellevue (bottom) flourish in Nebraska and explain local and regional history.

PRISONER OF WAR CAMPS—Several communities in Nebraska were sites of World War II prisoner-of-war camps. Several thousand Italian and German POWs were held in the state from 1943-45.

THE DEADLY FAT MAN—This is a replica of the atomic bomb, referred to as "Fat Man," dropped on Nagasaki, Japan, August 9, 1945
to end World War II. This is one of the numerous displays at the
Strategic Air Command's Aerospace Space Museum in Bellevue.

INDEX

299

300

De Soto National Wildlife Refuge 200
de Villasur, Col. Pedro 4, 197
Deepwell Ranch 53, 54
Deer Creek Evangelical Lutheran Congregation 150
Dennis, Sandy 60
Dennis-Stephenson House 191
Dennison, William W. 191
Dept. of the Platte 22
Deshler 170
Deshler, John G. 170
Devil's Gap 127
Dey, Peter 24
Diamond Springs 103, 282
Dice, II. 150
Diceratherium 3, 129
Dillon-Peterson House 191
Dillon, Sidney 105
Dinohyus 3, 5, 129
District 81 School 178
District 10 School Museum 173
Dix 112
Doane College 149, 216, 271
Doane, Thomas 272
Dobytown 72, 76, 77, 281
Dodge 212
Dodge, Col. Henry 5, 197
Dodge County Historical Society 202
Dome Rock 127
Dorchester 269, 272, 273
Dorchester County Museum 269
Dorseys or Elk Horn Stage Station 99
Doughtery, Sgt. William 258
Douglas, David 233
Douglas County Historical Society 23
Douglas, James 164
Douglas, Stephan A. 6
Drips, Andrew S. 127, 128
Dull Knife, Chief 144, 239
Dunbar, John 36
Dungan, William O. 76
Dunn, F. 128
Dunning 256

Earth Science Museum 235
Edgar, William 236
Edgerton, Dr. Harold E. 56
Edison 157
Ehman Park, Gothenburg 88
Eight (Ashcan) School, art 86
Eisley, Loren 10
Elfreda Gross House 105

Elkhorn Station 282
Ellsworth, William 110
Elm Creek 80, 281
Elmwood 51, 52
Elyria 257, 258
Emery Brothers, Bob and Charles 165, 168
Emmet 218, 219
Emmet, Robert 219
Emmons and Brewster 242
Enders 134
Enders Reservoir 134, 141
Enola Gay 37
Enterprise Junior 30
Eppley, Eugene C. 16
Eppley Foundation, Eugene E. 16
Erma's Desire, sculpture 70, 111
Estelle Post Office 134
Eubanks, Lucinda 281
Eubanks, William and family 165-168
Evett, Kenneth 48
Ewing 208

Fairbanks, Arvard 19
Fairbury 155, 168, 170, 171, 173, 269, 275, 276, 280
Fairview 44, 46, 139
Falls City 185, 193, 194
Farmers Valley 53
Farwell 268
"Febold Feboldson" 87
Feeney, Joe 60
Ferguson Mansion 46
Ficklin, Benjamin F. 124
Ficklin's Springs Station 122, 125, 283
"The Fighting Norths" 203
Filley 177, 178
Filley, Elijah 178
Filley Stone Barn 177, 276
First Presbyterian Church 38
Fisher, Fred 66, 68, 252
Fisher, Jacob 69
Fisher, W. S. 134
Fisher Rainbow Fountain 69
Fitch House 144
Flanagan, Father Edward J. 9, 25
Florence 19, 32
Folsom Children's Zoo 50
Fonda, Henry 57, 60-62
Fonner Memorial Rotunda 61
Fontanelle 212
Fontanelle Bank 38
Fontanelle Forest 40
Ford, Gerald Rudolph and Dorothy 29, 30

301

302